Henry Seebohm

Siberia in Europe

A Visit to the Valley of the Petchora, in North-East Russia

Henry Seebohm

Siberia in Europe
A Visit to the Valley of the Petchora, in North-East Russia

ISBN/EAN: 9783337166854

Printed in Europe, USA, Canada, Australia, Japan

Cover: Foto ©ninafisch / pixelio.de

More available books at **www.hansebooks.com**

SIBERIA IN EUROPE.

SIBERIA IN EUROPE:

A VISIT TO THE VALLEY OF THE PETCHORA,
IN NORTH-EAST RUSSIA;

WITH DESCRIPTIONS OF THE NATURAL HISTORY, MIGRATION
OF BIRDS, ETC.

By HENRY SEEBOHM,
F.L.S., F.Z.S., F.R.G.S.

WITH MAP AND ILLUSTRATIONS.

LONDON:
JOHN MURRAY, ALBEMARLE STREET.
1880.

LONDON:
PRINTED BY WILLIAM CLOWES AND SONS, LIMITED,
STAMFORD STREET AND CHARING CROSS.

PREFACE.

The following pages contain the narrative of a trip, which I made in the year 1875, to the lower valley of the Petchora, in North-East Russia, in company with my friend J. A. Harvie-Brown, Esq., of Dunipace, a naturalist well known in ornithological circles for excellent field-work in various parts of Scotland, in Archangel, and in Transylvania. I have endeavoured to pourtray the character of the people with whom we came in contact with as little political or religious bias as possible, and to give as vivid a picture as I was able of a country widely different from our own, and possessing a climate of an almost opposite character to that of England. Little or nothing of importance has been added since my return home. I have given the reader credit for wishing to know something more of the birds we met with than we learnt on our trip, and I have endeavoured to give him an opportunity of satisfying his curiosity by foot-notes, to which he may refer or not as he likes. In some cases I have been obliged to correct errors of identification which we occasionally made; and I have introduced a chapter on the migration of birds, but inasmuch as this was principally written upon the island of Heligoland, it can scarcely be looked upon as padding.

Whatever merit the book may possess will doubtless be owing to the fact that it was for the most part written upon the spot. It is a faithful transcript of a stranger's first impressions of a part of Europe seldom or never visited by Englishmen, written at post stations whilst the horses were being changed, or in peasants' cottages, wrecked ships, or wherever our temporary quarters may have been. The accuracy which ornithological observations demand, made it imperatively necessary that what was seen should be at once recorded, and many a time eighteen or twenty hours' field-work have been followed by two or three hours' writing before we allowed ourselves rest. The general reader may perhaps complain that the book is too ornithological; but he must remember that an enthusiasm of some sort is necessary to lead the traveller into scenes where no hotels exist, where unknown difficulties have to be met, and which are absolutely virgin ground to the tourist. The writer also ventures to hope that the ornithological part of his little work may also interest the general reader. However dry the technical part of the subject may be considered, the study of Field Ornithology is a branch of Natural History which has always been a great favourite with Englishmen. Foreign writers may have produced more scientific works upon the subject; but the peculiarity of English ornithological research has been that, to a large extent, it is the work of amateurs, who make it a labour of love, whilst on the Continent most ornithological writers have been professional men connected with the various museums. An English ornithologist often begins by being a sportsman and ends by being a naturalist; and if closet natural history has been until perhaps quite recently carried to a higher point of scientific accuracy in Holland, Germany, and France, the British ornithologists, both of our own Islands and in India, have done the best field-work.

The results of our visit to this *ultima Thule* of Europe must be taken for what they are worth. We had no hair-breadth escapes to record, and our adventures may appear somewhat tame to a member of the Alpine Club; but the conditions of life in Siberia in Europe are so entirely different to those observed by the ordinary tourist, that our travels have at least the charm of novelty. It is true that we had to put up sometimes with hardships, but the recollection even of them is one of unmixed pleasure. Would that the narrative of our success might stimulate some of our junior ornithologists to follow in our steps. Much yet remains to be done. It is absurd to suppose that the ornithology of such a wide district could be exhausted in a single trip. Our information about those curious people, the Samoyedes, must be considered as only supplementary to, and confirmatory of, the account contained in Rae's 'Land of the North Wind,' or the more elaborate observations of Castrén and Schrenck. We neither of us make any claim to a scientific knowledge of ethnology, and the information on the subject contained in the following pages is merely such as interested us as tourists, and which, together with the greater portion of our ornithological observations, may prove interesting to the general reader.

CONTENTS.

CHAPTER I.

John Wolley — Unknown breeding-grounds — Birds of Archangel and Lapland — Voyages to the Petchora in the seventeenth century — Schrenck's visit in 1837 — Castrén's visit in 1842 — Keyserling's visit in 1843 — Pelzam's visit in 1874 — Hoffmansegg's visit about 1850 — Outfit — Letters of introduction .. .. Page 1

CHAPTER II.

London to St. Petersburg — Mode of heating railway carriages — Frozen Market at St. Petersburg — Bohemian waxwings — Moscow to Vologda — M. Verakin — Sledging from Vologda to Archangel — The Yemschik — Post-houses — The Samovar — Angliski Russ — Modes of yoking horses — State of the roads — Weather — Traffic — Scenery — Birds — Arrival at Archangel 7

CHAPTER III.

The white city Archangel — Decline of its commerce — Cheapness of living — Peter Kotzoff — Father Inokentia — Samoyede vocabulary — Their sledges — Their appearance — Samoyede names of birds — Their national songs — Election of their chiefs — Their ignorance of doctors or medicinal plants — Piottuch — Birds — The weather — Hasty departure from Archangel 15

CHAPTER IV.

Bad roads — Postal service in winter and summer — Changeable weather — Scenery — Pinega and Kuloi rivers — Snow plains — The forests — Birds — Samoyedes — Mezén — Polish exile — Snow-buntings — How caught — Jackdaws — We leave Mezén — The weather — Scenery — The Mezén river—The Pizhma—The roads—Piottuch's accident—The Via diabolica—Bolshanivagorskia—Break-up of the road—Polish prejudices—The villages—Curiosity of the peasants—Greek crosses—Love of ornament—Employment and amusements—Samoyedes—Birds—Umskia—First view of the Petchora—Arrival at Ust-Zylma. Page 23

CHAPTER V.

Ust-Zylma—Its streets—Its houses—Its manure—Its population—Its farms—Its churches—Our quarters—The banks of the river—The Old Believers—Their superstitions—Their crosses—Hospitality of the officials—Shooting-parties—Captain Arendt and Captain Engel—Snow shoes—Scarcity of birds—The snow-bunting—Mealy redpole—Winter
40

CHAPTER VI.

The Samoyedes—Reindeer—The tundra—Nomad life—Diseases of reindeer—Samoyede national character—Trip to Umskia—Bad roads—Birds—Easter Eve—Drunkenness—Snow—Our first bird's-nest—L'autre côte—Birds 54

CHAPTER VII.

Trip to Habariki—Samoyedes—Lassoing reindeer—Dogs—Birds—Samoyede sledges—Reindeer harness—The chooms—Samoyede hospitality—Marriage ceremonies—Funeral rites—Religion 63

CHAPTER VIII.

May-day—Snow-buntings—Jackdaws—Game—Birds of prey—Sunday at Ust-Zylma—A fire—Marriage ceremony—Tenure of land—The commune—Preparations for summer 78

CHAPTER IX.

Mild weather—Bear tracks—Saddle of bear—First rain—Six new migratory birds—Magpie's eggs—Cessation of the winter frost—Return of winter—A wild goose chase—Cachets—Night on the banks of the Petchora—The silent forest—A new bird 88

CHAPTER X.

Gulls—Species new to Europe—Fresh arrivals—Duck-shooting—Bird-life in the forest—Gulls perching in trees—Break-up of the ice on the Zylma—On the wrong bank of the river—Dragging the boats across the ice—Final break-up of the ice on the Petchora .. Page 98

CHAPTER XI.

Religious processions—Costumes of the peasants—A Russian holiday—Drunkenness—Prejudices of the Old Believers—Field-work—House-building—New birds—The Siberian chiff-chaff—Prices of provisions—Arrival of waders.. 113

CHAPTER XII.

Samoyede names—The Swedish mocking-bird—Toads—Birds resting on migration—Sparrow-hawk—The Petchora free from ice—A new song—Ceremony of blessing the steamer—Rambles in the woods—Arrival of the mosquitoes.. 124

CHAPTER XIII.

Trip to Habariki—Forest scenery—Tarns in the woods—Changeable weather—New birds identified in the forest—Golden eagle—Osprey—The hobby—The cuckoo—Yellow-headed wagtail—Bohemian waxwing—Great snipe—Terek sandpiper—Goosander—Smew—Black-throated diver 136

CHAPTER XIV.

Return to Ust-Zylma—Wedding of the engineer's son—Scarlet bullfinch—Last days at Ust-Zylma—Our boat—We sail to Habariki—Birds' eggs—Smew's eggs—Snipes in trees—Down the Petchora—Sedge warbler—Black-cock—Arctic tern—Willow swamps—We cross the Arctic Circle—A new bird—Arrival at Viski—The delta—Double snipe—Pustazursk—The tundra—Arrival at Alexievka 152

CHAPTER XV.

Alexievka—The timber rafts—The island—Nest and eggs—Buffon's skua—Sailing for the tundra—Description of the tundra—Its vegetation—Nests of Lapland bunting and red-throated pipit—First sight of the grey plover—Its nest—Watching by the nest—Shot at last—Omelette of grey plover's eggs—Birds seen on the tundra—Eggs collected during the day—Blowing eggs—Nest of the Petchora pipit .. Page 174

CHAPTER XVI.

The tundra near the Yooshina river—Golden plover's eggs—Various nests—Lapland bunting—Various birds—Richardson's skua—Various means of propelling our boat—The tundra near Stanavialachta—Eyrie of a peregrine falcon—Various nests—Abundance of willow grouse—Nest of the willow grouse—Visit to two islands in the delta .. 186

CHAPTER XVII.

Examination of nests—Excursion to Wasilkova—Search for breeding haunts of Bewick's swan—News from England—Grey plover's eggs—Flock of Buffon's skuas—Black scoter's nest—Watching for skuas' nests—Another nest of grey plovers—Scaup's eggs—The Zyriani .. 194

CHAPTER XVIII.

Second visit to Stanavialachta—Peregrine falcons—Plague of mosquitoes—Midnight on the tundra—Nest of the velvet scoter—Little Feodor sent in quest of the swan's skin—A Russian bath—Feodor's return—Identification of eggs of Bewick's swan—Mosquito veils—Our eighth nest of grey plovers—Our servants—Our ninth nest of grey plovers—The tenth nest 208

CHAPTER XIX.

Trip to the Golievski Islands—Shoal of white whales—Glaucous gulls—Dunlins and sanderlings—Black scoter—Dvoinik—Little stint—Curlew sandpiper—Snow-bunting—Overhauling our plunder—The Company's manager—Discussions concerning the stints—Probable line of migration followed by birds 226

CHAPTER XX.

Hybernation of birds—Migration of birds—Reed warblers—Origin of migration—Transvaal warblers—The mammoth age—Insect life—Lines of migration—Heligoland—Its ornithologists—Variety of birds—Wind and weather — The throstle-bushes — Migration by sight — Order of migration—Stray migrants—The yellow-browed warbler—Migration on Heligoland—Skylarks—Migratory instincts—Other facts of migration .. .. Page 242

CHAPTER XXI.

Trip to Kuya—The prahms—Travelling in a Bosposki—The birds we saw—Arrival of the *Triad* at Alexievka—We win over the manager—The *Ino*—Doing Robinson Crusoe in a wrecked ship—Nest of the long-tailed duck—Our first little stint's nest—The tundra—Sunset and sunrise—Little stint's eggs—The tundra near Bolvanski Bucht—Phalaropes—Interior of the tundra—Change of plumage in phalaropes—An early morning start—Confusion of time—The snowy owl—Two more nests of the little stint—A march of geese on the tundra—An old grave .. 262

CHAPTER XXII.

On short commons—Bad weather—A foraging party—Russian superstitions—Return of the steamer—Beautiful flowers—Arrival at Alexievka—Departure for home — Thunder-storm—Waterspout—Sea-birds—Hard fare—Copenhagen—Results of the trip 284

CHAPTER XXIII.

Summary of the trip — Summer in the Arctic regions — Circumpolar birds — Birds confined to the eastern hemisphere — Various ranges of birds—Migration of birds—Dates of arrival—Probable route—Conclusion 294

LIST OF ILLUSTRATIONS.

	PAGE
GREY PLOVER	1
OLD RUSSIAN SILVER CROSS	6
SLEDGING THROUGH THE SNOW	7
SAMOYEDE KNIVES	14
LITTLE STINTS	15
OLD RUSSIAN SILVER CROSS	22
UST-ZYLMA	23
OLD RUSSIAN SILVER CROSS	39
ANCIENT CHURCH OF THE OLD BELIEVERS	40
CHOOMS OF THE SAMOYEDES	54
LASSOING REINDEER	63
REIN RESTS	70
OLD RUSSIAN SILVER CROSS	77
A SPILL IN THE SNOW	78
OLD RUSSIAN SILVER CROSS	87
SHOOTING WILD GEESE	88
THE BANKS OF THE ZYLMA	98
OLD RUSSIAN SILVER CROSS	112
DIFFICULTIES WITH SNOW-SHOES	113
OLD RUSSIAN SILVER CROSS	123
WILLOW GROUSE	124
OLD RUSSIAN SILVER CROSS	135
THE FLOODED BANKS OF THE RIVER	136
OLD RUSSIAN SILVER CROSS	151
SAILING DOWN THE DELTA	152
PLOUGHING AT UST-ZYLMA	173

LIST OF ILLUSTRATIONS.

	PAGE
Alexievka from the Tundra	174
Old Russian Silver Cross	185
Stanavialachta	186
Old Russian Silver Cross	193
Grey Plover's Nest and Young	194
A Swan's Nest	197
Old Russian Silver Cross	207
Kuya	208
Watching Grey Plovers through a Cloud of Mosquitoes	211
Mosquito Veil	225
Little Stint's Nest, Eggs and Young	226
Old Russian Silver Cross	241
The Lighthouse at Heligoland on a Migration Night	242
View of Heligoland	259
Old Russian Silver Cross	261
Doing Robinson Crusoe at Dvoinik	262
Old Russian Silver Cross	283
Migration of Geese	284
Old Russian Silver Cross	293
From Mekitza to Kuya on a Rosposki	294
Our Headquarters at Ust-Zylma	303

MAP .. .. *at the end.*

OLD RUSSIAN SILVER CROSS.

GREY PLOVER.

SIBERIA IN EUROPE.

CHAPTER I.

John Wolley—Unknown breeding-grounds—Birds of Archangel and Lapland—Voyages to the Petchora in the seventeenth century—Schrenck's visit in 1837—Castrén's visit in 1842—Keyserling's visit in 1843—Pelzam's visit in 1874—Hoffmansegg's visit about 1850—Outfit—Letters of introduction.

THE history of British birds has been enthusiastically studied by ornithologists during the last half-century. In spring and autumn several species of birds annually visit our shores in considerable numbers, passing us in their migrations to and from unknown breeding-grounds. These migrations, and the geographical distribution of birds, have of late years

B

occupied a large share of the attention of ornithologists. The name of John Wolley stands pre-eminent amongst the discoverers in this department of science. His indefatigable labours in Lapland about twenty years ago are still fresh in the memory of the present generation of ornithologists, who will never cease to regret his untimely death. Notwithstanding his researches, there remained half-a-dozen well-known British birds whose breeding-grounds still continued wrapt in mystery, to solve which has been the ambition of many field naturalists during the past twenty years. These birds, to the discovery of whose eggs special interest seemed to attach, were the Grey Plover, the Little Stint, the Sanderling, the Curlew Sandpiper, the Knot,* and Bewick's Swan.

---

* The Knot (*Tringa canutus*, Linn.) was the only one of these six species of birds which we did not meet with in the valley of the Petchora. It probably breeds on the shores of the Polar basin in both hemispheres, but its eggs are absolutely unknown. On several of the Arctic expeditions the knot has been observed during the breeding season, but no eggs were obtained. Captain Fielden writes (Nares' 'Voyage to the Polar Sea,' Appendix, vol. ii. p. 212): "During the month of July my companions and I often endeavoured to discover the nest of this bird; but none of us were successful. However, on July 30, 1876, the day before we broke out of our winter quarters [in lat. 82½°], where we had been frozen in eleven months, three of our seamen, walking by the border of a small lake not far from the ship, came upon an old bird accompanied by three nestlings, which they brought to me. The old bird proved to be a male; its stomach and those of the young ones were filled with insects. . . . The knot bred in the vicinity of Discovery Bay, but no eggs were found there, though the young were obtained in all stages of plumage." During the winter the knot is almost cosmopolitan in its range. It is exceedingly common on the shores of Great Britain, and is more or less frequently obtained in various parts of Europe, Africa, South Asia, and even in Australia and New Zealand. On the American continent it is found on both coasts, occasionally straying as far as the South American shores.

In 1872 my friend John A. Harvie-Brown accompanied R. Alston on an ornithological expedition to Archangel, the results of which were published in the 'Ibis' for January, 1873; and in 1874, I went with Robert Collett of Christiania to the north of Norway. Neither of these journeys added any very important fact to the stock of ornithological knowledge; but in each case they considerably increased our interest in Arctic ornithology, and gave us a knowledge of the notes and habits of many Arctic birds which was of invaluable assistance to us on our subsequent journeys. The difference between the birds found at Archangel and those at the north of Norway was so striking that we, as well as many of our ornithological friends, were convinced that another ten degrees east would bring us to the breeding-ground of many species new to North Europe; and there was a chance, besides, that among these might be found some of the half-dozen birds which I have named, the discovery of whose breeding-haunts was the special object of our ambition.

My friend Harvie-Brown had been collecting information about the river Petchora for some time, and it was finally arranged that we should spend the summer of 1875 there together. We were under the impression that, ornithologically speaking, it was virgin ground, but in this we afterwards discovered that we were mistaken. So far as we were able to ascertain, no Englishman had travelled from Archangel to the Petchora for 250 years. In that curious old book called 'Purchas his Pilgrimes,' published in 1625, may be found the narrative of divers merchants and mariners who visited this river between the years 1611 and 1615 for the purpose of establishing a trade there in furs and skins, especially beaver, for which Ust-Zylma on the Petchora was at that time celebrated.

In 1837 Alexander Gustav Schrenck visited the Petchora under the auspices of the Imperial Botanical Gardens at St. Petersburg, and published voluminous information respecting the botany and the ethnology of this district.

In 1842 Castrén was sent out by the Swedish Government and collected much valuable information about the Samoyedes and the other races of North-East Russia. The following year, Paul von Krusenstern and Alexander Graf Keyserling visited the Petchora, and published an important work upon the geology and physical geography of the country, but none of these travellers seem to have written anything upon the subject of birds beyond a mere passing mention of ducks and geese. In St. Petersburg we learnt that Dr. Pelzam, from the museum at Kazan, visited the Petchora in 1874, but from information we obtained on that river, it would appear that he spent most of his time in dredging and paid little attention to birds. In Archangel we made a more important discovery. We there met the man who had been guide to Hencke and Hoffmansegg some twenty or five-and-twenty years ago. From him we learnt that those naturalists had spent a year or more on the Petchora, had there collected birds and eggs, and had been very successful in finding all that they were in search of. We cannot, however, learn that these gentlemen published anything respecting the birds of the Petchora. They seem to have collected chiefly as a commercial speculation, and to have sent their spoils to a dealer in Dresden, through whom some rare eggs, doubtless from this district, found their way to Mr. Dunn, of Orkney, and were subsequently distributed amongst English collectors. In consequence of the trade jealousy of the dealers these eggs were sold without authentication, and hence possess no scientific value whatever; therefore, practically, the Petchora may be considered to have been virgin ground to the ornithologist.

Our outfit was simple. We determined to be trammelled with as little luggage as possible. Besides the necessary changes of clothing we took each a pair of Cording's india-rubber boots, which we found invaluable. To protect our faces from the mosquitoes, we provided ourselves with silk gauze veils, with a couple of wire hoops inserted opposite the bridge of the nose and the chin, like little crinolines. These simple *komarniks* proved a complete success. On a hot summer's day life without them would have been simply unendurable. Of course the heat and sense of being somewhat stifled had to be borne, as by far the lesser of two evils. Our hands we protected by the regulation cavalry gauntlet. We took two tents with us, but had no occasion to use them. Our net hammocks served as beds by night, and sofas by day, and very luxurious we found them. We each took a double-barrelled breech-loader, and a walking-stick gun. Five hundred cartridges for each weapon, with the necessary appliances for re-loading, we found amply sufficient. The only mistake we made, we afterwards found, was in not taking baking powder, nor sufficient dried vegetables and Liebig's extract of meat.

A portable cooking apparatus, heated by spirits of wine, was occasionally useful, but as a rule we found that a wood fire with a substantial stewpot and frying-pan answered the purpose best.

In travelling in Russia, it is of the utmost importance to be on good terms with the officials, and we were most fortunate in obtaining the best introductions. Our warmest thanks are due to Count Schouvaloff for his kindness in giving us letters that ensured us a welcome such as we could not have expected, and which added very largely to the safety and success of our trip.

OLD RUSSIAN SILVER CROSS.

SLEDGING THROUGH THE SNOW.

CHAPTER II.

London to St. Petersburg—Mode of heating railway carriages—Frozen market at St. Petersburg—Bohemian waxwings—Moscow to Vologda—M. Verakin—Sledging from Vologda to Archangel—The Yemschik — Post-houses — The Samovar — Angliski Russ — Modes of yoking horses— State of the roads —Weather—Traffic—Scenery—Birds—Arrival at Archangel.

We left London on the 3rd of March, 1875. A journey of four days and three nights, including a comfortable night's rest at Cologne and a few hours each at Hanover and Berlin, landed us in St. Petersburg. In Belgium it was cold, but there was no snow. In Germany we saw skaters on the ice, and there were patches of snow in shady corners. As we proceeded eastwards the snow and cold increased, and in Russia the whole ground was from one to two feet deep in snow, and sledges were the only conveyances to be seen at the stations. As far as Cologne the railway carriages were heated by the ordinary hot-water foot-warmer, and very comfortable they were, with a temperature outside of about 40°. From Hanover to Berlin the carriages were heated with charcoal fires under the seats, and the sense of oppression from foul air was so intolerable, that we were only too glad to shiver with the windows open and the thermometer down to 20°. From Berlin to the frontier the carriages were heated by steam pipes, with an arrangement for regulating the heat, and although the temperature outside continued the same, we were able to keep a comfortable temperature of 60° without any sense of suffocation. In Russia the carriages were heated with wood fires, and we kept up about the same temperature without any sense of discomfort, although the thermometer had fallen to 5° outside. At Wirballen our letters of introduction saved us from an immensity of trouble and formality, thanks to the courtesy of M. de Pisanko and the other officials.

We spent four days at St. Petersburg, sight-seeing and completing the preparations for our journey. The morning after our arrival was the last day of the "butter fair," and we were very much amused and interested, especially with the ice slide, which is one of its great features. A most interesting sight to us was the frozen market. Here, one stall would be full of frozen pigs, there another, laden almost mountain high with frozen sides of oxen and deer. Part of the market was occupied by rows of stalls, on which the frozen fish lay, piled up in stacks. Another portion devoted to birds and game, heaps of capercailzie, black grouse, hazel grouse (the *rabchik* of the Russians), willow grouse (the *koropatki* of the Russians), &c., stacks of white hares, and baskets full of small birds. Amongst the latter we were anxious to secure some Bohemian waxwings, in order, if possible, to throw some light upon the vexed question of the difference between the sexes of their species. We bought a dozen of the most perfect skins for eighty kopecks. There were not many waxwings in the market, and all those we bought proved, on dissection, to be males. In winter these birds go in flocks, and it would seem that the sexes flock separately, as is known to be the case with many other species.

On the evening of the 10th of March we left St. Petersburg, and travelled by rail all night to Moscow, where we spent a day. In the frozen market there we were told that waxwings were seen only in autumn. Jackdaws and hooded crows we found very abundant in Moscow. We left in the evening, and travelled per rail all night and the whole of the next day, reaching Vologda at midnight.

We had previously written to the English consul in Archangel, and he was kind enough to buy fur dresses for us, and send them on to St. Petersburg. He also commissioned M. Verakin, a Russian merchant in Vologda, to furnish us with a sledge and provisions for the journey. M. Verakin treated us most hospitably, would not hear of our going to an hotel, and gave us every assistance in his power. Unfortunately, he spoke only his native Russ, but at last he found us an interpreter in the person of the German servant of the Oberst Gendarme, and we were able, through him, to convey our thanks to our host for his kindness to us.

From 8 A.M. on Sunday morning, the 14th of March, to Thursday at noon, we travelled by sledge day and night from Vologda to Archangel, a distance of nearly 600 English miles. Our sledge was drawn by three horses, driven by a peasant called the "yemschik." Both horses and drivers were changed at each station. There were thirty-six stages, varying in distance from fifteen to twenty-seven versts (ten to nineteen English miles). The horses were generally good, small, tough, shaggy, animals, apparently never groomed, but very hardy. We had but one lazy horse out of the 108 which we employed on the journey. Another broke down altogether, and had to be left on the roadside to follow as best it could. That this treatment was not a solitary instance, was proved by the fact that, on one of the stages (the one of twenty-seven versts), we passed two horses which had evidently broken down, and had been cast aside in the same way, and were lying dead and frozen on the road. The drivers were very civil and generally drove well, urging on the horses rather by the voice than the whip, often apparently imitating the bark of a wolf to frighten them, and at other times swearing at them in every variety of oath of which the Russian language is capable. The yemschiks were perfectly satisfied with a *pour-boire* of one kopeck per verst. The horses were charged three kopecks per verst each. There was generally a comfortable room at the stations, and the station-masters usually came out to receive us. Sometimes we did not quit our sledge, but if we were hungry we carried our provision-basket into the station-house, ordered the "samovar," and made tea. The samovar is a great institution in Russia. Provisions are not to be had at the station-houses, but we always found a samovar and we were generally able to procure milk. The samovar is a brass urn, with a charcoal fire in a tube in the centre, and boils water in a few minutes. We found that about a dozen words of Russ sufficed to pull us through very comfortably. Arrived at a station, we generally allowed the station-master to have the first say. As soon as a convenient opportunity occurred we interposed, "*tre loshed say chass*," which being interpreted means "three horses immediately." We then produced some rouble notes, and asked, "*scolco*," how much? The station-master would again begin to talk Russ. We offered the amount due as appeared from the list of stations which had been provided for us by M. Verakin at Vologda. This proving satisfactory, we proceeded to pay the yemschik his backsheesh. The station-master once more began to talk volubly in Russ. We waited until he had done, and then asked innocently, "*fameelye?*" The station-master nodded his head and said, "*da da*" (yes). We then said, "Brown Seebohm Angliski Vologda nah Archangelsk." After the changes had been rung upon our names, it generally ended in our having to copy them upon a piece of paper for the station-master to write in his book; and the new yemschik having by this time got his team in order, we settled ourselves down again, cried "*kharashaw!*" all right! and started off. With slight variations this course was repeated at each station. Our horses were yoked in divers ways: of course one was always in the shafts. The other two were sometimes yoked one at each side of the shaft-horse; sometimes one on the near side, and the other in front; sometimes side by side in front of the shaft-horse; and sometimes all three were in single file. The roads in the Archangel province, where the snow-plough was used regularly, were generally very good. In the province of Vologda, where the snow-plough seemed to be unknown, the roads were at least twice as bad as the imagination of an Englishman could possibly conceive. On the good roads the sensation of travelling was very pleasant, not unlike that in a railway carriage. On the bad roads our sensations were something like what Sancho Panza's must have been when he was tossed in the blanket. Our luggage was tightly packed with hay, and ourselves in fur, else both would have suffered severely. At first we expected to be upset at each lurch, and took for granted our sledge would be battered to pieces long before the six hundred miles to Archangel were completed, but, by degrees we began to feel reassured. The outriggers of our sledge were so contrived that the seat might approach, but not quite reach, the perpendicular; and after we had broken a shaft once or twice, and seen the cool businesslike way in which our yemschik brought out his axe, cut down a birch-tree and fashioned a new shaft, we began to contemplate the possibility of the entire dissolution of our sledge with equanimity. The weather was very changeable; sometimes the thermometer was barely at freezing point, sometimes we had a sort of November fog, and occasionally a snowstorm, but nearly half the time it was clear and cold with brilliant sunshine. The last night and day it was intensely cold, from 2° to 4° below zero. There was a considerable amount of traffic on the roads, and we frequently met long lines of sledges laden with hides, tar barrels, frozen sides of beef, hay, flax, &c. Many peasants were sledging about from place to place, but we saw very few travellers with government horses. The country was covered with about two feet of snow. It was rarely flat, at first a sort of open rolling prairie land with plenty of timber and well studded with villages. Afterwards it became more hilly and almost entirely covered with forest. In many cases the road followed the course of a river, frequently crossing it and often continuing for some miles on its frozen surface. The track was then marked out with small fir-trees stuck into the snow at intervals. During the whole journey we met only one person who could speak either English, French, or German. This was at Slavodka, where we bought some fancy bread and Russian butter from a German baker, from Hesse Cassel. Jackdaws and hooded crows were the commonest birds in the open country, feeding for the most part upon the droppings of the horses on the roads. They were in splendid plumage and wonderfully clean. Many of the jackdaws had an almost white ring round the neck and would doubtless be the *Corvus collaris* of some authors, but, so far as we were able to see, this cannot be considered as a good species. We frequently saw almost every intermediate variety in the same flock. During the first few days we noticed many colonies of nests in the plantations, but whether these would be tenanted by rooks later on in the season, or whether the hooded crow breeds in colonies in this country, we were not able to ascertain. We occasionally saw ravens and magpies, the latter becoming more common as we travelled farther north. In the opener country we frequently spied small flocks of yellow-hammers on the roads, and now and then a pair of bullfinches. In driving through the forest we occasionally caught sight of a crossbill, pine grosbeak, marsh tit, jay, or great spotted woodpecker. On one occasion we had an excellent opportunity of watching a small covey of willow grouse, almost as pure white as the snow upon which they were running. In the villages sparrows were common enough. At Vologda, we are under the impression that they were all the house sparrow. In the villages through which we passed after the first day they were certainly all tree sparrows. Upon our arrival at Archangel we were most hospitably entertained by the British Consul, Charles Birse, Esq. We were delighted once more to sit down to a good dinner, to enjoy the luxury of a Russian bath after our long journey, and have a good night's rest in a comfortable bed.

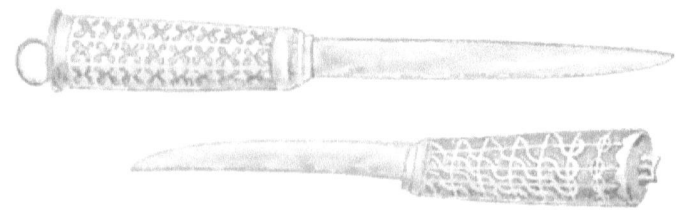

SAMOYEDE KNIVES.

LITTLE STINT.

CHAPTER III.

The white city Archangel—Decline of its commerce—Cheapness of living—Peter Kotzoff—Father Inokentia—Samoyede vocabulary—Their sledges—Their appearance—Samoyede names of birds—Their national songs—Election of their chiefs—Their ignorance of doctors or medicinal plants—Piottuch—Birds—The weather—Hasty departure from Archangel.

WE spent nineteen days in Archangel completing the preparations for our journey, and picking up what information we could respecting the great river Petchora, and the routes thither. Everybody looked upon our expedition as a most formidable undertaking, but all were anxious to give us every assistance in their power. There is an excellent German club in Archangel, and we dropped a few roubles in practising *crassnum pa bielemo* and *bielum pa crassnemo** with billiard balls large enough for Hercules to have played with. Archangel must have been christened in winter, indeed the odds are at least seven to five that such was the case. Most of the houses are painted white, the streets were white, the Dvina was white, and as far as the eye could reach the whole country was white. The principal street, the Troiski Prospect, is a long straight road flanked with low houses, separated by gardens. All the houses are constructed of wood, except in the centre of the town, where many of them are plastered bricks. The population is said to be from fifteen to seventeen thousand in winter, increasing in summer to about half as many more. Archangel seems to be declining in importance as a commercial centre, doubtless in consequence of its isolation from the railway system of Russia. The number of large firms does not increase, and there are now only three export houses of importance. The chances of commercial success are consequently small, and most of the young men who can afford it leave the city. The cost of living is small. House rent is very cheap, and provisions equally so. For example, best joints of beef can be bought in winter for 3d. per lb., in summer at 3¾d. White bread costs 4½d. per lb., but brown bread can be had for ¾d. Butter is 7½d. per lb. Milk (unskimmed) 1d. per quart, and cream 3¾d. per pint. Game is ridiculously cheap; capercailzie, 7½d. each in autumn, 1s. 7d. each in winter; hazel grouse 4½d. per brace in autumn, 11¼d. in winter; hares 3d. each, and salmon 9d. to 1s. 3d.

---

* Red upon white, and white upon red.

per lb. In spite of the long and severe winters, the price of fuel is not a very important item. Wood, sufficient to serve a small family for a year, costs about 10*l*.

For some days we sat in commission, examining witnesses on the Petchora, the British Consul kindly acting as interpreter for us. We got the best information from Peter Kotzoff, a Russian pilot, who showed us a chronometer which was presented to him by the British Government for assisting in the rescue of the crew of the *Elizabeth*, which was wrecked at the mouth of the Petchora. He was for some years a pilot on the great river, and acted as guide to Count Wilczee on his return journey overland from the Austrian-Hungarian Arctic Expedition. Another interesting acquaintance which we made was that of Father Inokentia, the present archpriest of Archangel. He lived seventeen years in the Petchora, principally east of Ishma. He was sent out by the Russian Government as a missionary amongst the Samoyedes, to convert them from their so-called idolatrous faith to the Greek Church. He told us that he remembered meeting with Schrenck, and that Castrén stopped some time at his house, at Kolva, on the river Ussa. He left the Petchora, in 1847 so that his information was somewhat out of date. Father Inokentia seemed to be a jolly fat friar of the old school, and was very kind and patient in answering our numerous questions. How far he succeeded in his mission it is difficult to say. Most of the Samoyedes on the west side of the Ural now profess to belong to the Greek Church, but we were repeatedly informed that many of them still secretly retain their old cliefs, and continue to practise their ancient rites. We went through most of the Samoyede vocabulary given in Rae's 'Land of the North Wind,' and found it to be on the whole correct. No doubt in districts so widely separated as the Kanin peninsula, and the valley of the Ussa, considerable differences of dialect must be expected. But perhaps the most interesting information which we obtained respecting this curious race of people, was that which we got from the Samoyedes themselves. We got our first glimpse of them at St. Petersburg, where we found a single *choom* erected on the ice of the Neva. These were probably poor Samoyedes, owning only a few reindeer, and earning a scanty living during the long winter by selling various articles made from the skins and horns of reindeer, and picking up a few kopecks by giving curious strangers a ride in their national sledges.

Near the villages round Archangel there were several Samoyede chooms. Two or more families were wintering about fifteen versts from Archangel, and came almost every day in their sledges to the town. On one of our shooting excursions we chartered a couple of these sledges to take us to an island on the Dvina, and thoroughly enjoyed this novel mode of travelling. The reindeer were very tractable, and we skimmed over the surface of the snow at a rapid pace. We had long conversations with several Samoyedes, the Consul of course, acting as interpreter, and we invited them to the Consul's house, where they gave us freely all the information they could respecting themselves and the traditions of their race. They spoke Russian well and were by no means devoid of intelligence. They were all small men,

with dark straight hair, thin moustache and beard, and little
or no whiskers. They wore their hair hanging over the forehead, like a south country English peasant. Their features
were irregular, wide flat noses, high cheek-bones, and thick
lips. The under jaw was coarse and heavy, the eyes brown,
small, and skewed like those of the Chinese, and not unfrequently sore. They had small hands and feet, and wide
round heads, with sallow complexions. We took some of
them to the museum, where they recognised many of the
stuffed birds, and tried to describe their habits and imitate
their notes. They gave us the following Samoyede names
of birds in the Petchora district:—

Sandpiper	Suitar.
Willow Grouse	Hoad-jy'.
Swan	Chouari.
Goose	Yebtaw.
Black Goose	Parden Yebtaw.

They told us there were two species of swans in the
Petchora, the larger one common and breeding there, the
smaller one rare, and appearing only in autumn. They
represented the Snowy owl as found on the " tundra," * but
did not recognise the Lapp or Ural owls. We found later
on, that these statements were substantially correct. On
one occasion the Samoyedes favoured us with some of their
national songs, a monotonous chant which reminded me
very much of the songs of the peasants of the Parnassus.
One, which was translated for us, was a sort of Ossianic ditty,
relating how the singer intended to make a journey with

---

* Peat-moss. See page 55.

reindeer, how he would select the four fleetest bull reindeer from his herd, how he would always be at the head of the party, how he would get plenty of vodka, how he would barter his skins, and how he would take care not to be cheated in the transaction. One of the Samoyedes told us that they have a chief, residing in the Ural, who is answerable to the Emperor for the annual tribute, and that at his death his son succeeds him, unless he is thought not worthy to be made king. In this case another chief is elected by ballot, by putting pieces of wood into a "*pimä*," or boot. It is right to note, however, that other Samoyedes whom we questioned had never heard of this Ural chief. The Samoyedes have no doctors, and use no medicinal plants, nor do they employ any other medicines, unless the outward application of goose or swan fat for frost bites may rank as such.

At Archangel we were fortunate enough to secure the services of M. Piottuch, a Polish exile, whom we engaged to go with us to the land of the Samoyedes in the double capacity of interpreter and bird-skinner. He spoke Russian and bad French, and since Alston and Harvie-Brown's visit to Archangel in 1872, he had spent a considerable part of his leisure time in shooting and skinning birds. Accompanied by Piottuch we made several excursions on snow shoes into the neighbouring woods, but saw remarkably few birds. Archangel contains a great number of sparrows; most of the farmyards abounded with them. Once or twice we identified a tree sparrow, but by far the greater number were the common house sparrow, many of the males being in splendid plumage. The next commonest bird was certainly the hooded crow. They were remarkably tame. In the market we sometimes saw half-a-dozen perched at the same time on the horses' backs, and we could almost kick them in the streets. They are the scavengers of Archangel. Pigeons were also common, now wild, but probably once domesticated. They look like rock-doves, a blue-grey, with darker head and shoulders, two black bars on the wing, and a white rump; but in some the latter characteristic is wanting. These pigeons are never molested, and are evidently held to be semi-sacred, like those in the Piazza di San Marco in Venice, or in the court of the Bayezidieh mosque in Stamboul. Jackdaws, ravens, and magpies were frequently seen. In the woods we found the mealy redpole, the marsh tit, an occasional bullfinch, a pair of lesser spotted woodpeckers, and a solitary hawfinch. Some white-winged crossbills and waxwings were brought alive into the town, but the peasant who had the waxwings asked eight roubles a pair, so, of course, we did not buy them. We were told that these birds were common near Archangel until towards the end of November, when they disappear as the weather becomes more severe.

During our stay in Archangel we had considerable changes in the weather. Soon after our arrival it was very cold, and on one or two occasions we noticed the thermometer as low as 27° below zero. If the weather was windy we felt the cold keenly, but at the lowest point there was not a breath of wind, and wrapped up in our furs we suffered from nothing but an attack of icicles on the moustache. Occasionally we had slight snowstorms, but brilliant sunshine was the rule, and we found the clear, dry air most invigorating. After April had set in the weather became more cloudy, and the thermometer once registered 37° in the shade. No signs of frost having been visible by the 6th, we made hot haste to be off before our winter road should break up, taking leave of our kind friends, Mr. and Mrs. Birse, with great regret. It has rarely been our lot to be received with such genuine hospitality as was shown us by this estimable gentleman and his lady.

OLD RUSSIAN SILVER CROSS.

UST-ZYLMA.

CHAPTER IV.

Bad roads—Postal service in winter and summer—Changeable weather—Scenery—Pinega and Kuloi rivers—Snow plains—The forests—Birds—Samoyedes—Mezén—Polish exile—Snow-Buntings—How caught—Jackdaws—We leave Mezén—The weather—Scenery—The Mezén river—The Pizhma—The roads—Piottuch's accident—The Via diabolica—Bolshanivagorskia—Break up of the road—Polish prejudices—The villages—Curiosity of the peasants—Greek crosses—Love of ornament—Employment and amusements—Samoyedes—Birds—Umskia—First view of the Petchora—Arrival at Ust-Zylma.

THE journey from Archangel to Ust-Zylma on the Petchora is between seven and eight hundred English miles. There are about forty stations, the distance between each being somewhat greater than that on our previous journey. Had we left Archangel a fortnight earlier, before the sun was powerful enough to soften the surface of the snow, we might have accomplished the journey in much shorter time. As it was, we took three days and three nights to reach Mezén. We stopped one day and two nights in this, the frontier town of Siberia in Europe; and the remainder of the journey occupied five days and four nights. A fortnight later the snow became impassable, the winter road was broken up, the horses at the stations in the uninhabited portions of the country, a distance of 250 versts, were sent home, and for two months the valley of the Petchora was as effectually cut off from all communication with civilised Europe as if it had been in the moon. The last 150 miles had become a series of uninhabited, impassable swamps, across which no letter, no messenger, no telegram, ever came. The postal service was suspended until the floods in the river, caused by the sudden melting of the snow, had sufficiently subsided to make it possible to row against stream. The summer route from Mezén to Ust-Zylma is up the Mezén river to its junction with the Peza, up that river to its source, across the watershed, a porterage of sixteen versts, by horses, to the source of the Zylma, and then down that river to the Petchora.

We left Archangel on a Tuesday evening, in two sledges or "pavoskas;" Harvie-Brown and I, with part of the luggage in one, drawn by three horses, and Piottuch, with the remainder of the luggage, in the other, drawn by two horses. That night and the whole of the following day were warm, the thermometer standing at 44° in the shade. In the sun it once went up to 70°. The wind was south-west, and in our inexperience we began to fear that summer would be upon us before we reached the Petchora. Our progress was slow, and at this time, including stoppages, we did not average much more than seven miles an hour. On Wednesday night we had a smart frost, and began to congratulate each other on the chance of our progress being more rapid. But we soon found that we were out of the frying-pan into the fire. The great traffic to and from the fair at Pinega had worn a deep rut for the horses' feet in the track, and one runner of our sledge would persist in running in it, which threw the sledge so much out of the level that the outrigger or projecting spar, which is necessary to prevent the sledge from being upset every five minutes, was continually ploughing into the snow which formed a bank on each side of the road. As long as the snow was soft it was of little consequence, but when the crust was hardened by an hour or two of frost, the outrigger of the sledge went "scrunch" into it with a sound almost like that of a man turning wood in a lathe, and our progress was as much impeded by this unwelcome brake as it had been by the giving way of the snow under the horses' feet. On Thursday afternoon the sun was again hot, but fortunately it froze again at night. Friday was dull all day, with a slight thaw, and we reached Mezén at 4 P.M. and found the roofs dripping.

The scenery on the route was much more varied than we had expected to find it. Most of the way we sledged through the forests, a wide space being cleared on each side of the track; but sometimes the trees came close up to the road, which was hilly and winding, and we seemed to be lost in a dense wood. Perhaps the most picturesque part of the journey was whilst we were ascending the Pinega river and descending the Kuloi, which we repeatedly enjoyed for some versts at a time. The Pinega river is very broad, with what looked like cliffs of oolite on each side, surmounted by pine forests. The Kuloi river is narrower, and there are no cliffs of any importance, the trees coming down to the edge of the ice. When we passed the Kuloi near its source, soon after leaving Pinega, the river was flowing through a strip of open country. In several places it was free from ice, and on two occasions we saw ducks swimming upon the open water. About thirty versts before reaching Mezén we crossed an immense plain of snow, as flat as a lake, extending east and west as far as the eye could reach. In almost every instance the flat plains were destitute of trees, being no doubt swamps or marshes, too wet for timber to grow in, whilst the hills were invariably covered with forests. We found that the roads were always deep in the forests. Our horses had firm footing, but the outriggers of the sledge "scrunched" unpleasantly. In the open plains the sides of the road were low, any deep tracks which might have been made being no doubt soon filled up again by the drifting snow, and we got on at a rapid pace so long as the snow did not give way under the horses' feet. The forests were principally spruce fir, and very spruce these fir-trees looked, as if they had just been combed and brushed, in striking contrast to the haggard larches, whose leafless branches were clothed with black and grey lichen like a suit of rags, and were torn and twisted by the winds into wild fantastic shapes, reminding one of a sketch by Doré. In many places birches and Scotch fir were common, and occasionally we saw a few willows. There were very few birds. The hooded crow was the commonest, principally close to the villages. Now and then we saw a jackdaw or a raven or a pair of magpies. As we proceeded farther east, sparrows became less plentiful, but we noticed both species, the house and the tree sparrow. Soon after leaving Archangel we met with a flock of snow-buntings, and they gradually became more frequent as we neared Mezén, especially on the rivers. They seemed to be slowly migrating northwards, following the course of the rivers, where there was always a chance of their finding some open water. Not far from Pinega we got out of the sledge to chase a pair of great spotted woodpeckers, and succeeded in shooting the female. We also saw a pair of Siberian jays, but, not being provided with snow shoes, we found it was no use attempting to follow the birds into the forests through the deep snow. Soon after leaving Pinega we saw a bird sitting on a cliff, and after a short chase shot it, and found it to be a common crossbill, a bird which, curiously enough, we did not meet with afterwards. A stage or two before reaching Mezén, we saw a second pair of Siberian jays, and surprised a fine male capercailzie not far from the road.

At Pinega we found a party of Samoyedes from Kanin, with about twenty sledges, and we passed a larger party about halfway to Mezén. We met with no difficulties. Once or twice, on our arrival at a station during the night, we were told that there were no horses to be had, that they were all out; but on the presentation of the "Crown

Padarozhnas," with which General Timarsheff (the Minister of the Interior at St. Petersburg) had kindly provided us, horses were forthcoming at once. We paid for five horses on one occasion when we had only four, and at Pinega the stationmaster tried to make us take six, but our obstinate refusal to do so, lest it should become a precedent in future, prevailed.

We reached Mezén on the 10th of April, and spent an interesting day in this frontier town of Siberia in Europe. The Ispravnik, to whom we had letters from the Governor of Archangel, called upon us and invited us to take tea at his house. He spoke a smattering of French, but had asked a Polish exile of the name of Bronza to meet us. Mr. Bronza spoke excellent German, and we endeavoured to get some information from him about the Samoyedes; but he was so full of his own grievances, and so utterly without interest in Russia and everything Russian, that we soon gave it up in despair. Poland is evidently the Ireland of Russia. Both the Irish and the Poles seem crazy on the subject of homerule, and in many other points show a similarity of temperament. They are both hot-blooded races, endowed with a wonderful sense of humour, and an intolerable tolerance of dirt, disorder, and bad management generally.

At Mezén we were much interested in watching a large flock of snow-buntings. Their favourite resort was the steep bank of the river, where they found abundance of food in the manure which was thrown away. In a country where there is abundance of grass in summer, and very little corn is cultivated, and where the cattle have to be stall-fed for seven or eight months out of the twelve, manure apparently possesses very little value, and hundreds of cartloads are annually deposited on the steep banks of the river, where no doubt it is washed away when the river rises with the floods caused by the sudden melting of the snow in May. The snow-buntings were also frequently seen round the hole in the ice on the river, where the inhabitants of Mezén obtained their supply of water. In both places the boys of the village had set white horsehair snares, and seemed to be very successful in their sport. At this time of the year these birds are fat and are excellent eating. We were told that in a fortnight they would be here in much greater numbers, and would be sold for a rouble the hundred, or even less. None of the birds we got were in full summer plumage, yet they looked extremely handsome as they ran along the snow like a wagtail or a dotterel, or fluttered from place to place with a somewhat scattered, butterfly kind of flight. We occasionally saw them hop, but they generally preferred to run. The most interesting fact which we observed was that the snow-bunting occasionally perches in trees. We saw two in the forest, one of which perched in a spruce fir.

We found jackdaws very numerous at Mezén, but Piottuch told us that it is only during the last four or five years that this bird has been seen in this neighbourhood. He said that it is now a resident there. Piottuch in the days of his exile lived some years at Mezén, and had a considerable circle of acquaintance there, who made merry on the occasion of his revisiting them.

We left Mezén on Sunday morning at nine, glad to get away, as Piottuch's old friends were too many for him, and far too hospitable; and he was drinking more champagne than we thought prudent. During the last four-and-twenty hours we had had violent wind and snowstorms, but the morning had cleared up, the sun shone brilliantly and it was not cold. But at night snow came on again and continued till Wednesday evening, when the weather suddenly cleared up again; and the thermometer fell from freezing-point to zero. During the three days, about four inches of snow had been added to the couple of feet already on the ground. Travelling during even a slight snowstorm is by no means so pleasant as when the sun shines on a mild day; but travelling in a sledge with the thermometer at zero is decidedly unpleasant, even with brilliant sunshine and no wind. If you expose your face to the air your nose is in danger, then the icicles that form continually upon your moustache are anything but comfortable; and the condensation of your breath upon your neck wrappings is always irritating; and if you subside altogether into your furs the sense of semi-suffocation is almost as bad. On the whole, however, we did not suffer so much from the cold as we expected.

The scenery on this journey was more varied than any we had previously met with. We alternated between forest, river, and open plain. The Mezén is a fine river, half a mile or more wide, with steep banks of what looked like red chalk about a hundred feet high, clothed with forest to the edge, which is continually crumbling away and letting the pine-trees slip into the water. At intervals, and often with remarkable regularity, the cliffs were cut away down to the water's edge, probably by small temporary rivulets born of the melting snow. The Pizhma is a much smaller river, not half the size of the Mezén, and without rocky cliffs on the banks. There are two Pizhmas, both of which we travelled on. Both rise in the lake of Jam, the Petchorski Pizhma flowing north-east into the Zylma just before that river enters the Petchora, and the Mezénski Pizhma flowing south-west into the Mezén. On the rivers the roads were always good, except in one part of the Mezénski Pizhma where the river is very narrow and the current was very strong. In one place we almost shuddered to see open water rushing along within nine feet of the sledge. Not long afterwards we stuck fast, and had to get out of the sledge on the snow in the middle of the river. It was nearly midnight and very cloudy. Piottuch with his lighter sledge had got safely over the dangerous part and stood grinning at us, as the yemschiks hacked the frozen snow off the runners of our sledge with their axes; and having added his two horses to our team, placed two little fir-trees across the path and flogged the horses until they dragged the machine through the snow and water on to firm ground. We had our revenge, however, shortly afterwards. A few stations farther on Piottuch's sledge came to grief, one of the runners breaking completely in two in the front. He was some distance in advance of our sledge, and when we overtook him at the station he came to us with a very long face to tell us of the "*très mal chose.*" We soon set him upon his legs again. We bought a peasant's sledge for a rouble and a half, took off the sides, and removing the runners from the broken sledge lashed the two together with a strong cord. Piottuch started in high glee again, assuring us that his sledge was "*beaucoup plus bon*" than ours. The effect of the alteration was, however, to raise the level of his outriggers a few inches, which made all the difference between safety and danger. He was soon fast asleep as usual, for he had not yet quite slept off his Mezén champagne, when his sledge gave a greater lurch than it was wont to do and capsized, waking him with a shower of portmanteaus about his ears; and he was dragged out of the deep snow by the yemschik amidst roars of laughter on our part.

As before, we found the roads in the open plain always good. These plains were a dead flat, with a tree or two here and there. The rut worn by the horses' feet was not deep, and the path was almost level with the side. We glided along smoothly and luxuriously. The roads in the forest were bad beyond all conception. The banks were high, and were always in the way of the outriggers, which "scrunched" against them with a most irritating sound. Both laterally and vertically they were as winding as a snake. Sometimes our sledge would be on the top of a steep hill, our first horse in the valley, and our third horse on the top of the next hill. The motion was like that of a boat in a chopping sea, and the sledge banged about from pillar to post to such an extent that we scarcely felt the want of exercise. The Russian forest road is not a *via mala*, it is a *via diabolica*.

At Bolshanivagorskia upon entering the station-house we found the room occupied by a party, and the samovar in full operation. Fancying that some of the party looked English, I inquired if any of them spoke German, and the least Russian-looking gentleman among them replied that he did. I informed him that we were Englishmen, travelling from London to the Petchora, and I added that we were glad to find some one on the route with whom we could converse. I then asked him if he and his party were also travelling. He replied that they were stationed there for some time. I then asked if his name was Rosenthal. He said it was, and a hearty laugh followed at the success of my guess. We enjoyed his astonishment for some time, and then explained that we had been told by the Ispravnik at Mezén that there was only one man in the district who could speak German, the forest engineer, Herr Rosenthal. We spent an hour pleasantly together. Like every one we met who had not been to the Petchora, he exaggerated the dangers and difficulties of the journey. He was engaged in measuring the timber felled on Rusanoff's concession on behalf of the Russian Government, who receive so much per tree according to the quantity of available wood in it.

On the other hand, it is possible that we may have underestimated the dangers and difficulties of our journey, seeing we had the good luck to pull through them so well. The roads were certainly giving way, and it may have been a happy accident in our favour that the weather changed again when it did. On one occasion the crust of snow not being firm enough to support the horses, they all three suddenly sank up to their bellies. Of course they were utterly helpless. We feared for a moment that our journey had suddenly come to an end, and that we had hopelessly stuck fast. We alighted from the sledge which had not sunk in the snow. The two yemschiks set to work in good earnest, and we doffed our malitzas and followed suit. The horses were unharnessed, and we soon succeeded in making them struggle out on to firm ground. We had no difficulty in pushing the sledge after them, and were soon ready to start again. All this time Piottuch stood calmly by, never offering for a moment to render us the smallest assistance. The Russians we always found equal to any emergency, and ready to lend a helping hand on such occasions as an Englishman would. The Poles, on the contrary, seem to be a helpless, shiftless race of people, with a contemptible prejudice against manual labour. A similar accident did not happen again. We had many a stumble, but no irretrievable fall. Our horses were sure-footed and wonderfully plucky, and we seldom had a really bad animal. We started with five horses for the two sledges, which we reduced to four the latter half of the journey, and on one or more occasions we accomplished a stage satisfactorily with only three. The country is very thinly populated. After leaving Mezén the villages were small, and during the last 150 miles there were no villages at all, only a single station-house, where a change of horses could be obtained, and which would shortly be deserted altogether for the summer months. As we were the first Englishmen who had travelled on this road during the lifetime of any of the villagers, our appearance naturally excited great curiosity, and when we stopped at a station in the village to change horses, a crowd quickly gathered round the sledges. We found the peasants very inquisitive, asking the

English names of various articles. They were extremely
good-natured, enjoyed a broad joke, laughed heartily at our
pigeon-Russ, and were, so far as we could judge, perfectly
honest. We left our sledges with all our luggage, wraps,
&c., unprotected, sometimes for an hour, at the station where
we stopped for a meal, and on no occasion had anything been
stolen. In the villages on this part of the journey we noticed
a number of crosses, generally one or two at the entrance,
and one near the centre of the village. They were made of
wood, and were about ten feet high, the ordinary Greek
double cross, with an oblique foot-bar, and most of them were
protected by a wooden roof to keep off the snow. Both the
roof and the cross itself were, as a rule, elaborately carved,
and the whole face of the cross was covered with inscriptions
(no doubt Slavonic) in about three-inch letters. Sometimes
in the poorer villages the crosses were not carved, and the
inscription and ornamentation were simply painted upon the
wood, generally in various colours. The Russian peasantry
in Siberia in Europe seem to be fond of ornamentation.
The majority of the houses are built with the gable end
to the street, and in the centre of the gable is a window,
opening on to a balcony. This balcony, the framework of
the windows, the ends of the rain-gutters, and the ends of the
ridge of the roof, were often elaborately carved and fretted,
and sometimes painted in gay colours. In nearly all the
villages we noticed a conspicuous arrangement of railings for
the drying of flax, hay, or corn. In the station-houses we
found the men, and sometimes the women, engaged in spin-
ning flax, making nets, or weaving coarse linen. In the

station, however, where there was no village, a draught-board of very rude construction evidently served to while away the long winter evenings. Several times during the journey we saw Samoyedes, or Syriani, sledging along with their reindeer, and in many places the snow was ploughed up some distance from the road, showing that the reindeer had been seeking for food. As we neared Ust-Zylma we passed several of the chooms, or reindeer-skin tents, of these curious people by the roadside. During the greater part of the journey few birds were to be seen. In the villages magpies were the commonest birds, and occasionally we saw a few pigeons, hooded crows, and tree-sparrows. On the banks of the river flocks of snow-buntings were common. In the forests we saw a few capercailzie.

At Umskia, where we were fortunately detained six hours for want of horses, there was an abundant supply of birds. This station is a solitary house on the banks of the Petchorski Pizhma, about fifty-four versts from Ust-Zylma. The great attraction for birds in this place was doubtless the hole in the ice of the river, which had to be kept open to supply the station with water, and the dung which the horses dropped during the few hours they fed and rested outside the station. We shot five Siberian jays,* and had

---

* The Siberian jay (*Perisoreus infaustus*, Linn.) has not been met with in the British Islands. It is a resident bird even in the coldest districts which it inhabits, extending across the eastern hemisphere from the Arctic circle in Scandinavia, as far south as latitude 50°. Eastwards it ranges as far as Kamtchatka, and in the valley of the Yenesay extends southwards to latitude 50°. In the valley of the Petchora we did not observe it farther north than latitude 65°. After the autumn moult these birds seem to be half feathers; light fluffy feathers only one remove from down, which must render them capable of resisting any amount of cold.

some opportunity of watching their habits. They were not at all shy, and were fond of perching upon or clinging to the trunks of the pines, and sometimes we saw them run up the stems like a woodpecker. The song was by no means unmusical, a low warble like that of the starling, but not so harsh. These birds are early breeders, and the song is probably discontinued soon after incubation has begun, as we did not hear it afterwards, though we frequently came across the birds. Out of the five birds which we shot only one proved to be a female, with the ovary very small. There were a few snow-buntings always to be seen, but we did not think it worth while wasting powder and shot upon them, as we had selected a score of handsome birds out of a lot brought to one of the stations by a peasant who had snared them. We could have bought almost any quantity alive or dead at ten kopecks the score. I shot one by accident as it was feeding under a larch-tree in company with a Siberian jay, a couple of bullfinches, and half-a-dozen other snow-buntings, and a few redpoles. Harvie-Brown shot another as it sat perched upon the branch of a larch, in order to be able to produce the skin of a bird shot perching, as the fact that they do ever perch in trees has been disputed. We had abundant opportunity of seeing these birds in trees. We saw as many as three or four in one tree at the same time, and frequently observed them fly from one tree to another. We saw plenty of bullfinches,* and shot five males in brilliant plumage. They

---

* The Northern bullfinch (*Pyrrhula rubicila*, Pallas) differs from the common bullfinch in being somewhat larger, in having a stouter bill, and in having the red of the under parts more scarlet in colour. It is not known to

were all in pairs. We fancied that the call note of these bullfinches differed from that of our bird. Speaking from memory it seemed to us to be louder and harsher, by no means so plaintive, and not badly represented by the word 'kak.'

After leaving Umskia we looked anxiously out for the first glimpse of the distant Petchora, and it was not long before we crossed a low range of hills, from the ridge of which we had a view of the mighty river. As we sledged down the Zylma, and finally reached its junction with the Petchora, the vastness of this river impressed us beyond all our expectations. We were 300 miles from its mouth, and to our left the huge flood stretched away in a broad white stream as far as the eye could reach, and fifteen times as wide as the Thames at Hammersmith Bridge. On the opposite bank, a mile and a half off, we could discern the churches and houses of Ust-Zylma, round which the river swept to our right. Piottuch had arrived at the town some hours before us, and we found comfortable apartments in the house of a Russian peasant, of the name of Boulegan, where we were visited by M. Znaminski, the Preestäff of Ust-Zylma, and drank a toast (the success of our visit to the Petchora) in a bottle of excellent Crimean champagne. The total course of the mighty river covers nearly one thousand miles,

---

occurred in the British Islands. It breeds in the south Arctic and north temperate regions of Europe and Asia, from Scandinavia eastwards as far as the watershed of the Yenesay and the Lena, beyond which it is represented by a somewhat nearly allied species, *P. griseiventris* (Lafr.). It winters in South Europe and South Siberia. In the valley of the Petchora we did not see it farther north than latitude 65½°.

It rises in the Urals, north of the government of Perm, not far from the important town of Tcherdeen', which lies upon the watershed of the Petchora and the Kah'ma. It drains nearly the whole of the north-western slope of the Ural Mountains, and flows almost due north, till its junction with the Ussa; here the river is a mile wide, and the Ussa is the larger stream of the two. The Petchora at this point makes a bend west; but after receiving the waters of the Zylma, it resumes its northward course, till it falls into the Arctic Ocean by a number of mouths opposite the islands of Nova Zembla.

OLD RUSSIAN SILVER CROSS.

ANCIENT CHURCH OF THE OLD BELIEVERS.

CHAPTER V.

Ust-Zylma—Its streets—Its houses—Its manure—Its population—Its farms—Its churches—Our quarters—The banks of the river—The Old Believers—Their superstition—Their crosses—Hospitality of the officials—Shooting-parties—Captain Arendt and Captain Engel—Snow shoes—Scarcity of birds—The snow-bunting—Mealy redpole—Winter.

Ust-Zylma* is a long, straggling village, lying on the narrow strip of flat land, on the north and east bank of the Petchora, where that river makes a sudden bend from west

---

* In 'Purchas his Pilgrimes,' the narrative of the voyage of Josias Logan, who wintered in the valley of the Petchora in 1611, contains the following description of this town : " Ust-Zylma is a village of some thirtie or fortie houses, and standeth in the height of 66° and 30 minutes. They have corne growing there, both barley and rye, and their barley is passing faire and white almost as rice."

to north, about 300 miles from its mouth. Each homestead is a farmhouse with outbuildings, including almost always a bath-house. They are irregularly scattered over the ground, sometimes at considerable distances apart, and sometimes in clusters. There is a principal road, which meanders through the village for perhaps two miles, with numerous side branches, which one might by courtesy call the main street; but its general appearance is as if the houses had been strewed about at random, and each peasant had been left to make a road to his nearest neighbour as best he could. Towards the centre of the village there is here and there a wooden causeway, like those in Archangel. We found the wooden *trottoir* all but indispensable when the thaw set in. When we reached Ust-Zylma the streets were covered with a thick layer of frozen manure. The yards round the houses were in a still worse condition, and when the sun was hot it was difficult to walk dryshod in consequence of the pools of liquid manure, which filled every depression in the ground, and no doubt very frequently soaked into the wells. This manure makes Ust-Zylma one vast dunghill, and would probably produce much disease, were it not for the fact that it is frozen for nearly seven months out of the twelve, and is in most years carried away soon after it thaws by the floods of the Petchora, which generally overflows its banks, when the snow melts all at once with the sudden arrival of summer. It not unfrequently happens at this season of the year that half the village is under water, and the peasants have to boat from house to house. All the houses are built with this contingency in view. The bottom story is generally low, and consists of a suite of lumber rooms, where the cattle are often housed in winter. The dwelling rooms are on the second story, generally reached by a covered flight of stairs outside the house, reaching from a porch below to a gallery, which leads round the house. Upon this porch, staircase, and gallery a good deal of skill in wood carving is often expended. The winter is long, and the length of time during which the cattle are stall-fed so great, and the amount of land available for cultivation so small, that there is always a large surplus of manure, which the peasants do not think worth the cost of preservation. The cattle are fed principally upon hay, which is cut upon the low lands on the other side of the Petchora. These lands are flooded every spring, and any manure placed upon them would speedily be washed off; nor is it needed, as the river itself is the great fertiliser in these low-lying districts, exactly as the Nile is in Egypt. Of course, to accumulate so much manure in the streets, the traffic must be large. Long strings of sledges were often to be seen drawing hay, pine logs for building, and smaller timber for firewood. In the summer nearly every peasant turns fisherman, and catches salmon and other fish in the Petchora with a seine net. Neither farming nor fishing seems to be very profitable. It is very easy to get a living, but there is no market for surplus produce. Beef fetches only 1½d. per lb. retail. Most articles that are worth the cartage, such as furs, feathers, down, frozen meat, tar, &c., go to Pinega fair, and some are even sent as far as Nishni Novgorod; but the cost of transit absorbs the profit. Now and then you meet with a merchant who has accumulated a handsome fortune; but the peasants are on the whole poor, and will doubtless remain so until railway communication with Moscow is opened, or steamers run regularly from the mouth of the Petchora, either of which projects seems at present to be hopelessly impossible. The population of Ust-Zylma does not probably exceed 1500 or 2000, increased in winter by Samoyedes, who erect their chooms in the neighbouring forest. When we reached Ust-Zylma, and for a week or more afterwards, a great migration of these curious people was going on, and we often saw a score or more of their sledges in a day, and sometimes there would be as many reindeer as horses to be seen in the streets.

The flat country on the banks of the Petchora, upon which the village is built, does not extend more than a few hundred yards. The land then rapidly rises, and these slopes are cultivated for some way up the hillside. We found the peasants busily employed in carting manure in sledges, and spreading it on the snow. The monotony of the long village is broken by three churches, one a very ancient and picturesque structure, in some places rather artistically ornamented. This was formerly the church of the Old Believers, but it is now too rotten for use, and a more modern-looking building has been erected. The third church is that of the Orthodox Greek Church. All the houses in Ust-Zylma are of course built of wood, solid balks of timber with moss and tar in the joints, and notched into each other at the corner, and more or less carved and ornamented in various places. Sometimes the slopes of the hills are relieved by a large tree which has been left standing, and here and there is an old windmill. Beyond the cultivated ground is the forest clothing the hilly country stretching away north, the trees gradually dwindling in size as far as the Arctic circle, beyond which lies the mysterious "tundra."

Our quarters in Ust-Zylma were two excellent rooms on the second floor of the best house in the village, for which we paid two roubles a month. No doubt we could have had them for half the money if we had taken them for six months. The house was built by M. Sideroff, the founder of the Petchora Timber-trading Company, and was afterwards sold to M. Boulegan. Our windows looked out across the street on to the Petchora, which we calculated from two rough trigonometrical observations to be a mile and a half wide. At Ust-Ussa, 200 miles higher up the great river, its width is said to be nearly a mile. A little beyond the limits of the village at each end, the flat land on the bank of the river ceases, and the forest comes up to the edge of a cliff of sand, earth, and pebbles, varying from 50 to 100 feet high. This bank drops nearly perpendicularly on to the mud and pebbles on the edge of the river. In some places the pebbly strand was bare of snow, and we noticed pieces of granite, ironstone, and limestone. Some of the latter was full of fossil shells, and we found many pieces that looked like madrepore and fossil coral. Soon after the high steep bank of the river begins, the grand sweep which the Petchora makes round the village ends, and the river stretches away north-east for miles. The view from the top of the bank looking up the wide white river, is very fine. The high banks, too steep in most places for the snow to rest upon, and the dark pines on the top, form a striking contrast to the pure white snow on the ice below, down which for many versts may be seen the long winding line of diminutive fir-trees, marking the road, upon which the sledges of the travelling peasants look like black spots in the distance. It would, perhaps, be a very difficult subject to make a fine picture of, the effect on the eye being one of simple vastness, causing one continually to exclaim, " What a great river! What a big country!"

Most of the peasants of Ust-Zylma and the villages near are Old Believers, people who retain a very curious form of Christian superstition, closely allied to the Greek Church. Castrén calls them the " Raskolnicken" of Ust-Zylma. They have not a good reputation amongst the Germans, who have to hire labour for the timber trade on the Petchora. They are represented as crafty and faithless, and as few of them are employed as possible. Their chief characteristic appears to be that they make the sign of the cross with the thumb touching the second and third, instead of the fourth and fifth fingers, as is the fashion of the Orthodox Church. They have a curious prejudice against tobacco, and will not smoke it themselves nor, if they can help it, allow other persons to smoke in their houses. They seem to have Jewish superstitions against pork and hare, neither will they use any plate, glass, or other article from which persons not of their religion have eaten or drunk. If you offer them vodka in your own glass they will refuse it if they be strict Old Believers, but we must do them the justice to say that under circumstances of this kind many we met were superior to their superstitions.

But the most extraordinary feature of their religion is that it forbids the use of potatoes as food. They are said not to be very diligent in their attendance at church nor to be very much under the control of their priests, holding the doctrine that every man should be a priest in his own house, and should conduct divine worship there. Our host was very exemplary in this respect when he was sober, having an excellent religious library, and we often heard him and his family chanting Slavonic prayers. One of his books was a Slavonic MS., dating about 1740, and profusely illustrated with full-page coloured drawings, very carefully executed, although somewhat stiff. It appeared to be the history of some of the saints of the Greek Church. I tried very hard to buy this book, but nothing would induce M. Boulegan to part with it. In a corner of every Russian room is a sacred picture or "eekon," before which every one on entering the room bows and crosses himself several times before speaking to the host. Some of these pictures are very old, being handed down from generation to generation, and sometimes there is quite a collection of these "eekona," varied with brass and enamel triptychs of various ages and merit. Every peasant wears a silver or bronze cross. Some of these are of exquisitely delicate workmanship, frequently ornamented with enamel, and occasionally set with jewels. On the back of many of these crosses are elaborate Slavonic inscriptions. A wonderful fertility of resource is found in the designs of these crosses, which are always chaste and artistic, never florid in the ornamentation or wanting in harmony of parts. The great centre of all this religious art is, we were informed, the monastery of Onega, on the south shore of the White Sea.

A peculiarity which we were told marked the Old Believers of Ust-Zylma is a habit which the women have of uttering cries, not loud but frequently repeated. This habit or disease is called "equarter," and is brought on immediately by the smell of tobacco smoke. Whether the cry is voluntary, and is intended as a mark of disapproval, or as an exorcism against evil influences, or whether it be a form of hysteria allied to St. Vitus's dance, we were not able to ascertain.

The officials at Ust-Zylma received us with the greatest hospitality. In addition to the letters with which the Governor of Archangel had provided us, it so happened that Piottuch was an old friend of M. Znaminski, the Preestaff, or highest military officer. He had made his acquaintance some years ago, in the days of his exile in Mezén, and both being fond of a day's sport, they had fraternised as sportsmen ought to do. M. Sakeroff, the postmaster, was the other "swell chasseur" of Ust-Zylma, and these gentlemen were kind enough to plan several shooting-parties for our benefit. M. Znaminski was a stout handsome man, very dignified in his manners, but active in the field, and we were under very great obligations to him for his uniform kindness and hospitality to us. Another official who, as well as his charming wife, was most hospitable to us was the Public Prosecutor, M. Miranoff, the "Schlüdevatel" as Captain Engel always called him. We were also most kindly entertained by the "Maravoi," who appeared to be a gentleman of considerable education. Unfortunately none of these gentlemen spoke either

English, French, or German, so that our communication with them was necessarily very limited. Interpreting was certainly not Piottuch's forte. Any information we got through him was so largely mixed with his own ideas and opinions, that we soon ceased to attach much value to it, besides which his bad French was often as difficult to understand as the original Russ.

We got a great deal of information respecting the country and its inhabitants from two gentlemen in the employ of the Petchora Timber-trading Company, Captain Arendt, the manager or "Provalychik" in the Petchora, residing *pro tem.* at Ust-Zylma, and Captain Engel, the commander of the steamer belonging to the company, which was then lying in winter quarters at Habariki, about twenty-seven miles down the river. These gentlemen called upon us the day after our arrival, and we were indebted to both of them for innumerable acts of kindness.

One of our first purchases on our arrival at Ust-Zylma was a couple of pairs of snow-shoes, without which it is impossible to travel on the snow. No one can form the slightest idea how utterly helpless one is without snow-shoes when there is scarcely three feet of snow on the ground. To travel a mile would probably be a hard day's work, completely knocking one up. On snow-shoes we got along comfortably, at the rate of three miles an hour, and we soon became tolerably at home on them. They were about seven feet long and six inches wide, made of birch wood, and covered underneath with reindeer skin, with the hair pointing behind. This is absolutely necessary to enable one to ascend a hill, the hair preventing effectually any sliding backwards. The great difficulty with which we had to contend at first was to avoid treading on our own toes, but with a little practice we learnt to keep our shoes parallel. In going down hill we had to be careful lest our speed should increase to the point where we lost the control of our centres of gravity.

Every day we sallied out with our guns and snow-shoes in search of birds, but during the first week or so it was somewhat monotonous work, and we soon began to tire of winter. There were very few birds to be seen. In the village the hooded crow,* the magpie, and the tree-sparrow were common, and now and then we saw a raven. We took it for granted that these birds had been at Ust-Zylma all the winter. The peasants brought us frequently capercailzie and hazel grouse, which they shot with their rifles and offered us at twenty kopecks (about sevenpence) each for the capercailzie, and the same sum per brace for the hazel grouse. These birds are probably all residents, though Father Inokentia told us that the hooded crow was a migratory bird at Pustorzersk, arriving there about the 10th of May.

---

* The hooded crow (*Corvus cornix*, Linn.) breeds in Scotland, and is a winter visitant to England. The whole of Eastern Europe, including Denmark, Scandinavia, and Russia, and the whole of Western Siberia, including North Turkestan, eastwards as far as the watershed between the Obb and the Yenesay, may be described as a vast colony of hooded crows, with a few outlying settlements in Scotland, Italy, Greece, Palestine and Egypt. In other parts of Europe and North Africa it appears only as a winter visitant from the extreme north. Wherever the breeding range of this species adjoins that of the carrion crow, as, for instance, in Scotland, the valley of the Elbe, Turkestan, and the valley of the Yenesay, the two species appear freely to interbreed. In the valley of the Petchora we found it to be a resident in latitude 65½°, and a summer visitor in latitudes 67° and 68°.

The commonest bird at this season of the year in the streets of Ust-Zylma is undoubtedly the snow-bunting.* We were told that they arrived about the 1st of April. In spite of its abundance we could not help looking upon it with all the interest attaching to a rare bird. The brilliant contrast of the black and white on the plumage of these birds, then rapidly assuming their summer dress, was especially beautiful during flight. The flight itself is peculiar, somewhat like that of a butterfly, as if it altered its mind every few seconds, as to which direction it would take. It can scarcely be called an undulating flight. The bird certainly does rest its wings every few seconds, but either they are expanded when at rest, or they are rested for so short a time, that the plane of flight is not sufficiently altered to warrant its being called undulatory. The snow-buntings in Ust-Zylma were principally in flocks, but now and then we saw a couple of birds together which seemed to have paired, and occasionally, when the sun was hotter than usual, a solitary snow-bunting might be seen perched upon a rail attempting to sing, but we never heard them sing on the wing. Unfor-

---

* The snow-bunting (*Plectrophanes nivalis*, Linn.) is a circumpolar bird, breeding principally on the tundras of the Arctic regions beyond the limit of forest growth. It has been known to breed in Scotland, but is principally met with in the British Islands during hard winters. The snow-bunting is one of those irregular migrants which are driven southwards in severe seasons in larger or smaller flocks to Central Europe, South Siberia, North China, Japan, and the northern states of America. In the valley of the Petchora we did not find them breeding until we reached latitude 68½°. These birds seem to lead a roving gipsy life during winter, perpetually trying to migrate northwards with every appearance of milder weather, and perpetually driven southwards with each recurring frost.

tunately we did not get far enough north to meet with these birds at their breeding stations. In 1874, when Collett and I were in Norway, we found the snow-bunting breeding on the island of Vadso in the Varanger Fjord. We were too late for eggs, as this bird is a very early breeder, and the young were already in the nest by the middle of June; but we had many opportunities of watching the male birds. They would fling themselves up into the air almost like a shuttlecock, singing all the time a low and melodious warble, not unlike that of a shore-lark, or perhaps still more like that of the Lapland bunting, and they would immediately descend in a spiral curve with wings and tails expanded, and finish their song on a rock. Although we only once or twice heard the snow-buntings attempting to sing in Ust-Zylma, they were by no means silent birds, and were continually calling to each other. The call-note is a *zh*, not unlike that of the brambling or greenfinch. The alarm-note is a loud *tweek*. As they fly together in flocks they merely twitter to each other, not unlike purple sandpipers on the seashore.

Flocks of redpoles * were also common, but consisting of

---

* The mealy redpole (*Linota linaria*, Linn.) is a circumpolar bird breeding at or near the limit of forest growth, and visiting the British Islands somewhat irregularly in winter, being represented with us by a very nearly allied species, *Linota rufescens* (Vieill.), differing from the more northern form in being somewhat more rufous in the general colour of the upper parts. A nearly allied form, which is said to be still greyer in colour than the mealy redpole and of somewhat larger size, is found in Greenland, and has been named *L. hornemanni* (Holb.). Some writers make a fourth species, *L. exilipes* (Coues), which may be said to be intermediate between the Arctic and the Greenland forms. In the valley of the Petchora we found both *L. linaria* (Linn.) and *L. exilipes* (Coues), and came to the conclusion that the latter is nothing but the fully adult winter plumage of the

much smaller numbers than those of the snow-bunting. Many of the males were beginning to assume the carmine breast, showing great promise of beauty when the full summer plumage should be attained. We were informed that these birds arrived about the same time as the snow-bunting. On the outskirts of the town we met with a few small parties of yellow-hammers,* and occasionally heard their familiar song. These birds are probably also migratory. They were comparatively rare, and as we never saw any farther north, we may assume Ust-Zylma to be about the extreme limit of their summer range. The forests were remarkably silent. Often there was not a bird to be seen for miles. Once or twice we had a distant glimpse of a Siberian jay, a marsh tit, or a bullfinch, but we did not succeed in obtaining a shot. On the whole our first week in Ust-Zylma was not very encouraging from an ornithological point of view. After eight days' work our list of identified birds in the valley of the Petchora stood as follows:—

---

former. In winter this species is found at different times throughout the whole of Central and Southern Europe, occasionally straying across the Mediterranean. Eastwards it wanders as far as Turkestan, Southern Siberia, North China and Japan. On the American continent it winters in South Canada and the northern States. We did not observe this species in the valley of the Petchora further north than latitude 65°.

* The yellow-hammer (*Emberiza citrinella*, Linn.) is a common resident in the British Islands, as in most parts of Central Europe. Northwards it is a summer migrant, and in South Europe and North Africa it is principally secured in winter. The records of its occurrence east of the valley of the Obb appear to be unreliable. In the valley of the Petchora we did not observe it north of latitude $65\frac{1}{2}°$.

1. Hooded crow.
2. Raven.*
3. Magpie.
4. Tree-sparrow.
5. Snow-bunting.
6. Mealy redpole.
7. Yellow-hammer.
8. Capercailzie.
9. Hazel grouse.

—certainly a very meagre list. Notwithstanding such a bad beginning, we did not feel disheartened, but laid all the blame on the weather. We could not help smiling at our alarm in Archangel lest summer should come before we could reach the Petchora. Nearly three weeks had gone by, and summer and the summer birds seemed as far off as ever. The thaw made no progress. Sometimes it was hot enough in the sun in the daytime, and the glare of the sunshine on the white snow forced us to wear snow spectacles, but it always froze again at night, and if a few days' sunshine made any impression on the snow, a raw cold day, with a high wind and a more or less heavy fall of snow, made everything look and feel as winterly as before. Piottuch went over to Ishma with M. Znaminski, but did not shoot a bird. He told us that he saw two birds of prey, most likely hen harriers, and M. Znaminski informed us that we must not despair, as a swan had been seen flying over.

---

* The raven (*Corvus corax*, Linn.) is a circumpolar bird rapidly becoming extinct in England, though still breeding in some numbers in Scotland. It is a resident species throughout Europe, but is not found in Africa. Eastwards it extends throughout Asia from the Himalayas northwards, being replaced in China and Japan by a nearly allied species, *Corvus japonensis* (Bonap.). It appears to range throughout the continent of America as far south as North Mexico. In the valley of the Petchora we found it as far north as latitude 68°.

CHOOMS OF THE SAMOYEDES.

CHAPTER VI.

The Samoyedes—Reindeer—The Tundra—Nomad life—Diseases of reindeer—Samoyede national character—Trip to Umskia—Bad roads—Birds—Easter Eve—Drunkenness—Snow—Our first bird's-nest—L'autre côte—Birds.

DURING this comparatively idle time we picked up what information we could about the Samoyedes. Captain Engel, who was a wild harum-scarum devil-may-care fellow, and had been in most parts of the world, had seen a good deal of the Samoyedes. Some years ago he was wrecked in the lagoon of the Petchora, not far from the island of Varandai, had been hospitably received by these wandering people, had made his way across country to Kuya, and had remained in the district ever since. The information which we obtained from Captains Arendt and Engel may be summed up as follows:—

The Samoyedes* are a Mongolian race of people of nomad habits. They live almost entirely upon reindeer. In summer they live in tents made of birch bark; in winter their tents or chooms are made of reindeer skins. They eat the flesh of the reindeer, and drink its blood. Their dress is made of its skins, neatly sewn together with reindeer sinews. The wealth of a Samoyede consists entirely in the number of his reindeer; each knows his own by marks cut upon the animal's ear. In summer the Samoyedes live on the tundras. Some go to the Kanin peninsula, some to the Timanski Tundra or Malyazemlia, and others to the northern shores of the Great Tundra, the Bolshaizemlia of the Russians, the Arkya-ya of the Samoyedes. These tundras are naked tracts of slightly undulating land, rolling prairies of moor, swamp and bog, full of lakes and abounding with reindeer moss, upon which the reindeer feed. In summer the tundras are quite impassable for horses, but the reindeer, with their broad feet, will carry a sledge over places where it would be impossible for a man to stand. The Samoyedes are always on the tramp, seldom remaining long in one place. A considerable portion of their lives is spent in packing, unpacking and travelling. In winter the cold is too great for the reindeer to find food under the frozen snow of the Arctic latitudes, and in summer the poor animals would

---

* Pronounced Sam'-o-yade.

be driven frantic by the mosquitoes which swarm in the more southerly regions. In summer the Samoyedes occupy their spare time in shooting ducks and geese, making their clothes, reindeer harness, &c., and in winter they come down to the towns and villages—Kuya, Pustozersk, Ust-Zylma, Mezén, Pinega, &c., and barter their surplus reindeer, skins, horns, feathers, &c., with the Russian merchants for bread, vodka and other articles. Those that come down to the more southerly towns have learnt the value of money, and prefer to sell rather than barter. They used to be very clever with the bow and arrow, but now they all use old-fashioned small-bore flint-lock rifles. Some of the Samoyedes are very rich. A reindeer is worth about seven or eight roubles, or an English sovereign. Some of the Samoyedes are said to possess as many as 10,000 reindeer. Of late years the reindeer have suffered much from disease. Captain Engel was of opinion that this disease was allied to cholera. The animals turn dizzy, and run round and round like sheep attacked by "sturdy." The reindeer also suffer much from a hideous parasite. One day as we were passing a herd of them in the streets of Ust-Zylma, Engel took hold of one of the animals, and groping among the long hair on the small of the back, he presently squeezed out of the flesh one of these disgusting creatures. In a short time he produced a dozen of them. They varied in size from half an inch to an inch in length, the diameter being from half to a third of the length. The surface was covered with rudimentary scales. The lower part of the body was tapered, and the head rounded with two indistinct jaws. We did not notice even the rudiments of legs. They are no doubt the larvæ of some fly or beetle. Engel told us that they sometimes reached a length of four inches or more. Some herds of reindeer are perfectly free from these creatures, and others suffer very much from them.

The Samoyedes are acute and intelligent people, but on the whole they are not so sharp-witted as the Russians. They are good-natured and harmless, except when they are drunk, then they become quarrelsome and dangerous. They are passionately fond of vodka, a mild, and to us by no means palatable spirit, distilled from barley, and they easily become intoxicated. In some places they distil an intoxicating drink from mushrooms. If a drunken Samoyede quarrels, and calls for help, the other Samoyedes will at once help him. Engel's recipe for dealing with a dangerously drunken Samoyede is to supply him with more drink, when he speedily becomes maudlin and begins to sing. The Samoyede women are generally betrothed very young, about thirteen, and often have children at fourteen. Some Samoyedes have more than one wife, but this is very rare. The race is no doubt slowly dying out, and is to some extent becoming mixed. They are acquainted with the stars, and use them as a compass; but Engel told us of a very curious circumstance which came under his observation when he was brought across the tundra in the sledges of the Samoyedes. In stormy weather, when it was impossible to determine the direction, the Samoyede used to scrape away the snow down to the moss, which he examined, and altered his course accordingly. The Samoyedes do not live to be very old, but greyhaired old men and women are seen among them.

After we had been a week at Ust-Zylma without seeing any sign of summer or summer birds, we began to find time hang heavy on our hands. Picking up information about the Samoyedes and the Old Believers was such unsatisfactory work, from the contradictory nature of the reports, that we soon got tired of it, and longed for something better to do than shooting redpoles and snow-buntings. As we had not met with any Siberian jays or bullfinches at Ust-Zylma, we decided that the best way to while away the time was to go back again to Umskia for a day or two, in the hope of finding as many birds as we saw there before. We took the small sledge and a couple of horses, and travelled all the Friday night. The journey was a very eventful one. The sledge, it may be remembered, had turned over once with Piottuch, but he had travelled at least a hundred miles in safety afterwards, and we had almost forgotten the circumstance. We soon found out, however, that something was radically wrong with the crazy machine. It must have dropped its centre of gravity altogether on the *via diabolica*, for between Ust-Zylma and Umskia (a distance of thirty-six miles) we were upset and tumbled over into the snow no less than fifteen times. This was altogether a new experience for us, but we survived it without any damage, thanks to the thickness of our malitzas and the depth of the snow.

Arrived at Umskia we were disappointed to see so few birds. The Siberian jays had disappeared altogether. The snow-buntings were represented by a solitary individual perched upon the summit of a lofty larch. Occasionally two or three redpoles were to be seen, and at long intervals during the day a pair of bullfinches put in an appearance. We saw a pair of white-tailed eagles* soaring over the forest, but they never came within gun-shot. The day was cold, with only occasional gleams of sunshine and continual threatenings of snow, and no birds seemed to be feeding. We took a long walk on the road, and made several excursions into the forest and down the river on snow-shoes, but scarcely a bird was to be seen. At this season of the year it would seem that the most absolute silence reigns in these drear Siberian forests. In the afternoon we tightened up our "pavoska," and so far succeeded in restoring the centre of gravity that we returned home without a spill. We saw only two birds either in going or returning, a Siberian jay in going, and a capercailzie † in returning.

---

* The white-tailed eagle (*Haliaëtos albicilla*, Linn.) appears to be confined to the eastern hemisphere and Greenland, and is still occasionally found in the British Islands. It breeds in suitable localities throughout Europe and North Africa. Eastward it breeds throughout Siberia, and is occasionally met with in India and China. We frequently saw eagles both at Ust-Zylma and on our journey down the river. On the tundra we occasionally saw them as far north as we went. At Habariki we saw an eagle with a brown tail, which may have been a bird of the year of this species or an adult golden eagle (*Aquila chrysaetos*, Linn.).

† The capercailzie (*Tetrao urogallus*, Linn.) formerly inhabited the British Islands, afterwards became extinct, but has of late years been reintroduced into Scotland with great success. Where it has not been exterminated it is still an inhabitant of the pine regions of Europe and Asia as far east as Lake Baikal, where it appears to be replaced by a nearly allied species, *Tetrao urogalloides* (Midd.). In the valley of the Petchora the hen-birds of this species formed an important article of our diet. The peasants were glad to sell them at sevenpence each. The male bird is eaten freely by the Samoyedes, but is despised by the Russians as coarse eating.

On our arrival at Ust-Zylma at two o'clock on Sunday morning, we found service going on in the church in celebration of Easter Eve. We went with M. Znaminski to the 3 A.M. mass, and after service breakfasted with him, and at 7 A.M. turned into our hammocks for an hour or two's rest. The Easter holidays lasted three days, during which we saw plenty of eating and drinking, and some (but not much) drunkenness. The Russian peasantry in Siberia in Europe easily get drunk. They drink vodka neat, and two or three glasses are enough for most of them. There is one very curious circumstance about drunkenness in this part of the world. So far as we could ascertain, with the Russian peasants drunkenness never produces crime. When a Russian peasant is drunk, he is not quarrelsome like most Englishmen, but simply becomes obtrusively affectionate. He wants to embrace you, and kiss you, and be your very best friend. During these holidays when we were returning from the hospitable boards of our Russian or German friends in the small hours of the morning, we would occasionally meet one or two victims of excess of vodka lying in the snow, their malitzas being warm enough to prevent them from being frozen to death.

On the Sunday night there was a very heavy fall of snow. At least a foot must have been added to the depth. On the Monday morning the weather was very stormy, and the fresh fallen snow was drifted into hills and valleys. The change in the appearance of the town was wonderful. The vast dunghill of Ust-Zylma had put on its Easter holiday attire, and was once more pure as the driven snow. Everything was covered with a layer of white powder, dry as dust, and white as (the only possible comparison) white as itself. At night the effect was still more striking. The snow on the railings, on the house tops, and wherever it had been disturbed by footmarks, was white, and all the rest was a pale delicate cobalt-blue.

On Tuesday, 28th April, we got our first nest. It was brought in by some peasants. It was the nest of a Siberian jay, and contained four eggs. This bird is probably the earliest breeder in these parts, and no doubt winters in the Petchora district. The nest was not so flat as we expected, composed almost entirely of lichens, with a few pieces of matting, hair, and feathers. The foundation was made of slender pine twigs, and the inside was profusely lined with feathers.

The snowstorm having now ceased, we made an excursion on snow-shoes to an island in the Petchora, and afterwards visited the opposite bank of the river, *l'autre côte*, as Piottuch called it. It was remarkable how very few birds we saw. I twice came across a flock of bullfinches, all males, and shot three of them. I also saw and shot a solitary tit, very nearly allied to our marsh tit.* It is a greyer bird than ours, with

---

* The marsh tit (*Parus borealis*, Selys.) appears to be a resident bird throughout Europe and Northern and Central Asia, being replaced on the American continent by a nearly allied species, *Parus atricapillus* (Lath.). It is subject to considerable variation in colour, which has given rise to its being divided into several species, which are generally admitted now to be only deserving of subspecific rank. The British form, which is very brown on the back, and has the black of the head only extending to the nape, is also found in South Europe and, curiously enough, in China. In Scandinavia the subspecies *borealis* (Selys.) occurs, having the back much greyer. The form which we found in the valley of the Petchora, which extends eastwards

the white cheeks much whiter, and the black hood extending much farther down the back.

We saw frequent footmarks of hares, and found several snares set by the peasants to catch them. The next day we visited the same ground again. We did not see a single bullfinch, but caught a glimpse of a small spotted woodpecker. We crossed over to the banks of the Zylma, but the birch woods there produced nothing but a solitary marsh tit, which I shot. The woods round Ust-Zylma seemed to be absolutely empty of bird life. Our first eight days had produced only nine species of birds. During the following ten days we increased our list by only three birds—the bullfinch, the Siberian jay, and the Siberian marsh tit.

---

throughout the whole of Siberia, and which bears the name of *camtschatkensis*, has a still greyer back, and the black of the head extends below the back of the head on to the upper back. An intermediate form, however, occurs in Japan, in which the black of the head also extends on to the upper back, but in which the colour of the upper parts is almost as brown as in the British form. In the valley of the Petchora we did not see this species further north than latitude 66°.

LASSOING REINDEER.

CHAPTER VII.

Trip to Habariki—Samoyedes—Lassoing reindeer—Dogs—Birds—Samoyede sledges—Reindeer harness—The chooms—Samoyede hospitality—Marriage ceremonies—Funeral rites—Religion.

It was quite obvious that we should make little or no progress in our ornithological researches until summer came. We accordingly laid ourselves out to pick up further information about the Samoyedes, so that our time might not be absolutely wasted. We had not yet visited any of their chooms, or tents, and we were glad to learn from Captain Engel that there were several in the neighbourhood of Habariki. On Thursday morning we sledged over to that village, a distance of forty versts. The road was about two-thirds on the Petchora, and the remaining third across country, principally islands. It was so good that we accomplished the distance in four hours, stopping for half an hour midway to feed the horses. We scarcely saw a bird on the whole journey.

Habariki is a poor little village, without a church and containing not more than a dozen houses. The sandy banks of the river are about fifty feet higher than the level on which it is built, and keep it out of the reach of the floods that come with the thaw. The village was admirably adapted for the winter quarters of Sideroff's steamer, which lay below the bend in a little creek running back out of the Petchora, protected there from danger of being smashed to pieces by the blocks of ice that crash down on the breaking up of the river.

After a good lunch we hired two sledges and started in search of the Samoyedes with Captain Engel and a Russian, the engineer of the steamer lying frozen under the village. We had ascertained that there were some chooms about four versts off, but just as we arrived at the place we found everything ready for a move northward. The chooms were taken down and packed on sledges, and the reindeer, to the number of about 500, were collected together; and before we had been there ten minutes the order to march was given. We were informed that they were not going far that afternoon, and would probably erect their chooms in the course of the evening within a verst of Habariki, but that before doing so they were going to take out fifty of the reindeer which belonged to a Russian. We were anxious to see the operation of lassoing, and drove with the Samoyedes in our sledges to the place selected for the purpose. As soon as we left the road our horses stuck fast with the snow up to their traces, and we were soon glad to give up our almost ineffectual struggle to get along on foot, and seat ourselves on one of the reindeer sledges which soon brought us to the spot. It was admirably chosen—a large open space—perhaps half a mile across, sufficiently hollow to give it the effect of a natural amphitheatre surrounded by forest. In the centre was a slight elevation, where three or four sledges were stationed, commanding a fine view of the herd of reindeer gathered round. A little below us in the hollow were about a score of sledges with the women and the baggage.

The Samoyedes proved themselves expert in throwing the lasso. In the left hand they held a small coil of rope, in the right hand the larger half. The lasso was thrown with an underhand fling, and generally successfully over the horns of the animal at the first attempt. The left hand was then pressed close to the side so as to bring the shock of the sudden pulling up of the reindeer at full speed against the thigh. When a reindeer found itself caught, it generally made desperate efforts to escape, but was usually on its haunches gasping for breath in a few seconds. The Samoyede then hauled in the rope, or, if it was nearly out at full length, another Samoyede came up and began to haul it in nearer to the animal. When he was close to it he took hold of the horns, and with a side twist, brought the reindeer down on to the snow. The Russian to whom the fifty reindeer belonged then approached, and taking a thong of three-plait matting from a bunch at his belt, tied one of the animal's forelegs to the hind leg on the same side; crossing the feet, but keeping the legs parallel at the point of ligature.

As soon as the reindeer was left, he made wild efforts to rise and walk; and sometimes succeeded in hobbling a few paces. Finding his strength give way with his frantic efforts to escape, he generally rested with his foreknees on the snow for a time; and finally lay down quietly. A dozen reindeer were soon on the ground. The scene became quite exciting; the reindeer were wheeling round and round in circles. The dogs tied to the sledges barked furiously, and evidently wished to have a share in the sport. The dogs selected by the Samoyedes to help them to get within lasso range of the deer, rushed frantically about at the command of their masters, whose loud cries added to the excitement of the scene. Sometimes a herd of reindeer ran over a place where the snow was unable to bear their weight; and it was interesting to watch them snorting and plunging. As the number caught increased, the difficulty also increased of identifying and catching the remaining few of the fifty that belonged to the Russian, and the Samoyedes with the lassos were driven about in sledges at a rapid pace to get within reach of the animals they wanted. The deer kept together; if one ran out of bounds a dog was sent after it and soon brought it back again. In one respect the reindeer resemble sheep; wherever one goes, the rest try to follow.

In this herd the greater number were females (*vah'shinka*), with good horns; these they do not cast till they drop their young. A few were males (*horre*), their new horns just appearing. Those chiefly used in the sledges were cut reindeer (*bük*), also without horns. Some of the hornless animals leaped right through the lasso and others were caught by the leg.

The lasso is a cord about one hundred feet long, made of two thongs of reindeer skin plaited together, so as to make a round rope three-eighths of an inch in diameter. The noose is formed by passing the cord through a small piece of bone with two holes in it. The lasso passes freely through the hole, while the end is fastened to a little bone peg with a bone-washer to prevent it slipping through the other hole.

The dogs were all white except one, which was quite black. They were stiff-built little animals, somewhat like Pomeranian dogs, with fox-like heads and thick bushy hair; their tails turned up over the back and curled to one side. This similarity between the Pomeranian and Samoyede dogs is a rather curious fact, for Erman mentions a race of people who, he says, resemble the Finns, both in language and features, in a district of Pomerania called Samogitia inhabited by the Samaites.

The next morning we turned out of our hammocks at four and strolled in the brilliant sunshine, hoping to meet with some birds; but with the exception of the hooded crows, magpies,* snow-buntings, and redpoles, we met with none

---

* The magpie (*Pica rustica*, Scop.) appears to be a resident throughout Europe and Asia north of the Himalayas, extending across Behring's Straits to Western America, from Alaska to California. In the extreme north it is a partial migrant. In the valley of the Petchora we found it up to latitude $67\frac{1}{2}°$.

feeding. In the wood we saw an eagle, a pair of marsh tits, a pair of Siberian jays, and occasionally we marked a pair of ravens.

After breakfast we visited the chooms, and very picturesque they looked in the white landscape in the dazzling sunshine. Here and there a few willows dotted the undulating ground near a winding rivulet, in the centre of which ran a narrow stream of open water. The reindeer were not to be seen, all were away feeding. Two chooms stood a few feet apart from the rest; in front of these the sledges were drawn up, twenty-three in number; some light and elegant in shape, with four carefully hewn ribs on each side, and a low sloping back. In these the Samoyedes and their families travelled. Others were not quite so finely finished, and had only three ribs on each side; these were used for the lighter baggage, reindeer skins, malitzas, &c., covered over, in some cases, with a tarpaulin made of pieces of birch bark, neatly sewn together with reindeer sinew. Other sledges again were of much stronger and clumsier make, with only two ribs on each side, adapted for the heavy baggage. Some of these were a simple gantry upon runners, carrying casks of reindeer meat, others a wooden chest with an angular roof like the recognised Noah's ark model, containing loaves of black bread and other perishable articles.

The harness of the reindeer is very simple. The saddle is a plain band of tanned reindeer leather, about eight inches broad, hanging a few inches below the body on each side. About six inches from each end a double thong of reindeer skin is attached, and forms the belly band. The thong passes through the saddle, and is fastened to a button (*stchorlak*) made of reindeer horn or bone. These buttons are about two inches in diameter, with two oval holes near the centre for the thong to pass through. Some of these buttons are round, others square with the corners off, others hexagonal; and others again hexagonal with every alternate side concave, whilst some are merely irregular rhomboids. All the buttons are bevelled on the edge, and generally slightly hollowed to fit the curve of the reindeer's side. On the near side of the near reindeer is a piece of carved bone, into which the reins can be hitched, called *halsü* (the *h* pronounced slightly gutturally). This part of the harness is of divers shapes and patterns, and seems to be especially the part on the ornamentation and variation of which the Samoyedes expend their spare time and taste.

The simplest form is a hook, to receive the reins. A more elaborate one is a double hook, the reversed hook being obviously added only for the sake of ornament. Others again have the double hook, with a variety of ornamental carving added. On the off side of the saddle, opposite the *halsü*, is a leather loop to which the bridle rein of the next deer is attached. The collar is a narrow band about three inches wide, also of tanned leather, passing round the neck. The two ends of this collar are fastened together by the trace which passes from the sledge, between the hind legs of the deer, between the body and the belly-band that hangs rather loosely, then between the forelegs to the breast, where it passes through the two ends of the collar, and is secured to a bone peg or *paysik* of simple construction. The head-piece or halter (for no bit is used) is called *syahney*. That of the leading deer consists of a square straight piece of bone or horn, about four inches long on the right cheek, under the root of the horns with a hole at each end, and a second piece of horn, a semicircular or half-round section bending nearly rectangularly, not quite in the middle. This piece of horn is hollowed or deeply

REIN RESTS.

grooved on the flat side, and has a hole bored through at each end, and a third hole about half an inch from that one at the long end. The position of this piece of horn is with the short end halfway across the forehead and the long end in a similar position to the straight piece of horn on the other side of the head. Both pieces were more or less ornamented with simple carving; they are fastened together, the ends about a couple of inches apart by a short thong of plain or plaited leather passing through the holes at one end of each piece, and tied across the forehead. To the other ends of the pieces of bone, plain thongs of leather are attached, one passing behind the horns, the other under the neck. Through the third hole, in the long side of the bent piece of horn passes a thong fastened to the single rein, either with a simple tie or with an intervening swivel made of horn, called by the Samoyedes the *sürnyah*. The head-pieces of the other deer are slightly different. The bone pieces under the horns are slenderer, both slightly curved and both alike. They are tied together across the forehead, as is the head-piece of the leading deer, but the other ends are tied to the apex of a piece of bone or horn, shaped like an isosceles triangle, with the angles cut off square, the angle at the apex being very obtuse, and the basal line slightly concave. These triangular pieces are placed nearly over the jugular vein, and are fastened at one end under the neck, and at the other at the back of the head. The bridle-rein is attached at one end to the thong passing at the back of the head, and the other to the saddle of the deer to the left or near side. The wood or bone blind pulley through which the traces run, is called *pate-chay*, it is so arranged that any deer not doing its fair share of the pulling drops behind against the sledge. The animals are urged on by a long pole, with which they are hit or poked; it is called the *toor*, and the bone button at the end of it the *toor-mahl*. Behind each sledge, on each side, there is a thong of leather passing through a hole, pierced through one end of a bit of bone about nine inches long. A second thong of leather forms the link connecting this to a second bone, which can be fastened to the headpiece of the deer of the following sledge, which thus requires no driver. This rude chain is called the *poo-in-ah*. The swivel is occasionally a brass one, bought from the Russians; now and then a brass ring is seen on the head-piece; sometimes tassels of plain leather shaped like luggage labels, and stained vermilion, ornament it.

The chooms were shaped like ordinary regulation tents, about twelve feet in diameter and height; they were supported inside by some thirty slender birch poles, converging to a cone, tied together in a bunch at the top. This skeleton was covered with old, dirty and much patched reindeer skins, sewn together and lined with coarse and half rotten canvas, probably old sails. Some cords of twisted reindeer sinew strengthened the structure, and an opening about a foot wide was left at the summit of the tent to serve as a chimney. We drew back the covering overlapping the opening used as a door, and entered. Snow, heaped up to the height of about a foot, protected the choom from bottom draughts. A wood fire burned in the centre upon a thin metal plate; an ordinary gipsy kettle was suspended over it by a simple arrangement. Mats of slender birch bark, woven together every six inches by a warp of string, were placed on either side of the fire; over these were stretched another mat made of some kind of rushy grass. Around were packed various articles of clothing, wooden bowls and spoons of Russian origin, a Russian box containing a china tea-service; a heap of entrails of reindeer, part of which were doubtless stewing in the kettle, and sundry other articles. Exactly opposite the door there hung one of the Onega bronze bas-reliefs of saints or Virgins, framed in a rudely carved piece of wood, shaped somewhat like a cross.

After purchasing some reindeer harness, we were invited to drink a cup of tea, and to eat a kind of spiral biscuit. Our hostess had just been sewing; a steel needle, a tailor's thimble, and thread of reindeer sinew, lay in a corner of the tent. The smoke annoyed us when we stood up, but we did not feel it much when seated. The Samoyedes sat cross-legged on the ground; and tea was served on a little table, just large enough to hold half-a-dozen cups, and whose legs were not more than six inches high. As usual, we found our hosts very ready to give us any information we asked them.

The Samoyedes never seemed annoyed at our taking notes among them; they struck us as a good-tempered, somewhat phlegmatic race. They carried old-fashioned Russian flint-lock rifles, but we could not rouse their interest in our breech-loaders; they do not appear to work much in metals. They always carry a knife, no doubt of Russian make, but they are very ingenious in making handles, and in ornamenting them. Patterns of various kinds of elaboration are carved upon them, and the patterns filled up with melted tin. They use a small saw; a rude form of brace and bit, and also the indispensable axe.

Like the Russians, the Samoyedes have beautiful white and regular teeth. They are very fond of chewing the resin which they get from the Scotch fir, which doubtless assists in keeping the teeth clean.

As we are now on the subject of this strange race, we may as well insert here some details we gathered a few days later, after our return to Ust-Zylma, from a Samoyede, who drove up in his reindeer sledge from a choom near Habariki. Our interpreter was a Polish Jew, banished by his father to Siberia, because he had adopted the religion of the Greek Church. He translated the Samoyede's bad Russian into worse German.

We were informed that when a young Samoyede desires to marry, and has come to some understanding with the damsel of his choice, he visits her father's choom, and with a short stick taps him, and then the mother of the maiden, on the shoulder. He then demands the girl in marriage, and offers the father and mother a glass of vodka, which he has brought with him. As a token of his goodwill the father drinks the vodka; he tells the young man he has no objection, but that he must ask the girl's consent. The preliminary ceremony of asking papa having been gone through, the young man retires. A few days later he comes again to the choom; this time accompanied by what servants he has, and provided with plenty of vodka. His retinue remain outside, while he enters the choom, and seats himself by the side of his lady love. The father hands the young man a glass of vodka; he drinks half, and hands the half-full glass, under his left arm, to the girl, who finishes it. The father then gives his daughter a glass of vodka, who in like manner drinks half of it, and presents the remainder with her left hand under her right arm to her lover, who drains the glass. After this the father hands a piece of raw flesh to the young man who eats it, and then takes a piece from the floor, eats half, and presents the other half under his left arm to the girl to finish. She, in her turn, takes a piece of raw flesh from the floor, eats half, and likewise hands the other half under her right arm to the young man to finish. Then follows the eating and drinking that in barbarous, as in civilised nations, is considered necessary to ratify the ceremony. Before night an old man, called a *shamman*, a kind of magician or medicine man, carrying a drum, visits the choom; of him the bridegroom asks certain questions concerning his bride. If the old man knows nothing against her he begins to play upon his drum, and the marriage is completed. If, however, the magician speaks evil of the girl, then the young man has the option of leaving her there and then, or if he be still enamoured of her charms, it is open to him to bargain with her father to take her for a month or a year on trial. At the expiration of the time agreed upon, if the pair suit each other, they consider themselves married for life. On the other hand, should they not agree, they can separate at the end of the time specified; but in that case the man must provide for any children born within the period. After the marriage festivities are over, the young couple are left alone in the choom of the bride's father.

It is customary for the bridegroom to present his bride with the skin of a black fox. The girl's father gives his son-in-law a choom, with all its appurtenances, and five, ten, twenty or thirty reindeer, according to his wealth. If the bridegroom be rich, he gives his father-in-law money to the amount sometimes of two hundred roubles.

Since the adoption of the Russian faith by the Samoyedes they bury their dead. Previous to their conversion, when one among them died he was fully dressed and, in his best malitza and soveek, he was laid flat on his back on the snow or the tundra, according to the season of the year. His favourite *bück* reindeer was killed and laid by his side, with his best harness and his driving pole and bow.* The choom is taken down at once, and the camp is broken up amidst much weeping and lamentation. If possible the place is never revisited. The Samoyedes believe that if the dead man's property were not left with him his spirit would follow them.

The Samoyedes used to have wooden idols, to which they sacrificed reindeer.† In order that the reindeer may reach the unseen god, of whom the wooden idol is evidently considered but the symbol, it must be killed in a peculiar fashion. A running noose is made in the middle of a cord and put round the horns of the deer; a Samoyede holds the two ends. Another noose is put round the animal's hind feet, and while he is thus held at full stretch, he is stabbed in both sides with two pieces of wood (not with a knife); then the spirit of the reindeer is supposed to be sent to the god.

---

* Captain Hall, in his 'Life with the Esquimaux,' mentions a similar custom existing among them. The Innuits seal up their dying in snow-huts, or *iglos*, where they are allowed to die alone. The blubber lamp, the fishing and hunting instruments of the dead, are always laid by his side, and the place is abandoned.

† William Govedon, who wintered at Pustozara, 1614–1615, tells us that the Samoyedes had then "no true knowledge of God, but worship blocks and images of the deuill, unto which they strangle tame deere."—See 'Purchas his Pilgrimes,' lib. iii. ch. 12.

The greater number of Samoyedes have adopted the Russian faith, and have been baptized into the Greek Church, but many of these still retain their ancient beliefs, and sacrifice to their idols, while in the more easterly parts of the Great Land of the Samoyedes, many have not yet been "converted."

OLD RUSSIAN SILVER CROSS.

A SPILL IN THE SNOW.

CHAPTER VIII.

May-day—Snow-buntings—Jackdaws—Game—Birds of prey—Sunday at Ust-Zylma—A fire—Marriage ceremony—Tenure of land—The commune—Preparations for summer.

On May-day the thaw continued in real earnest. A warm wind and a hot sun made great havoc with the snow. All traces of the heavy fall of the previous Sunday night soon disappeared, and a considerable portion of the old accumulation of winter melted. Ust-Zylma became once more a vast dunghill; and on the hills, where the snow in some places lay exceptionally deep, it was too soft to bear our weight even on snow-shoes. We attempted our usual ramble in the woods at the back of the town; but travelling was very laborious, and we returned to our quarters with broken snow-shoes, and without having remarked anything of special interest. With the exception of a yellow-hammer, which was making a feeble attempt to sing, we scarcely saw or heard a bird. One effect of the thaw was to banish the snow-buntings from the town to the country. Although this bird is thick-billed, and undoubtedly feeds on grain and seeds during the winter, it appears to change its diet to some extent during the breeding season. When I was in Lapland I found it nesting amongst the rocks on the island of Vadso, in the Varanger Fjord. Not far distant, down by the shore was the great whaling establishment of Mr. Foyne, where an average of three whales a week were cut up. The snow-buntings visited the yard constantly, which abounded with insects attracted by the offal; and the stomachs of some which I shot and skinned proved to be full of insects.

During this sloppy season we confined our walks pretty much to the town itself, carrying our walking-stick guns in case a new bird should turn up. On the 3rd of May we were rewarded by seeing for the first time a pair of jackdaws.*

---

* The jackdaw (*Corvus monedula*, Linn.) is a resident throughout Europe and in many parts of North Africa. Specimens from Eastern Europe frequently are much whiter on the collar, and may be considered as a sub-species, *collaris* (Drumm.) which extends eastwards as far as the watershed of the Obb and the Yenesay, southwards through Cashmere to North-West India; still farther to the east a more distinct or nearly allied species is found — *Corvus dauuricus* (Pall.) — distinguished by having the collar still whiter, and also by having the vent white. The variety which we found in the valley of the Petchora was the *Corvus monedula*, subspecies *collaris*. We found this bird common on our journey as far as Mezen, and afterwards only met with a solitary pair at Ust-Zylma.

It was contrary to law to shoot in the streets, and the birds were within a stone's-throw of the house of the public prosecutor. I shot one of them, as I thought very cleverly on the sly; but I found that my attempt at concealment had been a failure, for a day or two afterwards, whilst discussing our walnuts and wine with the chief magistrate at the public prosecutor's hospitable table, we were kindly cautioned to shoot as little as possible in the streets.

The liberal hospitalities of our friends helped to beguile the time during the thaw; and occasionally the peasants offered us birds, which provided variety for our larder, and sometimes interested us and found employment for Piottuch. We bought four capercailzies for eighty kopecks from one of our friends the Samoyedes, who had shot them with ball. Hazel grouse* were also frequently brought in to us, at twenty kopecks per brace. They are most delicate eating, and are thought by many gourmands to be the finest game that can be brought to table.

Winter returned on the 4th of May, when a raw west wind brought a heavy storm at noon; after which snow and bitter cold continued, with occasional high wind, till the

---

* The hazel grouse (*Bonasa betulina*, Scop.) is not found in the British Islands, but inhabits the pine forests of Arctic and north temperate Europe and Asia, as far east as Japan, where it is a partial resident, wandering from forest to forest in the winter season rather than migrating. In the valley of the Petchora these birds were sold to us by the peasants, but, curiously enough, we never chanced to come across them ourselves. I afterwards shot plenty of them on the other side of the Ural Mountains. This bird, the *Hjerpa* of the Norwegians and the *Ryab'chik* of the Russians, is considered by many epicures to be the finest game that comes to table—even superior to our own grouse.

8th. We went out, notwithstanding, struggling on snow-shoes across deep ravines and through bushes and plantations. We also made an excursion within the island, in search of birds. For some days the snow-buntings remained outside the town, in such immense flocks, that when they rose the whirring of their wings could be heard at some distance. On the 6th, the snow drove them back into Ust-Zylma; also small parties of redpoles, that follow the buntings very much as the starlings follow rooks.

When we first met with the flocks of snow-buntings we found them to consist principally of males, but as the season advanced the females largely predominated. On the 4th of May we saw a white-tailed eagle and a hen harrier,* and on the following day we had an excellent sight of a merlin. Magpies were as abundant as ever, but, like the snow-buntings, they had moved into the country, and on the 5th we discovered a nearly completed nest in a spruce fir, built about five feet from the ground. The birds were most vociferous, and used every artifice to decoy us away from their property.

On the 8th of May summer seemed farther off than ever. The day before the weather had been very changeable—alternately warm, snowing, hailing, sleeting, with an occasional gleam of sunshine, and a cold wind, but on the

---

* The hen harrier (*Circus cyaneus*, Linn.) has not yet been exterminated by the gamekeepers from the British Islands. It breeds in the Arctic and north temperate regions of Europe and Asia, visiting South Europe principally in winter, at which season of the year it is found in North Africa as far south as Abyssinia. It also winters in Persia and India and South China. In the valley of the Petchora we found it as far north as latitude 68½°.

whole a thaw. The next day the morning was bitterly cold, with the north wind blowing hard. In the afternoon the wind veered to the west, with a heavy fall of snow. At midnight the wind dropped, the sky became clear, the thermometer went down to 16°. The landscape was again white and frost-bound. It looked exactly like mid-winter, except that at that hour of night we could see to read a newspaper out of doors. The climate of these regions is very curious at this time of the year. The change is sudden and violent —the leaping from mid-winter into summer, without any intervening spring.

We strolled out in the morning, not expecting to see anything new. We shot a tree-sparrow and a yellow-hammer, and were returning home somewhat disheartened, in spite of our unexpectant mood at starting, when a hen harrier suddenly put in an appearance. He did not, however, come within range, and we went into a little valley, there to wait for him or a chance raven. By-and-by a small hawk crossed in front of us. We followed it up the hillside, caught sight of it again, watched it alight on a heap of manure, quietly stalked it, and shot it. It turned out to be a female merlin.*

---

* The merlin (*Falco æsalon*, Gmel.) still breeds in the British Islands and throughout North Europe, wintering in South Europe and North Africa. Eastwards it breeds throughout Northern Siberia, occasionally straggling as far south as Scinde and North-West India in winter, passing through Mongolia on migration, and wintering in South China. On the American continent it is replaced by a very nearly allied species—*Falco columbarius* (Linn.). In the valley of the Petchora we observed it as far north as latitude 68°. The merlin is a regular summer migrant to the moors of South Yorkshire and North Derbyshire, where it would commit sad havoc among the young grouse, if it was not relentlessly persecuted by the gamekeepers, who keep a close watch

Whilst we were carefully putting it away, the eagle passed almost within shot of us. In one of the cottages a peasant

upon its well-known breeding-places. It arrives upon the moors towards the end of March or beginning of April, and feeds principally upon the smaller birds frequenting the district (the meadow pipit, gray linnet, twite, &c.), which its rapid powers of flight enable it easily to fly down without resorting to the manœuvres which the clumsier sparrow-hawk is compelled to take advantage of. These moors are the constant breeding-place of three species of hawk—the kestrel, the sparrow-hawk, and the merlin. The kestrel hovers over the ground at a considerable height, and pounces down on a mouse, and occasionally a lizard or a young grouse, as the pellets they cast up abundantly testify. The sparrow-hawk skims over hill-tops or hedges, or round rocks, and comes upon its prey unawares. The merlin, on the contrary, fairly flies it down. The site selected for a nest varies in different localities with many species of birds. On the moors in the neighbourhood of Sheffield, however, the sparrow-hawk invariably builds in a tree; the kestrel as invariably chooses a cleft in a rock, and the merlin always builds upon the ground. The date of nidification is evidently chosen with relation to an abundant supply of food for the young, as in the Cyclades Eleonora's falcon postpones its operations until August, so that the young may be fed upon the flocks of quails returning southward on their autumn migrations; the merlin lays its eggs about the middle of May, so that the voracious young may be fed upon young grouse. A slight hollow is chosen amongst the tall ling; whatever roots or dry grass may chance to be upon the spot are scratched into the rudiments of a nest; and the only materials actually selected by the bird appear to be a few slender twigs of ling to form the outside of the structure, and which are generally broken from the heather overhanging the nest. The site is usually sloping down to a stream and commanding a good view of the moor, and a patch of heather some couple of hundred yards square has often contained a merlin's nest every year for the last dozen years, whilst no other breeding-place could be found nearer than eight or ten miles. I watched two of these breeding-places on the Sheffield moors — one near Ashopton and the other near Strines— for many years, and was well acquainted with the gamekeepers in both localities. There would be nothing extraordinary in this if it could be proved that the same pair, or their descendants, annually visited and occupied the same breeding-stations; they might easily be supposed to have obtained a vested right in the estate and to have defended it successfully against all comers. But every year the gamekeepers in both localities shoot or trap one or both of the parent birds—generally both—and in no case for more than ten years have they ever allowed

showed us the skin of an eagle-owl.* The next evening we strolled out on the banks of the Petchora. Brilliant sunshine flooded the earth, not a cloud was in the sky; but it was cold and winterly as Christmas. Flocks of magpies and of hooded crows were almost the only birds we saw. They passed us on the wing, evidently going to their resting-places in the woods.

The week had not brought us many birds, but we knew summer was at hand, and we waited patiently. Meanwhile we mingled with the inhabitants of Ust-Zylma and observed their ways. Sunday seemed among them a day devoted to

the young birds to get away. They have found out by experience that it is of no use to shoot one of the birds before they have begun to breed, because in such case the survivor finds another mate in a few days. They shoot or snare the cock-bird as soon as they can after the hen has begun to sit. In the neighbourhood of the nest are little rocky elevations on the ground, which the cock-bird uses as feeding-places, and which are easily found by the feathers of young grouse and other small birds scattered round them. Upon these knolls traps are set, and as soon as the cock-bird is caught, the hen is easily shot off the nest. For several successive years I have seen this done, and taken the eggs myself, but curiously enough, in the summer of 1872 no merlins appeared in either locality. The only way in which to account for the selection every year of the same locality by a fresh pair of birds seems to be to suppose that the merlins mi-

grate *en masse*, and that as they pass each recognised breeding-place, if the former occupants are not there to take possession, another pair immediately occupy it. The facts of the case seem to warrant the conclusion that the selected sites for breeding are well-known to a large circle of merlins; otherwise it is difficult to account for the choice always falling upon the same site, out of an indefinite number of others apparently equally eligible.

* The eagle owl (*Bubo maximus*, Flem.) has almost become extinct in the British Islands, but is still a resident in the mountainous districts of most parts of Europe, and is occasionally found in North Africa. Eastwards it is found throughout Siberia and China, and has been met with in the Himalayas. We did not meet with this owl in the valley of the Petchora, but twice saw skins of birds of this species shot at Ust-Zylma.

calling, and many sledges would drive up to the house where we were, from the neighbouring villages. The peasants combined business with these visits to town, and we bought one Sunday four skins of the white fox and one of the grey fox for nine roubles and a half, from one of Boulegan's visitors.

Once we had an opportunity of seeing the people of Ust-Zylma turning out to extinguish a fire. A small conflagration burst out in the house of Captain Arendt. All the villagers trooped to the spot, armed with axes, wooden shovels, and boat-hooks. It is the law that in case of fire every peasant should assist in putting it out. On each house a board is nailed up, on which is roughly sketched the article its inhabitant must furnish to assist in extinguishing the flames. The people keep to their primitive ways and habits. We watched a peasant one day shooting at a mark with a flint-lock rifle. The barrel was very thick, and the bore the size of a large pea. He carried a spiral coil of lead, and, when the unsophisticated fellow wanted a bullet, he bit a piece off with his perfectly white regular teeth, and chewed it into a rough bullet. His gun, which he told us was worth five roubles, was ornamented all over the stock with by no means unartistic carvings.

On one occasion we assisted at a wedding in the Orthodox Greek church. The marriage ceremony took place in the afternoon, and was sufficiently imposing. The priest met the couple at the vestibule of the church. After going through a form of prayer, he presented the bride and bridegroom with a lighted taper, which he had first crossed over their bowed heads; the rings likewise were crossed over their heads, as were also a pair of gold crowns before being placed upon them. The Bible and the crucifix were kissed. A silver cup of wine was quaffed by the plighted pair, each drinking from it alternately. Censers of incense were swung. The priest, the happy couple, and the assistants bowed and crossed themselves continually, and between each part of the ceremony prayers were offered.

We were not very successful in our attempts to obtain accurate information as to the tenure of land. It was sometimes difficult to reconcile conflicting statements. Most of our informants, however, agreed that they or their ancestors were formerly serfs of the crown, that after their emancipation the land remained the property of the crown, and was leased to the village or commune at a nominal rent. The affairs of the commune are managed by a parliament or town council, composed of every householder, electing a mayor or "starrester" (literally, oldest man), whose term of office is three years, and who is responsible to the Government for the rent or taxes payable by the commune. Every three years a redistribution of land takes place, the arable land being divided amongst the householders in lots proportionate to the number of individuals living in each house. Five hundred roubles will build a handsome habitation in Ust-Zylma. We were informed that every peasant was annually entitled to a fixed number of cubic yards of firewood without charge, and to a limited number of balks of good building timber, which he was free to sell if he did not require to use it.

The evident near approach of summer was the signal for unusual exertions on the part of the peasants. Procrastination seems to be a Russian national vice. Now when the horses were nearly worn out by long feeding upon bad hay, and when the roads were very heavy by reason of the thaws, the poor animals had to work double time. A quantity of last year's fodder still lay on the flat land on the other side of the Petchora, which, if left, would inevitably be swept away when the frozen river broke up; the cattle had now to be taken across the ice and housed in a place of safety, there to wait until the floods subsided on these flat stretches, and the new rich pasture had begun to spring up. The women and children had also to be transported across, to look after the cattle; whilst the men went down the river to fish, leaving Ust-Zylma as deserted for three months as a winter village in the Parnassus.

OLD RUSSIAN SILVER CROSS.

SHOOTING WILD GEESE.

CHAPTER IX.

Mild weather—Bear tracks—Saddle of bear—First rain—Six new migratory birds—Magpie's eggs—Cessation of the winter frost—Return of winter—A wild goose chase—Cachets—Night on the banks of the Petchora—The silent forest—A new bird.

On the 10th of May, for the first time we had real summer weather, which continued for some days. It thawed in the shade, as well as in the sun; as there was not much wind, however, the snow melted slowly. We drove up the Zylma and took a long walk in our snow-shoes, returning across the island; but the pine and birch woods were still almost deserted. We shot a pair of marsh tits, heard the cry of a great black woodpecker, and saw four wild geese flying over our heads. On the island we fell in with a small flock of shore-larks * and succeeded in shooting four, while feeding upon the bare places on the banks of the island. We also started a pair of wild geese and a large owl, probably the snowy owl, which alighted on a heap of snow in the middle of the Petchora. Its flight resembled that of the glaucous gull, but it occasionally skimmed close to the snow for some distance.

We traced along the snow the footprints of a bear and its cubs, about a day or two old. The traces of Bruin's presence had an added interest to us, from the fact, that for the last two days we had been breakfasting and dining on a saddle of bear, and most excellent we had found it, much better than beef. The animal, we had been feasting on, was about a year old; it had been turned out of its place of hybernation by some woodcutters, who had cut down the tree at the root of which it was sleeping. I bought the skin and had an excellent hearth-rug made of it.

Summer now seemed to have suddenly burst upon us in all its strength, the sun was scorching, the snow in many places melted so rapidly as to be almost impassable. The mud banks of the Zylma were steaming from the heat. On

---

* The shore-lark (*Otocorys alpestris*, Linn.) is a circumpolar bird breeding on the tundras beyond the limit of forest growth, migrating southwards in autumn and occasionally visiting the British Islands on migration, or during winter. It winters in the south of Europe, North China, and the southern states of North America.

the 12th of May, about noon, the weather grew hazy, with a very conspicuous halo around the sun, like a dull circular rainbow; the wind was warmer than it had yet been, and in the afternoon there came on a steady rain, the first rain we had seen since we left home. Sancho Panza says that one swallow does not make a summer; but the arrival of six species of migratory birds within two days ought to have some significance. On the 11th we saw for the first time a pair of swans. The same day on the half open land, between the Petchora and the Zylma, we saw some flocks of wild geese, and, near a pool of water on the ice, half-a-dozen Siberian herring-gulls.* Their cry seemed to me to be

---

* The Siberian herring-gull (*Larus affinis*, Reinhardt) was first described from a bird obtained in Greenland, where it is probably only an accidental visitor. When we visited the valley of the Petchora, little or nothing was known of its history or geographical distribution. It had long been confused with the lesser black-backed gull and the Mediterranean herring-gull. The colour of its mantle is intermediate between that of these two species. From the former it may easily be distinguished by the pale wedge-shape pattern on the first few primaries, and from the latter the fact that the tarsus is longer instead of shorter than the foot is an additional mark of distinction, besides the difference in colour.

When I was in St. Petersburg in the autumn of 1877 I carefully examined the magnificent series of gulls in the museum of the Imperial Academy of Science, and discovered that this species appears to breed in the extreme north of Europe and Asia, from the White Sea to Kamtchatka. Middendorf obtained it in the breeding season on Bear Island, south of Solovetsk in the White Sea. Harvie-Brown and I obtained eggs in the valley of the Petchora, about latitude 68°. Finsch and Brehm found it in the valley of the Obb. I found it breeding abundantly in the valley of the Yenesay, between latitude $70\frac{1}{2}°$ and $71\frac{1}{2}°$. Middendorf brought home skins from the Boganida and Taimyr rivers, near the North-East Cape, and Kittlitz obtained it in Kamtchatka. The European and West Siberian birds probably winter on the shores of the Arabian Sea, since it was obtained by Karelin both on the spring and autumn migrations in the Caspian Sea, and abounds in winter at Kurrachee, where Hume records it ('Stray

exactly the same as that of the common and Mediterranean herring-gulls. On the 12th came a little detachment of white wagtails * in the village, we shot six during the day. In each instance, they were on the roof of the houses. We also shot a redstart,† occupying the same position. Another new arrival was the meadow pipit, of which we shot a solitary example. The shore-larks had already been some days in Ust-Zylma, and by this time were in large and small flocks in the fields on both sides of the town. All those we shot proved to be males. Three or four small hawks, probably merlins, were hovering about, and a snowy owl ‡ was

---

Feathers,' 1873, p. 273), under the erroneous title of *Larus occidentalis*, (Audubon). It has not hitherto been obtained in the British Islands, but several examples have occurred during winter on Heligoland, and a sharp lookout should be kept on our shores.

* The white wagtail (*Motacilla alba*, Linn.) is a comparatively rare bird in the south of England, but is common on the continent of Europe, breeding in the south only at high elevations, but extending northwards beyond the limit of forest growth. In some parts it is said to be resident, but the Arctic birds migrate into South Europe and North Africa in winter. Eastwards it extends throughout Siberia as far south as about latitude 59°, and as far east as the watershed between the Yenesay and the Lena. There appears, however, to be a somewhat isolated colony breeding in the mountains round Lake Baikal, crossing Mongolia and West China on migration, and wintering in India. In the valley of the Petchora we met with it up to latitude 68°.

† The redstart (*Ruticilla phoenicurus*, Linn.) is a common British bird during the summer, arriving early in April. It breeds throughout Central Europe, extending northwards beyond the Arctic circle. In South Europe it is rarely seen except in spring and autumn, though a few remain to breed at high elevations. It probably winters in Northern and Central Africa. In Asia its range during the breeding season extends eastwards as far as the valley of the Yenesay, the Asiatic birds wintering in Persia.

‡ The snowy owl (*Nyctea scandiaca*, Linn.) is a circumpolar bird breeding principally within the Arctic circle, and occasionally straggling in winter to the British Islands, various parts of Central Europe, South Siberia, Mongolia, and the United States of America. In the valley of the Petchora we found it as far north as we went.

brought in to us, apparently just killed. A white-tailed eagle, his white tail looking grey against the snow, was perching on an ice block in the Petchora; and at a little distance off we could distinctly see a raven picking a bone. Morning and evening we watched the gulls, without being able to get a shot at them. The redpoles had disappeared altogether, and we saw the snow-buntings only once or twice. The signs of coming summer were surrounding us, small flies were on the wing, twice we came upon a tortoise-shell butterfly; we visited the magpie's nest, which we had discovered some days previously in a pine-tree, and found that it contained seven eggs. But even the approach of summer has its accompanying drawbacks: we had to give up at this time all hope of more winter posts, and two months might elapse before the summer ones would arrive. This break in the communication with civilised Europe is one of the sorest trials to be endured by explorers in these districts.

The little spurt of mild weather, however, turned out to be a delusion. Our six species of summer migrants proved no more reliable than Sancho Panza's solitary swallow. On the 13th a strong gale from the north brought winter back again, and drove away our newly arrived visitors to more genial latitudes. The snow-buntings and the shore-larks became very wild during this spell of bitter wind; towards evening it dropped, and when we came in upon a flock of the former, they were so tame that they allowed us to walk about, within ten and sometimes five yards of them. The flock was composed mostly of females; one male, that we observed amongst them, was in more mature plumage than any we had yet seen. Birds of prey appeared in unusual numbers. We saw hen-harriers, both male and female, numerous merlins, which often perched upon the heaps of manure in the fields, and for the first time we saw a peregrine falcon.* Piottuch was fortunate enough to shoot a fine snowy owl on the goose ground, between the Petchora and the Zylma. A hard frost in the night, followed by a cold east wind, with bright sunshine, was most unfavourable to the arrival of migratory birds. We were deliberating as to what would be the least unprofitable mode of spending the day, when the Preestaff sent in to inquire if we would join him and the postmaster in an excursion four-and-twenty miles up the Petchora to shoot geese. These were the two "swell chasseurs" of Ust-Zylma, and we accepted their invitation gladly. We ordered a horse and sledge, packed up provision, tents, and wraps, and were soon *en route*.

About halfway we descried two swans on the snow of the Petchora. We started our sledge in pursuit, approaching the birds in a spiral curve, we came within range, fired, and missed. The birds, very large and very white, flew about a verst across the river, and again alighted. Here they were joined by a third swan. Slowly again we crept up in a spiral curve within range; this time two rifles fired, and

---

* The peregrine falcon (*Falco peregrinus*, Tunst.) is a circumpolar bird still found in Great Britain, although rapidly becoming extinct. It breeds more or less regularly in every country in Europe, and winters in Africa, occasionally straying as far south as the Cape. It also breeds throughout Asia and North America, wherever suitable localities are found; and has been found in winter as far south as the Argentine States of South America. In the valley of the Petchora we met with it breeding in latitude 68°.

both missed; a third time the rifles came within range, but with no better result; after which the swans flew right away.

We then visited a small lake close to the banks of the Petchóra, but it was completely ice-bound, and declared to be "necayt dohbra" (good for nothing). Finally, we selected a spot where there was open water in two places. Geese flew about in small flocks, at intervals during the afternoon, and we all expressed confident hopes of a bag after sunrise. The horses were taken from the sledge, a fire was lit, supper with unlimited tea followed, and was over by eleven. We then selected places, supposed to be favourable for the cachets; at each place a hole was dug in the snow, which was piled up to the height of three or four feet, and this snow wall was planted round with willow twigs. Cocksure (the nickname we gave to Piottuch, a bad pun on his name),* who by the way was in high glee, drove across the Petchora, with the postmaster, where he was "cocksure" of finding plenty of geese.

After a final cup of tea and a smoke, we separated at one o'clock, each departing to his cachet, to take, if he felt so inclined, a sleep in the snow for a couple of hours. I did not feel sleepy, and was curious to watch a whole night on the banks of the Petchora; so doffing my malitza, axe in hand, I set to work to turn my cachet into a turreted castle, some six feet high inside. It was a keen frost, and the surface snow was easy to hew out into square blocks, which I joined together, with soft snow from below; soon, my

---

* "Piatoukh" is the Russ for "a cock."

castle was one solid mass of frozen snow. The exercise kept me warm. I planted my last piece of willow twig and put on my malitza, just as the sun appeared above the horizon, amidst lake and vermilion clouds, behind the steep mudbanks on the other side of the Petchora. Behind me rose a thick wood of willow and decayed or decaying birch, a pine rising here and there between. Presently I spied, between my turrets of snow, a marsh tit silently searching for food on a willow; I changed one of my cartridges for dust, put my feet into my snow-shoes, sallied forth, and shot it. His mate soon began to call, and in half a minute I secured her also, and returned to my cachet.

An hour passed by; now and then I heard the distant "gag gag" of the geese, or the wild cry of some far-off swan, but nothing came within range of less than cannon shot of me. Fourteen large glaucous gulls slowly flew up the Petchora; I watched a pair of swans on the ice through my telescope, and listened to the distant call of some smaller gulls; whilst redpoles and white wagtails often passed over me, all flying up wind.

At length I got tired of waiting and watching, and made an excursion on my snow-shoes into the wood. All around was dead silence; nothing to be heard but the gentle rattling of the east wind amongst the leafless branches of the willows. The wood seemed as empty of bird-life as the desert of Sahara.

I returned to my cachet, and waited and watched with no better result than before. A flock of snow-buntings came fluttering up the Petchora, and alighted on some willow-trees; this was interesting. I now made an excursion to the cachet of my companions. I had forgotten to wind my watch, and made this an excuse for my visit. Halfway to it, I came upon a small flock of reed-buntings, amongst some willows, and missed a shot at one of them. My companion had stuck heroically to his cachet, but had had no better luck than mine. As we were chatting, we heard the note of a bird, which I took to be a redstart.

I followed the sound to some distance, but could not overtake the bird on my snow-shoes. Setting out to return to my cachet, I was interrupted by a flock of reed-buntings;* I got a shot at one, but the cap missing fire, away they flew. I was returning disconsolately by the side of a thick but narrow plantation, when I heard a "gag gag" through the trees, and descried seven geese, apparently flying straight for my companion's cachet. I fired, and down came a pair of bullfinches; the rest flying away ahead of me. I followed in pursuit, but without getting a second shot; on returning I learnt my companion's success. He had brought down a "bean goose." †

---

* The reed-bunting (*Emberiza schœniclus*, Linn.) is a resident species in the British Islands, and breeds throughout Northern and Central Europe and Northern Asia. Wherever the winter is severe it is a migratory bird, visiting South Europe, North Africa, Persia, Turkestan, India, and Japan. In the valley of the Petchora we did not observe it farther north than latitude 68°.

† The bean goose (*Anser segetum*, Gmel.) appears to be confined to the eastern hemisphere. It is doubtful if it has ever bred in the British Islands, but it is common in various parts during winter. It does not breed far south of the Arctic circle, frequenting principally the tundras beyond the limit of forest growth. In winter it is found in various parts of temperate Europe, occasionally crossing the Mediterranean into North Africa. In Asia its winter range appears to be confined to Asia

On my way to my cachet, I met another party of reed-buntings, one of which I bagged; then I sat in my hiding-place for an hour, waiting for geese that never came within range.

At eight I found I had taken a wink of sleep, I could stand it no longer, so set off in search of my companions, and bagging another reed-bunting and wagtail on my way, we returned together to our encampment, where we soon had the kettle boiling with "tchai."

The postmaster and "Cocksure" turned up as we were breakfasting, and reported a blank night. The Preestaff, we found afterwards, had fared no better. Deciding that we had had enough of this wild goose chase, we harnessed our sledges and returned home in a steady rain. Our horse was done up, and we were six hours on the road, through four of which we slept soundly, waking up just in time to bag a score of shore-larks.

Notwithstanding its inglorious results, we enjoyed our trip as a novelty, and had many hearty laughs, over divers "spills" out of and over the sledge. As ours was the only one that brought home a dead goose, the best of the laugh was on our side. We had, moreover, bagged a new migrant, and Cocksure had seen a black woodpecker * and a common snipe.

Minor, China, and Japan. In the valley of the Petchora we found it as far north as we went.

* The black woodpecker (*Dryocopus martius*, Linn.) is of extremely doubtful occurrence in the British Islands, but is a resident throughout Northern and Central Europe and Asia. In Eastern Europe its range is somewhat more southerly, extending to Turkey, the Ionian Islands, and Asia Minor. In Asia it does not occur south of Siberia. We did not succeed in obtaining a specimen in the valley of the Petchora, nor did we see it farther north than Ust-Zylma.

THE BANKS OF THE ZYLMA.

CHAPTER X.

Gulls—Species new to Europe—Fresh arrivals—Duck-shooting—Bird-life in the forest—Gulls perching in trees—Break-up of the ice on the Zylma—On the wrong bank of the river—Dragging the boats across the ice—Final break-up of the ice on the Petchora.

THE same evening, as we sat at the window of our rooms writing up our journals, and now and then looking up to glance through the rain at the ever-impressive scene before us, the great river Petchora, suddenly we descried upon the ice a flock of (it might be) two hundred gulls. In the twinkle of an eye, we had donned our indiarubber boots and were wading through the streets of Ust-Zylma. As we neared the birds we made sure, from their note, that the larger number of them were the common gull,* with (it might be) a dozen Siberian herring-gulls among them. We discharged four cartridges of our goose shot into them. Our broadside, fired from a distance, left one dead and one wounded on the field. The smaller species was undoubtedly the common gull with soft parts as follows:—

Bill and legs, gamboge yellow; inside of mouth, angle of gape, and round the eye, vermilion; irides, grey; pupil, blue-black.

It was not at first so easy to determine to what species the larger gull belonged. The soft parts were as follows:—

Bill and legs, straw yellow, with a large pale vermilion blotch on the angle of the lower mandible; inside of mouth, straw yellow, with a tinge of orange at the angle of the gape; irides, pale straw yellow; pupil, blue-black; round the eye, the colour of a Seville orange.

The colour of the mantle of these large gulls was intermediate between that of the lesser black-backed gull and the Mediterranean herring-gull, but the wing pattern resembled that of the latter species. Upon our return home, with the help of our friend Mr. Howard Saunders of London,

---

* The common gull (*Larus canus*, Linn.) appears to be confined to the eastern hemisphere, breeding both in the temperate and Arctic regions, being a resident in the former and migratory in the latter. It breeds in many parts of the British Islands, and in winter its numbers are increased by arrivals from the north, many of which wander as far south as the Mediterranean. Eastwards it is found as far as China, Kamtchatka, and Japan, but in America it is replaced by two very closely allied species, *Larus delawarensis* (Ord.), and *Larus brachyrhynchus* (Rich.). This species is less arctic in its range than the other gull which we met with in the valley of the Petchora. We did not find it further north than latitude 67½°.

the great authority on gulls and terns, we cleared up the difficulties surrounding this species, and finding that it had no colloquial name in our language we ventured to christen it the Siberian herring-gull. The species was not new to science, but we claim to have been the first to add it to the list of European birds.

Another species new to our list was the golden plover,* which also arrived in flocks. These birds were special objects of our attention, partly because they were a valuable addition to our larder, and still more so because we were anxiously on the look-out for the arrival of the grey plover, the eggs of which were one of the possible prizes which we hoped to obtain. All our efforts to obtain even a glimpse of the latter species on migration proved, however, in vain. As we subsequently met with them on the tundra, we can only suppose that they migrate to their breeding-quarters by a different route, probably following the coast line. If they do fly across country, they must travel at such a high elevation that they are rarely observed inland.

Wild geese and swans increased in numbers daily, and

---

* The golden plover (*Charadrius pluvialis*, Linn.) is another of the western palæarctic species, the eastern limit of whose range is bounded by the Himalayas and the watershed of the Yenesay and the Lena, being replaced in Eastern Siberia by a nearly allied species, *Charadrius fulvus* (Gmel.), and on the American continent by *Charadrius virginicus* (Burkh.), the two latter species being easily distinguished by having smoke-grey instead of white axillaries. Within this range it breeds in the north temperate and Arctic regions, including the British Islands. Some remain in South Europe to winter, but the majority appear to pass on to North Africa, a few migrating during the winter season as far as South Africa. The Asiatic birds winter in Beloochistan, some of them probably crossing Arabia into Africa.

about this time flocks of wild ducks began to fly up the Petchora. So far as we could judge they seemed to be principally pintail ducks, though we succeeded in shooting a teal.*

Pipits also began to arrive in great numbers. They were wild and difficult to shoot, apparently all flying up wind; evidently eager to continue their journey and rarely alighting on the ground. Both species were represented, but they appeared to migrate in separate flocks; and the red-throated pipit † was much more abundant than the meadow pipit.‡ We occasionally heard both species singing, but they were by no means in full song, being evidently intent on migration.

---

* The teal (*Querquedula crecca*, Linn.) must be considered as a palæarctic species, being only occasionally found in Greenland and the eastern coasts of North America. In the nearctic region it is replaced by a very closely allied species, *Querquedula carolinensis* (Gmel.). It is a resident in the British Islands, though its numbers are largely increased during the winter season. There are very few countries in Europe where it does not occasionally breed, and in winter it has been found as far south as Abyssinia. It breeds throughout Siberia, and winters abundantly in India, China, Formosa, and Japan. In the valley of the Petchora we did not find it north of the Arctic circle.

† The red-throated pipit (*Anthus cervinus*, Pall.) has been included in the British list, but apparently on insufficient evidence. It breeds on the tundras in the Arctic regions of both Europe and Asia, wintering in South-Eastern Europe, Algeria, Egypt, Nubia, and Abyssinia, and eastwards in Persia, India, China, and Japan. In the valley of the Petchora we found it as far north as we went on the mainland.

‡ The meadow pipit (*Anthus pratensis*, Linn.) is common throughout Arctic and temperate Europe, the birds inhabiting the colder districts migrating southwards to the basin of the Mediterranean. The records of its occurrence east of the Ural Mountains are very questionable. In the valley of the Petchora we found it a much rarer bird than the red-throated pipit, and only once met with it breeding in about latitude 68°.

Fieldfares * and redwings † also arrived and soon became very numerous; and in the flocks of shore-larks which continued to pass through the district, a few Lapland buntings ‡ were generally to be seen.

Flocks of shore-larks had by this time become more numerous, and consisted of males and females in nearly equal numbers. These birds were very tame, frequenting for the most part the fields at the back of the village,

---

* The fieldfare (*Turdus pilaris*, Linn.) is a regular winter visitor to the British Islands, having a somewhat more southerly breeding range than the redwing. It breeds in the Arctic circle, extending up to and occasionally beyond the limit of forest growth, and frequenting also in large colonies the various birch regions in north temperate Europe and throughout Siberia, as far eastwards as the watershed of the Yenesay and the Lena. It winters in Southern Europe, occurring very rarely in the Spanish peninsula, but crossing the Mediterranean to Morocco, Algeria, Egypt, and Nubia. In Asia it winters in Turkestan and Cashmere. In the valley of the Petchora we found it up to latitude 68°.

† The redwing (*Turdus iliacus*, Linn.) is a regular winter migrant to the British Islands, breeding at or near the Arctic circle, occasionally straying into Greenland, throughout the palæarctic region, though it appears to become very rare east of the valley of the Yenesay. It winters in western and southern Europe, occasionally crossing the Mediterranean into Algeria. In Asia it has been found sparingly in winter in Persia, Turkestan and North-West India. In the valley of the Petchora we found it as far north as latitude 68°. The redwing frequents the birch region and the upper zone of the pine region, occurring south of the Arctic circle, wherever these trees are found at a greater or less elevation. It is the most northerly in its range of any of the thrushes, being occasionally found on the tundra beyond the limit of forest growth. In these localities it breeds on the ground like a ringousel.

‡ The Lapland bunting (*Plectrophanes lapponicus* Linn.) is a circumpolar bird breeding on the tundras beyond the limit of forest growth, and occasionally straggling into England in winter. It winters in various parts of Europe, China, and the Northern United States of America. In the valley of the Petchora we found it passing through Ust-Zylma in great numbers, and did not meet with it again until we reached latitude 68° and latitude 68½°.

feeding and running about in the stubble, and occasionally attempting to sing on the ground. The snow-buntings and redpoles had disappeared, and in the streets their place appeared to be taken by white wagtails. Fresh flocks of these charming little birds in full breeding plumage arrived daily; and in a large flock consisting of thirty to forty birds, we noticed among them a green wagtail.*

Three whimbrels† passed over us. My companion whistled to them, so cleverly imitating their note that they approached within fifty yards of him, when he shot them. A peasant also brought us a rook.‡ the only one we saw during

---

* The green wagtail (*Budytes viridis*, Cuvel.) has not been found on the British Islands, being represented there and in the temperate regions of Europe by a nearly allied species, *Motacilla flava* (Linn.), which differs in having the colour of the head—and especially of the cheeks and the lores—paler, and in having a white eye-stripe. The former species breeds at or near the Arctic circle, throughout the palæarctic region, wintering in South Europe, North Africa as far south as Abyssinia, India, and China. In the valley of the Petchora we found it as far north as latitude $66\frac{1}{2}°$.

† The whimbrel (*Numenius phæopus*, Linn.) is very widely distributed, but appears to be confined to the eastern hemisphere and Greenland. In the British Islands it only breeds in the extreme north, visiting the remainder only in spring and autumn on migration. It is said to breed in South Russia, otherwise it is doubtful if it breeds very far south of the Arctic circle. In winter it is found throughout South Europe, the whole of Africa, and Southern Asia as far south as Australia. In the valley of the Petchora we did not see it further north than Ust-Zylma.

‡ The rook (*Corvus frugilegus*, Linn.) breeds in considerable colonies throughout Central Europe, extending eastwards in Asia as far as the valley of the Obb. To the north it becomes much rarer, seldom, if ever, reaching the Arctic circle. In England, as is well known, it remains throughout the year, but in countries where the winter is more severe it migrates southwards to both shores of the Mediterranean, the Siberian and Turkestan birds apparently wintering in Cashmere and North-West India. In East Asia it is replaced by a very nearly allied species, *C. pastinator* (Gould), which differs in

our journey. At this time we ascertained positively the presence of a bird which we had long suspected to be on the roof of the Preestaff's house next door to ours—a no less important bird than the common sparrow.* We shot two males and three females. This is an extraordinary instance of the extreme localness of birds. We never by any chance saw these common sparrows among the tree-sparrows † in our yard, nor had we any reason to think that they were to be found elsewhere in the town.

On the 19th we received an invitation from our friends the *chasseurs*, who had assisted us in our late wild goose chase, to join them in a duck hunt. M. Znaminsky had a *maisonnette* a few versts up the Zylma, which he turned to use on such occasions of sport. He and M. Sacharoff were already there. We accepted the invitation, and after sledging across the Petchora, and perhaps four versts up the Zylma, we reached our host's quarters at about 3 A.M. We had made a somewhat circuitous road up the Zylma, for

---

having the head and neck glossed with purple and not with green, and in having the bare place round the bill of much smaller extent.

* The common sparrow (*Passer domesticus*, Linn.) appears originally to have been confined to Europe, North Africa, and Asia as far east as the watershed of the Yenesay and the Lena, but it has been introduced in almost every British colony, the United States, many of the Pacific Islands, West Indies, New Zealand, Australia, &c. It is generally a resident species, except where the winters are very severe. In the valley of the Petchora we did not find it farther north than latitude 68°.

† The tree sparrow (*Passer montanus*, Linn.) appears to be confined to the eastern hemisphere, being a not uncommon resident in the British Islands, and is found throughout Europe, occasionally crossing the Mediterranean. In Asia it is found as far as the Pacific, extending southwards to North India, Burmah, and South China; being everywhere more or less a resident. In the valley of the Petchora we found it as far north as latitude 68°.

there were many ugly-looking places in the ice which had to be avoided. On arriving we dismissed our yemschiks, who returned to Ust-Zylma with orders to come with five sledges to fetch our whole party back on the following day at noon.

The shooting-ground was a flat piece of country, lying between the Petchora and the Zylma. It bore traces of its annual submersion for a week or two under the waters of the great river when it breaks up. The larger part was covered with a forest of birch, willow, and alder; many of the trees were dead, no doubt all life drowned out of them; and, all around, driftwood was scattered or accumulated in piles.

It was heavy work walking in these woods, or rather wading through the water and snow in them. Every now and then we came to a lake or an open swamp, or found ourselves on the banks of a "kooria" or creek where the snow had melted, and the walking was easier. Few or no trees grew by the side of these koorias; the banks of the Zylma also were bare; the forests near the Petchora being shaved off by the ice that sometimes mows down the stoutest trees as a man mows grass with a scythe. On the low ground between the Zylma and the forest land, pollard willows grew, many of which were knocked down by the floating blocks of ice.

It would be impossible to estimate the number of ducks we saw. They seemed to fly over us by hundreds and thousands. Small and large flocks continually passed us on the wing. In the evening the shores of the Zylma and a piece of open water opposite were almost black with them;

sometimes they filled the air like a swarm of bees. They were very wild, but the old pollard willows gave excellent opportunities for concealment, and a good shot would have made a heavy bag in a short time. My companion shot seven in about an hour; six pintails * and one teal. Nearly all these ducks were pintails; we identified hundreds through our glasses, and saw only a few teal.

My companion identified a small flock of shovellers,† one of which flew quite close to him. He also distinctly made out a pair of golden-eyes,‡ which came within shot while

---

* The pintail duck (*Dafila acuta*, Linn.) is another species of duck breeding in the Arctic regions of both hemispheres. In the British Islands it is a winter visitant, though a few may remain to breed. Its range in summer extends from the northern portion of the temperate region to some distance beyond the Arctic circle. It winters in various parts of Europe and North Africa, India, China, Japan, and Central America. In the valley of the Petchora we found this species abundant wherever we went.

† The shoveller duck (*Spatula clypeata*, Linn.) is a circumpolar bird tolerably common in the winter season in Great Britain, a few remaining with us to breed. Throughout Central and Southern Europe, and Africa as far south as Abyssinia, it appears to be a resident species, though the numbers in winter are largely increased by birds from the Arctic regions. In Asia its southern limit during the breeding season appears to be the mountains of Cashmere. It winters in India, Ceylon, South China, Formosa, and Japan. On the American continent its winter range extends almost to the equator. We met with it in the valley of the Petchora up to latitude 68°.

‡ The golden-eye duck (*Clangula glaucion*, Linn.) is also a circumpolar bird, but is replaced in Greenland and Iceland by *Clangula islandica* (Gmel.), a species which is also met with throughout the American polar region. In the British Islands it is only known as a winter visitant. From the peculiarity of its breeding in hollow trees it does not, of course, migrate beyond the northern limit of forest growth, and it is occasionally found breeding south of the Arctic circle. In winter it is found in various parts of Central and Southern Europe, sometimes crossing the Mediterranean. It has not been recorded from Persia or India, but in Eastern Asia it has been found as far south as China in winter, and in America in North Mexico

we were dining. Through the glass he also recognised a widgeon.* We also saw a few geese and swans. We met with the greenshank † more than once, and had a fine view of the peregrine falcon. A small flock of shore-larks and a few red-throated pipits, too busy migrating to stop to be shot, nearly complete the list of birds we saw in the open country.

I spent most of my time in the woods. Three weeks before we had made a long round through them on our snow-shoes, and found them deserted; not a bird to be seen but a solitary marsh-tit or an occasional "hoodie." Now in the early morning these woods were full of life and abounded in interest for the ornithologist. In the afternoon they were more quiet, and the interest was not sufficient to repay the

---

and Cuba. In the valley of the Petchora we did not meet with this species farther north than Habariki.

* The widgeon (*Mareca penelope*, Linn.) must be considered as a palæarctic duck, though its range extends eastwards beyond Behring's Straits to the coast of Alaska. In Great Britain it is a common winter visitant, occasionally remaining to breed. It also breeds in the northern portion of temperate Europe, extending northwards beyond the limit of forest growth. In Asia it appears to breed throughout Siberia, passing through Turkestan in spring and autumn on migration, and wintering in Scinde, India, South China, Formosa, and Japan. This bird is certainly the most abundant species of duck inhabiting the islands of the delta of the Petchora, but we did not see it farther north than latitude 68°.

† The greenshank (*Totanus glottis*, Bechst.) is confined to the eastern hemisphere, breeding in Scotland, but only known as a spring and summer migrant in the rest of the British Islands. It breeds on the fells of Norway and Sweden, and in Siberia south of the Arctic circle. It passes through Central Europe on migration, and winters on both shores of the Mediterranean and throughout Africa. It passes through South Siberia on migration and winters in India, the islands of the Malay Archipelago, Australia, China, and Japan. In the valley of the Petchora we did not meet with it farther north than Habariki.

toil of wading through water, snow, mud, and drift-wood. The commonest and noisiest bird was the redpole. Next to it strange to say, was the meadow pipit. This bird behaved in every way like the tree pipit, being occasionally seen on the ground, but mostly up in the trees; sometimes singing on the ground, sometimes when on the wing, oftener in the branches overhead.

We had just decided that these birds were, or ought to be the tree pipits, when we shot down half-a-dozen from among the branches, and finally satisfied ourselves that they were the meadow pipit. Our astonishment was still greater, however, when we beheld three gulls quietly perched upon the top of a tall birch in the wood. We watched them for some time, examining them through our glasses; at last they rose and flew over our heads, and by their cry we recognised them to be the familiar *Larus canus;* shortly afterwards we shot one.

Fieldfares and redwings were sprinkled through the woods; we could almost always hear the song of the latter bird, as well as the loose cry of the former, and its starling-like note before alighting. My companions saw a couple of redstarts chasing each other, and I followed a willow-wren,*

---

* The common willow-warbler (*Phylloscopus trochilus*, Linn.) is one of the most abundant of the numerous songsters which visit the British Islands every spring, arriving early in April. Throughout that month, as well as in May and June, its familiar song, like a peal of little bells, resounds in every wood and garden. This species breeds in Western, Central, and Northern Europe. I found it common in Norway up to the North Cape. Colonel Irby found it breeding abundantly near Gibraltar. It is said only to pass through Italy in spring and summer on migration. Mr. Danford tells me that it breeds in Transylvania, but Dr. Krüper informed me when I was in

which was in full song, for at least an hour, but did not succeed in shooting it. Many white wagtails flew past, and the reed-buntings were also common. Where the birches were largest we heard the tapping of the woodpeckers. We shot a pair of lesser spotted woodpeckers;* and of a pair of three-toed woodpeckers† that we saw, we succeeded in

Athens that it is only found in Greece and Asia Minor in winter. Captain Shelley says that it winters in Nubia and Egypt, and Canon Tristram records it as abundant in the oases of North Africa in winter. I have also seen skins collected in winter from the river Gambia, Damara Land, Cape Town, Natal, the Transvaal, and Abyssinia. In Siberia Finsch and Brehm found it in the valley of the Obb, and I constantly heard its song in the valley of the Yenesay up to latitude 70°. The Siberian birds are probably those which have been found wintering in North-Central, and South-Eastern Persia.

* The Siberian lesser spotted woodpecker (*Picus pipra*, Pall.) is very nearly allied to the smallest species of British woodpecker (*Picus minor*, Linn.), but differs in being larger and in having the whole of the underparts unspotted silky white, with the exception of the under-tail coverts, which are slightly streaked with black. The outside tail-feathers have two rudimentary cross-bars. The transverse bars on the back and rump are nearly obsolete. This species is the *Picus kamchatkensis* of Cabanis, Bonaparte, Sundevall, and Malherbe. I have shot it at Archangel as well as in the valley of the Petchora, and have seen

skins from the Yenesay, Lake Baical, and the Amoor. I have also in my collection examples from the islands of Sakhalin and Yezzo, north of Japan. Compared with the South European form it is an excellent species, but birds from Norway and Sweden are somewhat intermediate, being as large as the Siberian species, but in the colour and markings of the back and underparts scarcely differing from the South European form. In the valley of the Petchora we found the Siberian species not uncommon in the birch forests as far north as the latter extended, where they doubtless remain throughout the year.

† The three-toed woodpecker (*Picoides tridactylus*, Linn.) has probably never occurred in the British Islands, but is a resident species throughout Northern Europe and Asia, and the mountainous districts of Central and Southern Europe and South Siberia. In the valley of the Petchora we did not observe it farther north than latitude 67°. On the continent of America it is replaced by a species (*Picoides americanus*, Brehm) so nearly allied as to be considered by many ornithologists to be only subspecifically distinct.

shooting the male. We also shot a pair of marsh tits. Between this bird's habits and its note and those of our English bird I could distinguish no difference.

When I returned, on the morning of the 20th after a five hours' solitary ramble in the woods, I found the sportsmen still fast asleep. My entrance roused them, and we soon proceeded to make "tchai." We were sitting down to our pipes after our late breakfast, when we were startled by the appearance of M. Znaminski, who had just gone out, and who now came hurrying back in a state of great excitement, beckoning to us to come.

We seized our guns, expecting to see some great and rare bird; we rushed to the door, and there we paused and stood still, gazing before us in mute astonishment. Our road was in movement, and was going to Ust-Zylma at the rate of two or three miles an hour. There was no doubt about it, the Zylma was breaking up. The scene was wild and picturesque. In a few hours it was very impressive. The rush of ice had broken into the Petchora at the mouth of the Zylma. Here and there piles of it lay upon the banks. Finally it had blocked, and gradually the Zylma became a confused mass of jammed ice; tree trunks or an occasional ice-floe, thicker than the rest, formed where the water had been stiller and deeper, rising above the level. While the ice moved the sound was like that of a waterfall: as it cracked on the Petchora, the noise was as that of rumbling thunder. The water was rapidly rising, and our predicament was serious. It was obvious that no horses could reach us. The Russians, who at first did not realise the situation, soon began to look grave. We took council together, and we decided to transport ourselves and our baggage to some houses that stood on higher ground, halfway towards the mouth of the Zylma. It took us some hours to do this. We were beginning to make preparations for a week's camping in the midst of floods, when towards four o'clock we discerned in the distance the figures of our yemschiks. They were coming, but they were coming without horses. When they reached us we learned from them that the ice was broken up on both shores of the Petchora. They had come across in a boat; that they had dragged for a couple of versts in a sledge across the central field of ice, being forced to leave it on the shore five or six miles off. We determined to put the bulk of our baggage under the charge of two yemschiks, and to return with the other men in the boat.

We felt rather nervous as we entered the boats, and put to sea on the open water across which we had sledged so recently, and we had some little difficulty in finding a solid piece of ice on which to land. The central ice of the Petchora was evidently on the eve of being broken up. Every nerve was strained to drag the boats across the mile of ice, and relaunch them on the safe side of the river without a moment's unnecessary loss of time. It was past midnight, and at any moment the crash might come. The ice was obviously under great pressure. Cracks running for miles with a sound like distant thunder warned us that a mighty power was all but upon us, a force which seemed for the moment to impress the mind with a greater sense of power than even the crushing weight of water at Niagara, a force which breaks up ice more than a mile wide, at least three feet thick, and weighted with another three feet of snow, at the rate of a hundred miles in the twenty-four hours. It was eight o'clock in the morning when we landed in Ust-Zylma, and heartily thankful we were to find ourselves once more safe in our quarters. We were hungry and dead tired after the excitement was over, and after a hasty breakfast we were glad to turn into our hammocks. We slept for a couple of hours, when, looking out of the window, we found the crash had come; the mighty river Petchora was a field of pack ice and ice-floes, marching past towards the sea at the rate of six miles an hour. We ran out on to the banks to find half the inhabitants of Ust-Zylma watching the impressive scene.

OLD RUSSIAN SILVER CROSS.

DIFFICULTIES WITH SNOW-SHOES.

CHAPTER XI.

Religious processions—Costumes of the peasants—A Russian holiday—Drunkenness—Prejudices of the Old Believers — Field-work — House-building — New birds—The Siberian chiffchaff—Prices of provisions—Arrival of waters.

The 21st of May was St. Michael's Day, one of the greatest holidays in this country. A long procession of "Old Believers," consisting mostly of women and children carrying banners and pictures, wended its way through the town. The women were dressed in their best, and decked with all the jewelry that they possessed, some of which was very ancient and valuable. Many of the dresses, too, were antique; heirlooms handed down from mother to daughter.

Some of these were gorgeous—none were vulgar—the colours being always sober, rich, and clear. The wealthier peasants' wives and daughters were arrayed in velvet and gold, silk and satin, those of the poorer in linen and cotton, almost entirely of Russian manufacture. The women, as a rule, wore the "roobahkah," which is simply a shirt put over the fur "malitza," coming down to within a few inches of the ground; their *chaussures* consisted of Wellington boots, and their headdress of an orientally-coloured handkerchief, tied behind. We had already noticed this Eastern taste for colour among the peasantry. A few days before, an imposing wedding procession had passed our window. The larger number of the party was on horseback, two on each horse. All were brightly dressed: the men wore knots of ribbons on their shoulders; the women, gaily apparelled, had on various and curious head-dresses, ornamented with gold braid. Yet, for all their brilliancy, the colours did not look garish, a little touch of grey being always introduced to subdue the effect.

On St. Michael's Day it is customary to make presents to the Church. The peasants brought various sorts of offerings, cows, sheep, gloves, ribbons, &c., which were afterwards sold by auction. Then the afternoon was spent in merry-making. As is too often the case on a Russian holiday, the revellers all got more or less drunk.

We found the condition of things wonderfully altered at Ust-Zylma by the breaking up of the ice of the Zylma and the Pishma. Despite the map, the latter river flows into the Petchora, and is not a tributary of the Zylma. The thaw of the two rivers together had been too much for the Petchora. The ice was broken up for three or four versts on either side of the town; most of it had disappeared, it might be under the other ice. Already several boats were out, and the men were fishing in open water. The breaking-up of the ice went on steadily for days. By the 25th of May the great river was entirely free. Summer had come upon them as suddenly as usual, and the people were hard at work; the women and children carting manure on the land, using sledges, although the snow had disappeared, except where it lay in drifts; the men breaking up the ground with an antediluvian-looking plough, sowing corn broadcast, or harrowing in the seed with a wooden-toothed harrow.

A good deal of building was also going on. The year before, the peasants had made large earnings out of the fisheries, and were now spending larger sums than usual in erecting houses. We found the demand for labour was great, and wages were high. Few men could be got under 10s. per week. We spent our days, as usual, on the look-out for the arrival of new migratory birds, in watching the habits of those at hand, and in adding to our collection. We saw no snow-buntings after the 18th; the merlins disappeared with them. Nor did we see any gulls after the the 21st. The shore-larks and the Lapland buntings were also growing scarce. Occasionally small flocks of them would appear in the fields behind the house, sometimes so busy feeding as to allow us to approach very near them.

On the 21st of May we were surprised to find a pair of

wheatears.* In England they are the earliest birds of passage to arrive in spring, but of course they winter farther south than the snow-buntings and shore-larks, and we might reasonably expect them to arrive later in such northerly breeding-grounds.

On the 22nd we added another familiar British migrant to our list, the tree pipit,† a bird which usually arrives rather late with us. A more important addition to our list was, however, the Siberian chiffchaff,‡ a little warbler which was

---

* The wheatear (*Saxicola œnanthe*, Linn.) afterwards became rather common at Ust-Zylma. Farther north it was rarer, but we saw it as far as Dvoinik. In the British Islands the wheatear is one of the earliest summer migrants, arriving on the moors about the middle of March. This species breeds throughout Central and Northern Europe as far north as land exists, extending westwards as far as Greenland, and eastwards across Siberia into Alaska. In winter it is found in Northern Africa, and probably Central Africa; the Asiatic birds migrating to Mongolia, Northern India, and Persia.

† The tree pipit (*Anthus trivialis*, Linn.) is a common summer visitant to the British Islands, and to the northern and central portions of Europe and Asia, as far east as the watershed of the Yenesay and the Lena. As we only met with one example in the valley of the Petchora, in latitude 65½°, we were probably somewhat beyond the ordinary limit of its northern range. It passes through Southern Europe on migration, wintering in North Africa, and having been met with as far south as Katlirland. Eastwards it has been recorded from Persia and India; in the latter country it has, however, generally been confounded with a nearly allied species, *Anthus maculatus* (Hodgs.), which is also found in Eastern Siberia, China, and Japan, and differs in being much greener on the back, and more spotted on the under parts.

‡ The Siberian chiffchaff (*Phylloscopus tristis*, Blyth) winters in the plains of India and Beloochistan. A few remain to breed in the Alpine districts of the Himalayas and the Karakorum mountains, whilst the main body passes through Turkestan on migration to their summer quarters in Siberia, which extend from the valley of the Petchora to Lake Baical. We found it abundant on the willow-covered islands of the delta of the Petchora, and in 1877 I took several of its nests and eggs in the valley of the Yenesay. It is very similar in size and in the proportion of its primaries to the European chiffchaff, but the

frequenting some low willows, uttering a plaintive call-note, a single note repeated at intervals. We were under the impression that we were adding a new bird to the European list, but we afterwards found that our discovery had been forestalled by M. Meves, of Stockholm, who had found it some years previously in the government of Perm. A third specimen which we added to our list was a skylark.*
On our return home we found that M. Znaminsky had also been out shooting, and had bagged some very interesting birds for us; five green wagtails, three meadow pipits, two red-throated pipits, and a stonechat,† the latter not the European but the Indian species, and a new and interesting addition to the European fauna. M. Znaminsky's hunting-ground had been a marshy piece of land just behind the town, sprinkled over with small spruce firs, bushes of stunted birch, juniper, and dwarf rhododendrons (*Ledum palustre*). To this spot we betook ourselves the next morning, and found it to be a favourite resting-place of migratory birds.

---

latter is much greener above and much yellower underneath, and has dark brown instead of black legs.

* The skylark (*Alauda arvensis*, Linn.) is found all over the palæarctic region, from the British Islands eastwards into Siberia and North China, being a resident in the temperate regions; the Arctic birds migrating in autumn to South Europe, North Africa, North-West India, and North China. We only met with two examples, and therefore conclude that we were beyond its ordinary breeding-range.

† The Siberian stonechat (*Pratincola maura*, Pall.) differs from the British and European species in having a pure white unspotted rump and nearly black axillaries. The eastern form, found by us in Europe for the first time, breeds in the southern Arctic and northern temperate regions, from the valley of Petchora eastwards to the Pacific, wintering in Persia, India, Burmah, and South China. In the valley of the Petchora we did not see them farther north than latitude 66°.

We shot a red-throated pipit on the ground, solitary among a company of meadow pipits. We secured a green wagtail and a short-eared owl.* In that favoured spot the willow warblers congregated and were in full song; the blue-throated warblers were also there, but their song was not so full; it resembled sometimes the warble of the pipit, and sometimes that of the whitethroat. We secured, besides, a brace of golden plover and a reed-bunting.

During the afternoon we visited the skirts of the pine-forest in the valley, and there I shot two male wheatears. The day before a male and female wheatear had flown past me, and perched on the summit of a tall pine. Out of a spruce fir in the wood we now heard a loud, clear "chiff-cheff-chaff." We thought it was the cry of the chiffchaff; but we failed to find the bird. Shortly after we heard a warbler singing. For a moment we fancied it was a willow-wren; but before the song was half finished, we felt convinced that we were unacquainted with it. It was not unlike the chiff-cheff-chaff of our bird when it makes the third variation it occasionally does in its notes; but these notes were more musical, repeated rapidly without intermission, running into

---

* The short-eared owl (*Asio brachyotus*, Forst.) is a circumpolar bird, and is principally a winter visitant to the British Islands, a few, however, remaining to breed. It is found in summer in North Europe, but is only a winter visitor to South Europe and Africa, where it has occurred as far south as Natal. Eastwards it is found throughout Siberia, passing through Turkestan on migration, wintering in Persia, India, Burmah, and South China. On the American continent it breeds in various parts of Canada and the United States and in winter has been found as far south as Chili and the Falkland Islands. In the valley of the Petchora we did not meet with it much beyond the Arctic circle.

a song. This bird was also perching in a spruce fir, but a long shot brought it down. It proved to be the Siberian chiffchaff. For days afterwards we heard several of these birds singing, and, on further study of their note, we found it very distinct from the one of the chiffchaff. That of our bird is not badly represented by its name, with an equal accent on both syllables. The note of the Siberian chiffchaff is better represented by the word "chiv'it," with a decided accent on the first syllable. It is seldom uttered singly, but generally repeated "chiv-it, chiv-et," or oftener "chiv-it," followed by two notes of its song. The bird seemed very partial to the spruce fir, perching on its topmost bough. In comparing its habits and those of the willow-warbler, we found the Siberian chiffchaff easy to shoot, while the former was as wild as possible.

Another song that greatly roused our curiosity was a melodious whistle, reminding us both of the song of the blackbird and of the redwing. We expected the songster would turn out to be some rare Siberian thrush. The bird was by no means shy, so we had no difficulty in following its song, and in approaching within easy shot, as it perched sometimes on the top, sometimes near the summit of a spruce fir. Once we observed it hopping on the ground. We obtained six specimens, and were somewhat disappointed to find such melodious and thrush-like notes proceeded from the pine grosbeak.*

---

* The pine grosbeak (*Pinicola enucleator*, Linn.) is a circumpolar bird visiting the British Islands somewhat irregularly during winter. It breeds in the high north of the pine region, migrating southwards only in severe weather, being a more or less accidental visitor to most parts of Central and

It was a curious fact that the day following, on returning to the spot where we had seen and shot so many various birds, we found it deserted; there were nothing but willow-warblers on it. Red-throated pipits passed over singly and in flocks; but none seemed disposed to alight. In a plantation hard by, we heard a chaffinch sing; but we did not get a shot at it. We fell in there with a small flock of bramblings,* and secured a male that was not yet in full breeding plumage. On the following day a thick mist came up the Petchora, which cleared up about noon, and was followed by a north-west breeze with gleams of sunshine and threatenings of rain. Birds were few and sang little, the note of the warblers being almost the only one we heard. We had an excellent opportunity of identifying a white-tailed eagle, that came almost within shot of us. Two cranes† passed

---

Southern Europe. Eastwards it winters in South Siberia, occasionally wandering as far as the northern states of North America. In the valley of the Petchora we did not observe it farther north than latitude $65\frac{1}{2}°$.

* The brambling (*Fringilla montifringilla*, Linn.) appears to be confined to the eastern hemisphere, visiting the British Islands in flocks during the winter. It breeds throughout the northern portions of the palæarctic region frequenting the pine, and especially the birch forests at or near the limit of forest growth, wintering in most parts of Central and Southern Europe, and occasionally crossing the Mediterranean. Eastwards it winters in India,

North China, and Japan. In the valley of the Petchora we found it an abundant species up to the Arctic circle.

† The common crane (*Grus communis*, Bechst.) is confined to the eastern hemisphere, being replaced in America by two allied species, *Grus canadensis* (Temm.) and *Grus fraterculus* (Baird). The increase of population has caused the crane to become little more than an accidental visitor to the British Islands. It formerly bred throughout the whole of Europe, wherever marshes of sufficient extent and solitude were to be found, which principally remain at the present time in Spain, Arctic Europe, and Turkey. It winters in the basin of the Mediter-

over us, and I recognised them as birds I had seen two or three days before. By this time all the hooded crows and magpies had gone into the woods to breed, and the town was deserted by them. During the week there had apparently been an arrival of house-sparrows in Ust-Zylma, for they abounded in M. Zuaminski's yard. Strangely enough, we could not meet with any in other parts of the town.

On the 26th the weather changed; a cold north-east wind blew. It was a day unpropitious to bird-shooting. So little did we anticipate meeting with any, that we spent the morning in buying provisions for our journey. It may be useful to record the prices we paid :—

Salt beef	1.70	roubles per pud.	($1\tfrac{1}{2}$d. per lb.)
Butter	6.50	,,	,,	($4\tfrac{1}{2}$d. per lb).
Tea	2	,,	per lb.	(5s. per lb.)
Coffee	0.55	,,	,,	(1s. 4d. per lb).

We also bought a *nyelma*, or white salmon, for our present use. It weighed 15 lbs., and cost 10 copecks per lb. We were told that, later on, the price would be 5 copecks per lb. This fish sometimes reaches the weight of 60 lbs. We found it very nice eating, but we failed to recognise its boasted superiority to salmon. We acknowledge, however, that the cooking may have been in fault. In its stomach were several small fishes.

In the afternoon we went out in the cold wind, not expecting to shoot anything; but to our astonishment we found

---

ranean. Eastwards it ranges to Kamtchatka, wintering in Persia, India, and China. In the valley of the Pet- chora we did not discover its breeding-grounds, and met with it only at Ust-Zylma on migration.

a number of new birds in the town itself. We secured a wood sandpiper * out of a flock of four; a Temminck's stint,† of which there were several. We saw a barn-swallow ‡ twice, and shot a pair of ringed plovers. § We had also an

---

* The wood sandpiper (*Totanus glareola*, Linn.) is confined to the palæarctic region during the breeding season, being known in the British Islands as a somewhat rare visitor during migration, and having once been known to breed near Newcastle. It breeds in various places in Northern and Eastern Europe, including Holland, Denmark, Scandinavia, North Germany, and the whole of Russia. Eastwards it is found throughout Siberia and Turkestan. It winters in South Africa, Beloochistan, India, Burmah, and the islands of the Malay Archipelago, passing through China and Japan on migration. In the valley of the Petchora we did not see it farther north than latitude 68°.

† Temminck's stint (*Tringa temmincki*, Leisl.) is confined to the eastern hemisphere, breeding only on the tundras beyond the limit of forest growth. In the British Islands it is a comparatively rare bird, only found on migration. It winters in the Mediterranean, principally on its southern shores, and it extends as far south as the Sahara. It probably extends eastwards in the breeding season as far as Kamtchatka, and winters in India and China.

‡ The common swallow (*Hirundo rustica*, Linn.), one of our most familiar British birds, breeds throughout the whole of Europe and North Africa, migrating to South Africa in winter, a few only remaining in the oases of the Sahara. Eastwards it breeds in Northern and Central Asia, wintering in India and the islands of the Malay Archipelago. The Eastern form has been described as a different species, *Hirundo gutturalis* (Scop.), and may be considered as a subspecies connecting the European bird with the very nearly allied American form, *Hirundo horreorum* (Barton). In the valley of the Petchora we were probably at the extreme northern limit of the range of this bird, which only accidentally wanders as far north as the Arctic circle.

§ The ringed plover (*Ægialitis hiaticula*, Linn.) is confined to the western portion of the palæarctic region, not having been found farther east than the watershed of the Lena in the north and Turkestan and Persia in the south. In the British Islands it is common and resident. Northwards it is found as far as the mainland extends, and also in Nova Zembla, Spitzbergen, Iceland, and Greenland. It does not go into South Africa. It frequents the seashore as well as the inland rivers and lakes, and is a more or less partial resident throughout the greater part of its range; in the extreme north being found in the summer only, and in the extreme south in winter alone.

excellent view of two oyster-catchers.* All these were new arrivals. Many green wagtails were to be seen, and we shot four males and two females. In the village we met a shore-lark, the first we had seen for many days in the streets.

The unfavourable-looking day proved one of the most interesting we had yet had.

---

* The oyster-catcher (*Hæmatopus ostralegus*, Linn.) appears to be confined to the eastern hemisphere, only accidentally straying as far as Greenland; being represented on the American continent by a nearly allied species, *Hæmatopus palliatus* (Temm.). The Arctic circle appears to be the northern limit of its range, and it does not appear to visit South Africa, Australia, or New Zealand, being represented in the two latter countries by a nearly allied species, *Hæmatopus longirostris* (Gmel.). Throughout the greater part of its range the oyster-catcher is a more or less partial resident, being a summer visitant only in the extreme north, and a winter visitant in the extreme south. In the valley of the Petchora we found them in small numbers up to about twenty miles within the Arctic circle.

OLD RUSSIAN SILVER CROSS.

WILLOW GROUSE.

CHAPTER XII.

Samoyede names—The Swedish mocking-bird—Toads—Birds resting on migration—Sparrow-hawk—The Petchora free from ice—A new song—Ceremony of blessing the steamer—Rambles in the woods—Arrival of the mosquitoes.

WHILST we were waiting for the flood in the Petchora to subside sufficiently to make it safe for us to proceed down the river in a small boat, we met with a Samoyede somewhat more intelligent than usual, and from him we were glad to have an opportunity of learning the names of various articles connected with reindeer and sledging which we had collected.

It is somewhat difficult to express the exact sound in English characters, since almost every Samoyede word is pronounced either nasally or gutturally.

The Samoyede for sledge is *khăn*, the *kh* pronounced like *ch* in German, and the *n* like *n* in Spanish.

A reindeer is *tŭ*, the *u* like the German *ü*. There are three sorts of reindeer, *khŏ'-ra tŭ*, the entire male reindeer; *khăb'-tŭ*, the cut reindeer; and *yăh' tŭ*, the female reindeer. These adjectives are also used in reference to horses and other cattle.

The piece of leather over the body of the animal, which takes the place of our saddle, is called the *yōdé'-yĕ-nă*. The narrower band round the neck, in place of the collar, is the *pōdé'-yŭr*. The single trace attached to the lower part of the collar, and passing between the legs under the body, is called the *să*. The blind pulley, or pulley block without a pulley through which it passes, is the *pyăt-săy'*. The halter, or bridle without a bit, is the *syăhn*. The halter of the leading reindeer is the *nyĕs'-mĭn-dyĕ syăhn*. The halter of the other reindeer is the *pyĕ-lăy' syăhn*. The rein with which the leading reindeer is guided is the *mĕt'-ă-nyĕ*. The hook on the side of the saddle-band on which the rein rests is the *khăl-sōō-lă*. The swivel or universal joint by which the rein is attached to the halter is the *sŭr'-nyĕ*. A button which serves to fasten the trace to the collar, or the belly-band to the saddle, is the *păy'-sik*. The long pole with which the reindeer are driven is the *tōōr*, and the bone or ivory nob at the end of it the *tōōr-măhl'*. The rein connecting the leading reindeer with the one next to it, is the *pōō'-ĭ-nyă*. A lasso is called a *teēn-zāy'*, and the bone noose through which it runs is the *sāh'-mik*. The tent or choom is the *myāh'-kăn*, and a dog is called a *vŏ'-ĭ-nyĕ-hō*. The Samoyede who gave us this information was one of the poorer men of his tribe. All the richer families had migrated north with their herds of reindeer before the snow had melted. The poorer families remained behind, hanging on to the skirts of the Russians, helping them with their fishing, and receiving for pay such food as their employers chose to give them. One cannot help pitying these poor people. Their nation is gradually dying out. Like the North American Indians, they are doomed to destruction, for, like them, they cannot refuse spirits. In the struggle for existence they have no chance with the cunning Russian, who in all matters of business has no more conscience than a Greek or a Jew.

During this time the birds were few. On the 27th we took a walk in the forest, and the only ones that were singing were the willow warblers; an occasional pine grosbeak breaking in now and then. We secured, however, a pair of bramblings out of a flock. We shot a blue-throated warbler, a yellow-hammer, a female reed-bunting, a Siberian jay, a stonechat, and a red-throated pipit, and out of a number we brought down a brace of golden plover. We saw a solitary shore-lark, a gull (apparently the common species), and a fine male bullfinch. In the town we got a couple of wood-sandpipers; then the green wagtails were common, and we came upon a large party of Lapland buntings, all apparently females. In the evening the wind dropped, and a sharp frost set in. At midnight, when we went to bed, the thermometer marked only 30°. The next day was bright, but cold, with a light north wind blowing. We went for another long tramp through the pine woods: very few birds were to be seen. We shot a pair of grosbeaks, a fieldfare, and a blue-throated warbler.* We saw a Siberian jay, for whose nest we had a long search, which resulted in our finding two old ones. Whether these were nests of the Siberian jay or of the pine grosbeak, we could not, however, determine. Twice we heard the note of the Siberian chiffchaff, but we could not see or get a shot at the birds.

The smart frost returned during the night. In the morning, however, the wind veered round to the east, and it was warm; in the afternoon it was very hot. Five hours' hard walking through the woods in the early morning resulted in nothing. I did not bring down a single bird. My companion shot two blue-throated warblers; they had now grown as common as the willow warbler. The blue-throated warbler is not inaptly called the Swedish mocking-bird. Sometimes it is shy and retiring, seeking food in the densest thickets and bushes; haunting the marshy grounds, sprinkled over with small spruce fir, dwarf willows and juniper. But when newly arrived from its winter home,

---

* The blue-throated warbler (*Cyanecula suecica*, Linn.) has only twice been met with in the British Islands. It breeds within the Arctic circle, or at high elevations above the limit of forest growth, in both Europe and Asia, occasionally crossing Behring's Straits into Alaska. In Western Europe it is replaced by a nearly allied species, *C. leucocyana* (Brehm.) which differs in having the red spot in the centre of the blue throat replaced by a white one. The blue-throat winters in North Africa as far south as Abyssinia, India, and South China. In the valley of the Petchora we did not observe it farther north than latitude 68°.

and beginning to sing, it is an easy bird to see, and not difficult to shoot. On its first arrival, it often warbles in an undertone so low, that you fancy the sound must be muffled by the thick tangle of branches in which you think the bird is concealed, while all the time it is perched on high upon the topmost spray of a young fir, this very conspicuousness causing him to escape detection for the moment. His first attempts at singing are harsh and grating, like the notes of the sedge warbler, or the still harsher ones of the whitethroat; these are followed by several variations in a louder and rather more melodious tone, repeated over and over again, somewhat in the fashion of a song-thrush. After this you might fancy the little songster was trying to mimic the various alarm-notes of all the birds he can remember—the "chiz-zit" of the wagtail, the "tip-tip-tip" of the blackbird, and especially the "whit-whit" of the chaffinch. As he improves in voice, he sings louder and longer, until at last he almost approaches the nightingale in the richness of the melody that he pours forth. Sometimes he will sing as he flies upward, descending with expanded wings and tail, to alight on the highest bough of some low tree, almost exactly as the tree pipit does. When the females have arrived, there comes at the end of his song the most metallic notes I have ever heard a bird utter. It is a sort of "tingting," resembling the sound produced by the hitting of a suspended bar of steel with another piece of the same metal.

Our afternoon walk was more fruitful of result than had been our morning's. I had followed for some time the shore of the overflowing Petchora, when, after having bagged a brace of wood-sandpipers and a ring-dotterel, I crossed a sand-bank to a marshy pool. The muffled croak of numerous toads or frogs kept up a sound resembling that of gurgling water. On my approach the whole tribe disappeared and hid in the mud. After I had waited a while, three slowly put up their noses above the surface. I fired ineffectually upon the reptiles, but I started seven or eight sandpipers and a red-throated pipit, upon which I set off at once in pursuit of the last bird. I presently found myself on a marshy piece of ground, covered with grassy hillocks, in the narrow trenches between which pipits were sitting. As I walked on they rose at my feet on all sides, and I soon had half-a-dozen within shot. I brought down a bird with each barrel, re-loaded, and, as I walked up to my victims, there rose between me and them two or three pipits, who evidently preferred being shot to being trod upon. Unfortunately I had but two cartridges left, so, bringing down another brace, I went back to our quarters for more ammunition. On returning to the open marshy ground, I found the birds still there, and very soon secured another half-dozen. My last shot was a double one. As I was getting over the soil upon which some pipits had been sitting, a hawk rushed past clutching a bird in its claws. A dozen wagtails set off after it in vociferous pursuit. I followed more quietly, and soon had the satisfaction of laying a male sparrow-hawk * upon

---

* The sparrow-hawk (*Accipiter nisus*, Linn.) is a resident in the British Islands, inhabiting the whole of Europe and Northern Asia. In the extreme north it is a migratory bird, wintering in North Africa, India, and China. In the valley of the Petchora we only identified one example at Ust-Zylma.

K

its back, with a half-eaten sparrow beside it. Some wagtails remained perched upon the railing behind which the hawk had retired to finish the devouring of its prey. They uttered cries, which might be interpreted either as doubting the supposed escape of their foe, or as a pæan of rejoicing over its downfall. The sight of their enemy lying motionless on its back rendered them deaf to the sound of my gun, and blind to my presence. They remained undismayed within a few yards of me, not stirring until I had packed away the hawk. At this juncture my companion came up. He had been more fortunate than I had been, in his raid upon the reptiles. He had secured a couple, which we found to be a species of toad, with whitish and black spots and stripes on the back. At this pool I now secured a Temminck's stint, and my companion another pipit, making the eleventh shot that day. For weeks we had never succeeded in shooting more than one out of a flock. They had abounded during the last fortnight in the fields and in the open ground about the town. We had seen hundreds, and yet, during those two weeks, we had not secured more than five males and one female; now in a couple of hours we had bagged ten males and one female out of a single flock. We had found them wild, and seldom disposed to settle on the ground. It was curious that these pipits should have been so different from the others; but what was still more curious and interesting was their behaviour during the raid we made upon them. After repeated shots, bringing down several of their numbers, the remainder would get up, settle on the railings, on the adjoining house-roof, or perch upon the slender branches of a willow-tree hard by.

The same day I saw again the barn-swallow, which seemed to be the only representative of its species at Ust-Zylma. I watched a flock of shore-larks and Lapland buntings on the stubble. As a rule they ran along the ground like the wagtail, but I also marked both birds hopping for some distance.

For the first time, on Sunday, 30th of May, the Petchora was free from ice. The steady march-past of the frozen blocks had lasted just one week. The wind that day was warm, blowing from the south, but the sky was cloudy. A peasant brought us three young Siberian jays, and another rowed across the river, the bearer of a ruff,* the first we had yet seen; and of some eggs, six duck's eggs, doubtless those of the pintail, and four of the hooded crow. The following day the warm south wind continued, with sunshine and cloud. We took a long round in the valley, where a few days before we had seen so many Siberian chiffchaffs. The blue-throated warblers were singing lustily, but we failed to hear or see the bird we were specially in search of. As we were making our way home, through a

---

* The ruff (*Machetes pugnax*, Linn.) is confined to the eastern hemisphere. In the British Islands it is rapidly disappearing before the advance of cultivation and drainage, and is now rarely met with except on the spring and autumn migrations. It breeds throughout Northern Scandinavia, Holland, and North Germany, wintering in Africa as far south as the Cape. Eastwards it breeds throughout Siberia as far as the valley of the Yenesay, wintering in India and Ceylon. The records of its occurrence in China, Japan, and Kamtchatka appear to be doubtful. In the valley of the Petchora we found it as far north as latitude 68½°.

swamp thickly studded over with willows, birch, and fir, I heard a song quite new to me. It closely resembled that of the yellow-hammer, whose note is popularly supposed to say "lit, lit, lit, little bread and no cheese." This bird cried "lit, lit, lit, in as tay." I shot the strange songster, and brought down my first little bunting.* Twice during the day we visited the marshy spot, upon which forty-eight hours previously the red-throated pipits had swarmed, but we found it utterly deserted. The flock we had come upon was one evidently resting after a long stage of migration, and that had now resumed its northward progress.

The next day a second visit to the same spot brought the same result; not a red-throated pipit was to be seen upon it. On the 1st of June I saw a black scoter † for the first time, flying down the Petchora close past Sideroff's steamer. I

---

* The little bunting (*Emberiza pusilla*, Pall.) can only be considered as an accidental visitor to the British Islands, breeding at or near the northern limit of the pine region from the valley of the Dvina eastwards to the Pacific. It is a comparatively rare visitor in winter to South-Eastern Europe, migrating principally into India and China. We did not succeed in obtaining its eggs, which are almost unknown in collections, and it was not until I visited the valley of the Yenesay in 1877 that authentic eggs of this bird were brought to this country. We observed it as far north as latitude 68°, where, however, it had become extremely rare.

† The black scoter (*Œdemia nigra*,

Linn.) is confined to the eastern hemisphere, although it is replaced on the American continent by a very closely allied species, *Œdemia americana* (Swains.). It breeds abundantly in many parts of Scotland, and is a regular winter visitant to Ireland and England. Its breeding-range may be said to extend from the Arctic circle to beyond the northern limit of forest growth. In winter it is found in various parts of Europe, occasionally crossing the Mediterranean, whilst in Asia it has been recorded at that season of the year from the Caspian Sea and Japan, the American form only apparently migrating farther south to China. In the valley of the Petchora we observed this bird as far as the coast.

was on deck at the time, one of a crowd waiting to witness the ceremony of sprinkling the vessel with holy water ere it set out on its summer voyage. The ship had arrived the evening before, from its winter quarters in the bay behind Habariki. The ceremony was effective. Flags were flying, cannons firing, guests assembled; a breakfast was prepared, then came the procession of robed priests, candles burning and censers swinging; prayers were chanted, the crucifix was kissed, and then the sprinkling began. Everybody and everything was sprinkled with holy water from a ro 1, apparently made of fine gilt wire. The paddle-boxes were sprinkled, the deck was sprinkled fore and aft, the cabins were sprinkled, the sailors were sprinkled; the captain and the engineer each received a whisk from the brush, which made them wince, for at that moment a detachment of ice, probably from the Ussa, was passing down the river, chilling the water not a little. Then all was over except the breakfast, when a practical joke was played upon the guests. A course of bear-flesh was served up incognito, so deliciously cooked that all ate of it with gusto, suspecting nothing. Our amiable friend, the wife of the public prosecutor, alone suspected, but wisely kept her counsel.

After our dissipation we spent the evening packing skins, and retired to our hammocks about midnight; but whether owing to Captain Arendt's hospitality or to the effect of the arsenic in the skins, we could not sleep. At three o'clock, finding the sun had been up some time, we bethought ourselves that we could not do better than follow his example, so we accordingly arose; then shouldering our guns, we marched off to the Siberian chiffchaff valley. We chose good positions in the wood, and disposed ourselves to watch and wait. Before long I heard the distant "chivit" of the much longed-for bird, rising from the bottom of the valley. I pressed forward cautiously through the trees, and caught sight of the little warbler's white throat glistening in the sunshine, as it uttered its unpretentious song, perched on the top of a pine. I could not approach it nearer than within sixty yards without making a considerable *détour* to avoid the stream with its high mud walls, crumbling down on all sides, so I risked a shot. It was too far and missed. Meanwhile a second Siberian chiffchaff set up its "chivit." I started off in pursuit of the cry and soon came within shot of the bird, perched, as usual, on the summit of a spruce fir. I fired, ran to the tree, searched diligently through the moss at the foot, but found nothing. Whistling for my companion to come up, I began to run the tree over with my telescope, when, to my great delight, I caught sight of my bird lying dead on a spray within six inches of the top. We saw no more of these birds during the morning, but shot two wheatears that had by this time grown common, a pair of bluethroated warblers and a willow wren. Nearly all the green wagtails which we saw had more or less brown on the breast; they were doubtless last year's birds, that had not yet assumed the full mature plumage. On our return a peasant brought us three young ravens and some duck's eggs, probably pintail's. That day I recorded in my journal, with many groans, the arrival of the mosquitoes. Horrid-looking beasts, with bodies a third of an inch long, monsters, the *Culex damnabilis* of Rae, with proboscis, "*infernali veneno munita*." I foresaw that we should have opportunities enough to study the natural history of these blood-thirsty creatures to our heart's dicontent.

OLD RUSSIAN SILVER CROSS.

THE FLOODED BANKS OF THE RIVER.

CHAPTER XIII.

Trip to Habariki—Forest scenery—Tarns in the woods—Changeable weather—New birds identified in the forests—Golden eagle—Osprey—The hobby—The cuckoo—Yellow-headed wagtail—Bohemian waxwing—Great snipe—Terek sandpiper—Goosander—Smew—Black-throated diver.

WE were fast asleep the next evening when we were roused up by Captain Engel's invitation to go down with him by the steamer to Habariki to stay there three days. We had barely time to dress and fill our pockets with cartridges. The current of the river was in our favour; it was running at the rate of four miles an hour, and we accomplished the twenty-seven miles in two hours. Arrived at Habariki we scarcely recognised the place again. The snow had disappeared, all but a patch or two on the Timanski hills, fifty miles off. The Petchora, freed from ice, had risen some twenty feet or more, and had flooded the island in front of the village, the willows and pine-tree tops being just visible above the surface. Inland, half the country at least was under water, a vast network of lakes and swamps with the forest between. In some places the skirts themselves of the forest were flooded. As we had not brought our wading boots we had to confine our explorations to the woods. These proved an inexhaustible source of interest to us, and one in no wise lacking in variety. There was much beauty in these woods. Under foot spread a carpet of soft green moss and lichens, the thick moss predominating in the older and thicker parts of the forest, while the reindeer moss and the many-coloured lichens abounded in the younger and more open woods. Stray shrubs of arbutus and rhododendron, bushes of bilberry, crowberry, cranberry, the fruit of which was preserved by seven months' frost, clumps of carices and other vegetation decked the shady aisles. The monotony of the great pine forest was varied by the delicate hues of willow and alder thickets, by plantations of young pines and firs, by clumps of tall spruce and haggard old larches, while here and there a fine birch spread abroad its glossy foliage, or a gaunt Scotch fir extended wide its copper-coloured arms. All around lay strewn trunks and branches of timber, fallen or felled, in every stage of decomposition, from the hoary log, moss-covered and turned to tinder, to the newly-lopped branches of some lofty forest patriarch, whose magnificent boughs had been wantonly cut up to furnish firewood for

Sideroff's steamer. The most curious features in these forests were open and slightly hollow places, like tarns or half dried-up tarns, the bed carpeted with moss and a network of last year's *Potamogeton*. The shallow places were quite dried up, but the deeper ones had still a lakelet glistening in the centre. These hollows are doubtless filled with water when the Petchora reaches its highest flood point in June, and many are not yet dried up when an early winter sets in, and the remaining water becomes ice-bound.

Our three days' stay at Habariki was marked by very variable weather. Thursday was calm and warm, with bright sunshine. Friday, bitterly cold, with a strong gale from the north, and only occasional gleams of sunshine, and slight storms of rain and snow. On Saturday morning the gale had subsided, and the greater part of the day the sun shone, but a violent hailstorm fell during the afternoon, and in the evening we had a dead calm. Notwithstanding the generally unfavourable weather we saw a vast number of birds, and added to our lists in these three days more than half as many species as we had seen during the whole of our stay at Ust-Zylma.

We saw several eagles, but one only near enough for identification. It showed no traces of white on the tail, and we concluded it might be a golden-eagle or a white-tailed eagle of the first year. We identified an osprey* as it flew past us

---

* The osprey (*Pandion haliaetus*, Linn.) is a regular though rare visitor to the British Islands during the spring and autumn migrations. It is a circum- polar bird, and may almost be said to be cosmopolitan in its range, breeding both in Europe, Asia, Africa, America and Australia, and has been recorded

overhead. We fired at it, and it dropped a large bunch of damp moss, that it was doubtless carrying to its nest. On a bare larch trunk towering high above the surrounding wood we could see, about fifteen feet from the top, a large nest, which we presumed was that of the osprey.

I rose a dark-winged hawk from the ground, which I have no doubt was a hobby.* Some hours later we saw a similar looking bird, perched high on the naked branch of a dead larch; a long shot brought it down. It proved a fine male of this species.

Many of the ancient stems of the larches contained old nest-holes of woodpeckers, and the bark of some trees was riddled from top to bottom with small holes, evidently made by these birds when feeding. One of our sailors shot a male. We saw, soon after, a pair of three-toed woodpeckers, but did not then succeed in securing one of them. On another occasion, we heard the tapping sound of the woodpecker's beak; a tap, then a slight pause, followed by a rapid succession of taps, and after a second slight pause, a final tap. I imitated the sound, as well as I could, with a cartridge on the stock of my gun. The bird immediately flew to a dead larch trunk, close to where we were standing, and perched, its head thrown back listening, perhaps, some

---

from New Zealand. In the valley of the Petchora we were only able to identify it in latitude 65½°.

* The hobby (*Falco subbuteo*, Linn). is a regular summer migrant to temperate Europe and Asia, and still breeds in the British Islands. A few winter in South Europe, but most appear to migrate into Africa, occasionally straying as far as the Cape. Eastwards it winters in India and South China. In the valley of the Petchora we only met with it in latitude 65½°.

fifty feet from the ground. In this position it fell to my companion's gun. It was a female.

We heard the cuckoo's* familiar note repeatedly every day; the first time it was near midnight, soon after our arrival at Habariki.

The hooded crow and magpie were as abundant as usual in this part of Europe.

The Siberian jay was very common in the woods, and very noisy; all the more so, perhaps, for the number of young birds among them. I saw on one occasion an old jay feeding a young one. I shot the latter; it was in the full plumage of the first year. The old birds were very tame and easy to secure; their skins, however, were worthless, for they were in full moult. The body bore no appearance of it, but the wing and tail feathers were " in the pen." The flight of the Siberian jay is noiseless, resembling somewhat that of the owl, sailing with wings and tail expanded before alighting. These birds like ascending from branch to branch, close by the stem of a birch or fir. When they cannot hop from one bough to another, they ascend the trunk in the fashion of the woodpecker. This habit we both of us specially noted. We did not hear their song, but they were constantly uttering harsh loud cries; the notes of some reminded us of those of the peregrine at its nest; I thought others resembled the

---

* The cuckoo (*Cuculus canorus*, Linn.) is a summer visitor to the whole of Europe, passing through North Africa on migration, and wintering in Central Africa. On the Asiatic continent it appears to be also a summer visitor, but is found in the winter only in Southern India, South China, and the islands of the Malay Archipelago. In the valley of the Petchora we met with it up to the Arctic Circle.

scream of the woodpecker. During the season of incubation the Siberian jay seemed shy and silent.

A flock of tree-sparrows was always to be seen among the few houses in the village, sometimes perched on the railings, at other times gathered in a bunch on the roofs. We saw no evidence of their having begun to think about building.

The pine grosbeak was one of the commonest, if not the commonest bird at Habariki. I shot a male, on the naked trunk of a birch about nine feet from the ground; it was hopping round and round the stem, and when I aimed at it I never dreamt of its being anything else than a small spotted woodpecker.

The mealy redpole also was common.

The little bunting was not uncommon, but its shy and retiring habits would often cause us to overlook it. We rarely heard it sing, yet frequently noticed its quiet call-note. We also often came upon it, feeding on the ground near the swampy edge of the forest tarns, in company with yellow wagtails, fieldfares, and bramblings.

We saw several reed-buntings, and shot a male. They usually frequented the willows on the edges of the marshes and lakes.

The green wagtail was common, and still kept together in flocks; we constantly saw them in trees.

The yellow-headed wagtail * was a bird we had neither of

---

* The yellow-headed wagtail (*Budytes citreolus*, Pall.) has never been found in the British Islands, the valleys of the Petchora and the Volga being apparently the westward limit of its range. It breeds in the Arctic regions, extending northwards beyond the limit of forest growth, and in similar climates

us met with before. The alighting of a small party of five, on an alder bush, surprised us. We secured a male, but the remainder disappeared among some alders and willows growing on an impassable piece of flooded land close to the Petchora, which was also full of floating driftwood. So, unfortunately, we saw them no more.

We noticed a few white wagtails, principally near the village.

Fieldfares were numerous, sometimes in flocks, generally in pairs. They scarcely seemed to have yet begun to breed in earnest. We had two nests brought us, however, each containing one egg. We found plenty of old isolated nests, but no traces of colonies. The fieldfares were singing far more in the woods about Habariki than I had heard them doing during the breeding season in Norway.

The redwing was decidedly commoner than the fieldfare, and its rich wild notes constantly resounded in all parts of the forest. Its usually plaintive whistle was only occasionally heard, the note which it more frequently uttered resembled rather that of a song thrush, but very short. We shot one, to make sure that it was a bird of no other species. Its low warble often came following the notes just mentioned; but sometimes it came without the preliminary note, and once we heard it utter a loose alarm cry like that of the fieldfare. It is evidently an earlier breeder than the latter bird. We got four or five of its nests, containing four eggs each; one

---

at high elevations in Cashmere and near Lake Baikal, wintering in Beloochistan, India, and China. In the valley of the Petchora we found it breeding from latitude 66° to latitude 68°.

had five eggs. We found one of the nests in a spruce-fir built nine feet from the ground. As we did not see the bird upon it, we cannot consider the fact of its being the redwing's fully established; but in no instance did we find a nest nearer than eighteen inches to the ground. Nor is it likely that there would be any built lower in a country periodically flooded. All the redwings were in pairs; we saw no signs whatever of their habits being gregarious.

The blue-throated warbler was very common and tame, allowing us to approach near as it sang, perched on a low bush, or fed on the ground. It was in full voice, and the variety of its notes formed a perfect medley of bird-music. It frequented marshy ground, whether amongst alders and willows, or in the forests of pines or other trees.

We saw several handsome male redstarts.

We came upon a pair or two of wheatears in the open sandy pinewood near the village.

In the same locality we saw a few pairs of stonechats. Willow warblers were very abundant. I heard at Habariki for the second time, this bird utter a note different from any I had heard in England. It is doubtless analogous to the *t-r-r-r* of the chiffchaff, but it is very difficult to describe it exactly on paper. The nearest letters denoting it are perhaps *z-z-z*; it reminded me very much of the spitting of a cat. We heard the song and also the "chiv-it" of the Siberian chiffchaff several times, and succeeded in shooting one bird. When silent we always found it busily engaged feeding like a tit, usually among spruce-firs.

Of the Lapp-tit,* we saw two pairs and a few solitary birds. The note of the waxwing † had long been familiar to me, for

---

* The Lapp-titmouse (*Parus cinctus*, Bodd.) has never been found in the British Islands, but inhabits the Arctic pine forests of Europe and Asia, wandering southwards to a limited extent in the depth of winter. The eastern form, which has been described as a distinct species by Sharpe and Dresser under the name of *Parus grisescens*, differs only in being slightly paler in colour and less russet on the flanks, and is certainly not deserving of specific rank, the specimens which we obtained in the valley of the Petchora being intermediate between the two forms. The eastern form is extremely abundant in Siberia, and has been recorded from North China, but not from Japan.

† The Bohemian waxwing (*Ampelis garrulus*, Linn.) is only an accidental visitor to the British Islands, appearing, however, in some winters in large numbers. It is a circumpolar bird, usually breeding in the pine regions at or near the Arctic Circle. This bird is a very irregular migrant, wandering southwards on the approach of cold weather, and revisiting the north whenever a thaw of sufficient length occurs.

The winter of 1866-67 will long be remembered by British ornithologists as one of the great waxwing seasons. The whole year 1866 (the year of the cattle plague) was wet, the mild winter at each end being scarcely distinguishable from the cold summer between. On New Year's Day frost and heavy

snow set in. Early in November great numbers of the Bohemian waxwing made their appearance. The largest flocks were seen in Norfolk. North of that county many birds were shot at Scarborough, Newcastle, Berwick, up to Aberdeen and Inverness; whilst southwards they were obtained at Dover and Rye. I was fortunate enough to meet with a small party of these interesting strangers as I was walking down the Glossop Road to business into Sheffield on the morning of the 29th of December. My attention was arrested by three or four birds which flew across the road and alighted in a laburnum tree in Miss Ray's garden. I imagined from their flight that they must be starlings, but fancying that they showed white marks on the wing, I had the curiosity to step across the road to get a nearer view of them. The tree on which they alighted was only a few yards from the road, and I watched them over the wall for some time. I recognised them at once by their crests. They were very active, putting themselves in all sorts of positions, and did not seem at all disturbed by my scrutiny; and when at last they flew away, and I turned round to continue my walk I found that quite a small crowd had collected behind me, one of whom (apparently a Sheffield grinder, and consequently well up in pigeons and dogs) volunteered the information that they were French starlings. Two days later two specimens were shot

I had once kept a pair in a cage for some months. I was delighted to hear it once more resounding from the lofty spruce and larch trees in the forest. We succeeded in shooting one pair only; nor were they in very good plumage, having very few and small wax appendages on the secondaries. The eggs in the female were very large, and the testicles of the male very fully developed. It is therefore probable that they were on the point of building, if they had not already begun. As the yellow on the primaries was I-shaped and not V-shaped, I set him down to be a young bird. The male differed from the female in this pair in the following particulars. It was a larger bird, with longer wings and tail, and slightly larger crest. The black on the throat was

---

in Broomhall Park. Some months afterwards a German bird-fancier brought a number of singing-birds for sale. Among these were advertised as great curiosities a pair of "Russian nightingales." These birds turned out to be waxwings, which I bought and kept in a cage for some months. They were most voracious eaters, and the cage required cleaning several times a day. They were very active and restless—especially after the gas was lighted in the evening—and even when perched at rest seemed to be continually moving their heads about, as razorbills are in the habit of doing. If alarmed they would stretch out their necks to almost double the usual length. They were remarkably silent birds. The only note I heard was a sort of *cir-ir-ir-re*, very similar to a well-known note of the blue tit. Occasionally this succession of notes was repeated so rapidly as to form a trill like the song of the lesser redpole. The sexes of the waxwing may be best distinguished by the markings on the wings. In the female the white mark at the end of the primary quill feathers is confined to the outside web, and resembles the letter I, and is only slightly suffused with yellow. The wax-like appendages to the secondaries are comparatively small. In the male a similar white mark is continued at the end of the inner web, making the mark resemble the letter V. This mark is generally suffused with deep yellow, and the wax-like appendages are twice the size of those of the female. It must be borne in mind, however, that the male bears the plumage of the female until after the second autumn moult.

much deeper in tone, and much more sharply defined. The bar of yellow on the tail was much broader. The wax appendages larger, and there were more of them. The yellow on the primaries was more brilliant, and the white in the secondaries and on the wing-coverts larger. Finally, the chestnut on the undertail coverts was of a decidedly darker shade.

We saw one solitary barn-swallow, and shot it.

We came upon many droppings of the capercailzie, but did not see the bird. Several traps were set in the forest to catch the hen, for the cock is not eaten. The peasants call the latter gloo-khah', and the female ty-tyoh'-ra. Willow-grouse and hazel-grouse, we were told, were abundant in some seasons.

We saw one pair of golden-plover on the newly-sown cornfields behind the village. We noticed two or three pairs of ringed plover frequenting the ploughed land below Habariki, and the grassy banks of a little stream running out of the Petchora. We rose a pair of double snipe * from the young wood rising on the sandy ground beyond the fields; and we bagged one. These were the first examples we had yet seen of the species.

---

* The great snipe (*Gallinago major*, Gmel.) appears to be confined to the eastern hemisphere, but is only an accidental straggler to the British Islands, principally in the autumn migration. It breeds in Scandinavia, Central Russia, and Northern Siberia as far east as the Yenesay, passing through Southern Europe and Persia on migration, and wintering in South Africa. In the valley of the Petchora we only found it as far north as latitude $67\frac{1}{2}°$, from which we conclude that its northern breeding range does not extend beyond the limit of forest growth.

We did not succeed in securing a common snipe,* but we often heard their peculiar *tic-tuc* note, and the sound of their drumming high in air. My companion identified a snipe with his glass as belonging to this species; it was uttering the characteristic *tic-tuc*; and later, when it flew to the ground, it rose again with the zig-zag flight belonging to this bird. We were not a little surprised the first time we saw a common snipe perched upon the topmost upright twig of a bare larch seventy feet above ground. We soon grew familiar to the sight; indeed, after what we witnessed of the arboreal habits of birds we are not accustomed to see perching in this country, we ceased to feel surprise at the circumstance. The origin of this habit is doubtless due to the flooding of the great tracts of country by the annual overflow of rivers at the time of migration. We saw but one small flock of Temminck's stint, feeding on the marshy ground near one of the forest trees. We shot them all, hoping to discover the "little stint" amongst them, but we were disappointed.

We found the greenshank and dusky redshank † abundant.

---

* The common snipe (*Scolopax gallinago*, Linn.) breeds throughout the arctic and sub-arctic regions of Europe and Asia, from the British Islands eastwards to the Pacific. It winters in various parts of Southern Europe, Persia, India, and China. On the American continent a species is found (*Scolopax Wilsoni*, Temm.) which many ornithologists suppose to be identical with the European bird. In the valley of the Petchora we found it as far north as latitude 67°.

† The spotted redshank (*Totanus fuscus*, Linn.) appears to be confined to the eastern hemisphere, being comparatively rare in the British Islands, where it occurs only on migration, more frequently in autumn than in spring. It breeds in the northern parts of Scandinavia, both above and below the Arctic Circle, extending its range

but did not succeed in shooting an example of either species.

Wood sandpipers were common, frequenting the edges of the marshes and the forest tarns. This bird has a similar habit to that of Temminck's stint of elevating its wings when alighting, until they almost meet. There is a likeness also in the song of the two birds. The note of the wood sandpiper is more musical than that of the other species, except the latter one. We shot specimens from the summit of high bare trees sixty-five feet at least from the ground.

We shot half-a-dozen Terek sandpipers,[*] the first we had yet seen. The favourite resort of these pretty birds was the grassy margin of the stream before-mentioned, where they fed on the edge of the water and on the shoals of driftwood which lined it in many places. We also came upon them in the marshy ground round some of the forest tarns; they were extremely tame. Like the wood-sandpiper, they would allow us to come and talk within a few yards of them; letting us take up a position where, by a little patience, a double shot could be obtained. We thoroughly identified the ruff on the marsh, although we failed to obtain a specimen of it.

---

eastwards as far as Kamtchatka. It passes through Europe and North Africa, Turkestan, South Siberia, Mongolia, North China, and Japan, wintering in South Africa, Scinde, India, and South China. In the valley of the Petchora we did not meet with this species farther north than Habariki.

[*] The Terek sandpiper (*Terekia cinerea*, Gald.) has never been found in the British Islands, its breeding-range being apparently confined from Archangel to the Pacific. It is an occasional straggler in autumn into Western Europe, and winters in South Africa, India, the islands of the Malay Archipelago, Australia, China, and Japan. In the valley of the Petchora we did not meet with it above the limit of forest growth.

We saw a bean-goose, which had been shot a day or two before our arrival. We saw a pair of swans; and identified the skin and head of one shot by a sailor a week or two before our arrival, as belonging to the common wild species.*

Widgeons were by no means uncommon on the lake, on the larger forest tarns, and on the open water in the marshes. We shot a female off the nest, and took from it five eggs and the down: it was built under a couple of fallen trees crossing each other. The nest had been used the previous year, as old egg-shells were under the down. Several others were brought to us.

The pintail was the commonest duck about Habariki. We shot a female from the nest, taking nine eggs and the down. This nest also was under a prostrate tree, and not far from the widgeon's.

We had one nest of teal with down brought us, together with a male bird. They were not rare.

The golden-eye was a common duck; generally seen in pairs on the open water in the marshes, and the larger forest tarns. We shot a female, and took a perfect egg from her. A nest in the hollow stump of a tree some twenty feet from the ground was shown to us, and we were told that these birds bred there every year. The nest contained ten eggs and plenty of down.

---

* The wild swan (*Cygnus musicus*, Bech-t.) is a winter visitant to the British Islands, breeding on the tundras of Europe and Asia, from Lapland to the Pacific, wintering in various parts of Europe, Turkestan, and China. In the valley of the Petchora we found it as far north as we went.

We saw several goosanders;* one pair we distinctly identified on the water of the marsh behind Habariki.

The smew† was rather a common duck; we saw many pairs on the pools, the large marsh and the woodland tarns. We secured a fine male. We were told that they breed in low stumps of trees.

We identified the black-throated diver‡ for the first time on the 2nd of June. We saw it several times, and heard it flying overhead.

---

* The goosander (*Mergus merganser*, Linn.) is another of the circumpolar ducks which occasionally breed in Scotland, but is usually a winter visitant to the British Islands. Its breeding range extends across the northern portion of the temperate regions of Europe, Asia, and Africa, up to the Arctic Circle, and to the mountainous districts of Mongolia, Turkestan, and the Himalayas, where it finds a similar climate at high elevations. In winter the European birds seldom migrate across the Mediterranean. In India it does not appear to wander south of the Central Provinces. It passes through Japan on migration, and winters in South China, whilst on the American continent, Texas appears to be the southern limit of its wanderings. Habariki is probably about the northern limit of this species in the valley of the Petchora.

† The smew (*Mergus albellus*, Linn.) is one of the ducks which appear to be confined to the eastern hemisphere, and must be regarded as a somewhat rare straggler during the winter season through the British Islands. Its breeding range may be described as slightly south of the northern limit of forest growth. It winters in Central and Southern Europe, occasionally crossing the Mediterranean, Turkestan, North India, China and Japan. In the valley of the Petchora we did not meet with this bird farther north than Habariki.

‡ The black-throated diver (*Colymbus arcticus*, Linn.) is not an uncommon bird in the breeding season on the Scotch lakes and tarns. It frequents similar localities throughout the whole of North Europe and Asia. Its home is on the water, and it does not appear to indulge in any extended migrations. In winter it frequents the sea-coasts of England, the shores of the North Sea, very rarely straying as far as the Mediterranean. In the Black Sea it is very common in winter, also in North Japan. On the American continent it appears to be equally abundant, breeding in the Hudson's Bay territory, and wintering on the coast of California.

We occasionally saw one or two common gulls, and one pair of Siberian herring-gulls. In addition to the above-mentioned birds, we frequently saw others that we were yet unable fully to identify. Thus, we often came upon large sand-pipers on the marsh, whose cry was like that of the redshank; they were probably the dusky redshank. The breast was black and the rump barred. We also saw a large flock of ducks, of a heavy species, flying overhead, which we put down to be the eider-duck.

In the woods and forests of Habariki, we did not once meet with the raven, the bullfinch, or yellow-hammer; nor with any species of pipit or lark.

OLD RUSSIAN SILVER CROSS.

SAILING DOWN THE DELTA.

CHAPTER XIV.

Return to Ust-Zylma—Wedding of the engineer's son—Scarlet bullfinch—Last days at Ust-Zylma—Our boat—We sail to Habariki—Birds' eggs—Smew's eggs—Snipes in trees—Down the Petchora—Sedge warbler—Black-cock—Arctic tern—Willow swamps—We cross the Arctic Circle—A new bird—Arrival at Viski—The Delta—Double snipe—Pustazursk—The tundra—Arrival at Alexievka.

WE returned to Ust-Zylma on Sunday, the 6th of June, and attended the wedding of the son of the engineer of Sideroff's steamer. It took place in the church of the Old Believers; but the ritual did not differ much from that of the orthodox ceremonial. The bridal party afterwards sat in state in the house of Sideroff's manager. Coffee was first served, then sherry, afterwards champagne. All the quality (as an Irish-

man would say) were present, except the public prosecutor.
It was an exceedingly formal and slow affair; the only
feature of interest being the assemblage of villagers outside,
who sang a melancholy tune, while two or three couples
slowly walked round each other in a depressed fashion; the
gentleman taking hold of one of the lady's arms by the
elbow, the other arm interlaced in hers. The girls wore
their hair plaited in a pigtail behind, at the end of which a
cross-bar was attached, from which dangled half-a-dozen
broad ribbons like a banner screen. They kept their eyes
fixed on the ground as they danced, and lifted a handkerchief of many colours to their mouths. All the time vodka
was served from a tin-can; and through the afternoon and
evening, the part of the room near the door was filled with
an ever-changing crowd of peasant maidens, who came to
have a good stare at the bride and bridegroom; and having
gazed their fill, retired to make way for others, who entered
and did likewise.

The next morning a stroll up the chiff-chaff valley resulted
in nothing; but as we were returning home, I heard the
song of a bird that was quite new to me. Four notes loud
and clear. I shot the little songster, and it proved to be a male
scarlet bullfinch.* It was in company with another bird, but
this one escaped us. We heard the cuckoo in our morning

---

* The scarlet bullfinch (*Carpodacus erythrinus*, Pall.) is confined to the eastern hemisphere, breeding somewhat south of the Arctic Circle, and accidentally visiting the British Islands only in winter. Its breeding range extends from Finland to Kamtchatka. In winter it is a more or less irregular straggler in Europe, but is found abundantly in Persia, India, and China. In the valley of the Petchora we did not observe it farther north than latitude $65\frac{1}{2}°$.

ramble. Four eggs of the wood sandpiper were brought to us, and the next day four eggs of the oyster-catcher, one of which was slightly set. All that day we worked hard at our eggs; we had blown 143 in all, including the egg of a peregrine falcon, which a Samoyede brought us, on the 27th of May. He said he found it, in a nest built on the ground, containing three others, which he had the clumsiness to break. At night we turned out for a breath of fresh air, along the banks of the great river. During our walk we shot a pair of Terek sandpipers, the first we had yet seen in Ust-Zylma. We also brought down two Temminck's stints. We afterwards secured our solitary example of the little ringed-plover.* I shot at it as it rose from and again alighted upon a swampy, hummocky strip of tundra land. The next day a peasant brought us a fine cock willow-grouse,† our first,

---

* The little ringed plover (*Ægialitis curonica*, Gmel.) appears to be confined to the eastern hemisphere, being represented on the American continent by a very nearly allied species, *Ægialitis semipalmatus* (Bonap.). In the British Islands it is a comparatively rare straggler. It frequents the rivers and lakes of the three continents south of about latitude 60°, but not migrating so far south as South Africa or Australia. Towards the northern limit of its range, it is only a summer visitant, and at the extreme southern limit of its range it migrates north to breed. In the valley of the Petchora we did not shoot a second specimen, and must consider the example we obtained as one which had accidentally strayed somewhat beyond its usual northern limit.

† The willow-grouse (*Lagopus albus*, Gmel.) is a circumpolar bird inhabiting the tundras above the pine regions, where cover of birch and willow is to be found in the sheltered valleys. In the British Islands it is represented by our common red grouse, which differs from the willow-grouse in little beyond the fact that the latter bird has a white wing, and the whole plumage becomes white for the winter. In winter they form themselves into large flocks and migrate southwards into the pine regions.

clothed in about half its summer costume. We had also a nest given to us of the wheatear, with one egg in it, and the female bird caught upon it.

We had for some time been on the look-out for a boat in which to make the journey down the river, and by the exertion of Piottuch and the kind help of M. Znaminski, who was much interested in our expedition, we succeeded in obtaining one which suited us very well. A wooden cabin, not unlike a large dog-kennel, occupied the centre, and was just large enough for us to recline in at full length; and at the back of it was a covered space, where our baggage could be packed secure from the heavy rains which occasionally occur in summer. It had one mast, on which we could hoist a square sail whenever the wind was favourable. The current would of course usually be in our favour, but we were also provided with four oars, which though incapable of propelling her at much speed, would be useful in crossing the stream, and in giving her way enough to make the rudder of some use in a calm. We engaged four boatmen, two Russians, a Samoyede, and a half breed, all of whom possessed some knowledge of the river; and the latter having the additional advantage of being what passed in this district as an enthusiastic sportsman. We left Ust-Zylma on Thursday, the 10th of June, and sailed down to Habariki with a fair wind and a strong current. The banks of the river were covered with birch and spruce woods, alternating with willow swamps. On our way, we landed at several places, but met with nothing of special interest. Everywhere we found the blue-throat, the redwing, the brambling, the fieldfare, the little bunting, and the willow-warbler common. We saw a solitary sand-martin.* The peasants at Habariki had collected eggs for us; some of the redwing, the redstart, the hooded crow, and of various ducks. The best nest contained eight eggs. It had been found by two boys, who had divided the eggs and the down between them. Four of these eggs, cream-coloured, of a smaller size than the pintail's, were first brought to us, and with them some white down. The lad who brought them said he had found the nest in the old stump of a tree; and the fragments of rotten wood scattered in the down seemed to corroborate his statement. We then sent for the other sharer of the spoil; he had already sold the eggs, along with another duck's nest containing six eggs. On our inquiry as to what he had done with the down, he immediately went off for it, and soon brought it to us. It was white down containing small fragments of wood, the exact counterpart of the other portion in our possession. We found, however, that the down of the second nest was mingled with it. We had no difficulty in separating it, for it was brown, and evidently that of the pintail. Ultimately we purchased the batch of ten eggs from Sideroff's manager, who had bought them from

---

* The sand-martin (*Cotyle riparia*, Linn.) is an inhabitant of both hemispheres, being found northwards up to and occasionally north of the Arctic Circle, the southern limit of its breeding range being North Africa, Central Asia and North China, and the southern states in North America. It probably winters somewhere in Southern Africa, and is known to do so in India and Brazil. In the valley of the Petchora we did not find it farther north than latitude $67\frac{1}{2}°$. In the British Islands it is an abundant summer visitant, breeding in most sand-banks, both inland and on the sea-coasts.

the lad. Four exactly matched the four we had secured from his companion; the other six were the same in size but more greenish in colour, and similar to eggs of the pintail duck which we afterwards obtained. Upon showing the boys some skins of ducks, they at once identified the smew as the duck which belonged to the whiter eggs with the pale grey down. These eggs are extremely rare in collections, and we were not a little elated with our prize.

At three the following morning we shouldered our guns and went on shore. We had sat up late blowing eggs, but the excitement of finding ourselves in a locality where rare eggs and birds might be expected, made an attempt to sleep fruitless, and we decided to gratify our curiosity without further delay. We shot a Siberian chiffchaff singing and "chiviting" lustily amongst the pines; and heard several cuckoos. The snipes were drumming on the marshes, and three times we marked them perched high up on trees; once upon a dead trunk, and twice on the slender dead branches near the summit of larches. These trees were at least seventy feet high. To put an end to all dispute concerning their species, we settled the question by dropping a common snipe with a No. 4 cartridge. It was shot from the topmost twigs of a lofty larch, just budding into leaf. My afternoon walk, which was a long round on the marsh, resulted in very little. I rose a reeve from her nest, and shot her as she was silently shuffling off. The nest was a rather deep hole upon a grass tussock, lined with dry grass, and in it were four eggs and two feathers. A quantity of green-wagtails were running along the swampy ground, and perching freely upon the birches growing on the islands formed in the marsh. Their usual cry was a loud *ne* or *us*, but what seemed the call-note to the female resembled the sound *i-i-i-k*; the song is a low chatter like that of the swallow. Ducks were constantly coming and going to and from the open places on the swamp. The widgeon, judging from the frequency of its cry, seemed the commonest species; its loud *m-e-e-é'-yu* was continually to be heard.

In the evening we left the little village of Habariki, and proceeded down the river. All the next day we crept slowly down the mighty Petchora, a strong current in our favour, but the wind contrary, and with only a couple of oars propelling us along. The scenery was often interesting. The west bank, lofty and steep, was now and then clothed to the water's edge with forests of birches and pines; the east bank at that part was a dead flat covered with willows. Numberless islands studded the water, *kourias* running up amongst them, sometimes of great picturesqueness. The *tirrr'-eek'* of the Terek sandpiper resounded continually; and sometimes we heard the cry of the common sandpiper.* We shot a brace of the latter, the first we had secured; we found the species very wild. Two or three times during the day we pulled up on an island or on the mainland. On a

---

* The common sandpiper (*Totanus hypoleucus*, Linn.) is confined to the eastern hemisphere, being a regular summer migrant to the British Islands, Northern and Central Europe, and Siberia. In the basin of the Mediterranean and China it appears to be a resident, wintering in South Africa, Beloochistan, India, the islands of the Malay Archipelago, and Australia. In the valley of the Petchora we did not see it farther north than the Arctic Circle.

sandy island thinly covered with grass, we came upon a
party fishing with a seine-net; we watched and saw the net
twice drawn without result. On this island we shot a hen
harrier, a cuckoo, and a short-eared owl. A few gulls were
flying about, the common gull and the Siberian herring-
gull. As we pulled on, I saw a party of six waxwings flying
north. Willow-warblers abounded; I watched one for some
time, that allowed me to approach within six feet of it.
I noticed that some appeared to have a whiter throat and
a more rapid song than usual. One I heard vociferously
uttering a note unlike any that I have heard from the
willow-warbler, "tuz-zuk." These observations convinced
me that two species of willow-warblers exist in these parts,
and upon a careful examination of our skins afterwards I
found that I had shot an Arctic willow-warbler.* Swans,
geese, ducks, especially the latter, were to be seen in the
ponds behind the fringing belts of willows; amongst these
we clearly identified the scaup† and the black scoter. We

---

* The Arctic willow-warbler (*Phyllo-scopus borealis*, Blasius) breeds in the north of the palæarctic region from Finmark, across Asia to Alaska towards the northerly limit of forest growth, and in a similar climate in the sub-alpine districts of South-Eastern Siberia and Mongolia. It passes in great numbers on migration in spring and autumn along the coast of China and Formosa, and winters in the islands of the Malay Archipelago, Malacca, Tenasserim, and the South Andaman Islands. Although this is not the only species breeding in North-East Europe which winters in the Malay Archipelago, it seems highly probable, from the fact of accidental stragglers having been shot on Heligoland, that it may occasionally stray as far as the British Islands. The Arctic willow-warbler differs from the three British species in having a pale bar across the wings formed by the greater wing-coverts being nearly white at their tips. It has the minute bastard primary of the wood-wren, with a bill almost as wide and stout as that of a reed-warbler.

† The scaup-duck (*Fuligula marila*, Linn.) is also a circumpolar bird which

found six ducks' nests, most of which were those of the widgeon. In one of those dense willow swamps, lining the east bank of the river I found for the first time the sedge-warbler.* On several occasions, especially at night, we heard its harsh notes; but the bird kept very close, and was very difficult to see. I shot two; one was flying out of a birch-tree, in which it had descended, singing after the manner of the blue-throat. We also secured a red-throated diver,† the first added to our list. We saw a rough-legged buzzard,‡ the only one of the species we clearly identified. It was sitting in a low willow-tree; we shot it, as we silently drifted past, about midnight. We lay to, soon after, anchoring in a

---

visits the British Islands only in winter. Its breeding range extends up to the limits of forest growth, and southwards in Europe throughout Scandinavia. It winters throughout temperate Europe and North Africa. It has not been recorded from Turkestan or Persia, but is mentioned as a very rare winter visitant to India, and is found in great numbers during the cold season in Japan. In the valley of the Petchora we found it as far north as latitude 68°.

* The sedge-warbler (*Acrocephalus schœnobænus*, Linn.) is a common summer visitant to the British Islands, breeding throughout Europe and Siberia as far east as the valley of the Yenesay, and wintering in South Africa. In the valley of the Petchora we found it as far north as latitude 68°.

† The red-throated diver (*Colymbus septentrionalis*, Linn.) is a still more widely-distributed bird than the black-throated species, being found, like it, in the breeding season in the northern portions of both hemispheres, wintering on the shores of the British Islands, the coasts of the Baltic and North Seas, sparingly in the Mediterranean, on the coast of China, Japan, Formosa, and on the American continent in California and the coast of New Brunswick. In the valley of the Petchora it was certainly the least abundant of the two species.

‡ The rough-legged buzzard (*Archibuteo lagopus*, Gmel.) is an irregular winter visitant to the British Islands. It breeds in Arctic Europe and Asia as far east as the watershed of the Yenesay and Lena. It winters in various parts of South Europe and Turkestan. This was the only occasion on which we were able to identify this bird in the valley of the Petchora.

little creek. A steady rain began to fall, which continued
all the following day; we just managed to creep down to
the river Yorsa, where again we pulled up *en route*. We
saw very few birds, but in the evening we got on shore ; and
a turn in the rain was not without result. We seemed
entangled in a network of willow swamps, lakes, and *kourias*
running out of the winding Yorsa. Here and there rose
a few taller willows and birches. After a while we came
upon a little house, the abode of the hay-cutters in autumn,
which our boatmen were now glad to make use of for the
night; all around it were long straggling meadows, upon
which the grass was just beginning to come up. My companion shot a second yellow-headed wagtail, a male; he
saw the female, but lost her. He also saw a small owl, probably Tengmalm's owl. I secured a fine male goshawk,*
the only one we identified on our journey. It was in a
thick alder-bush when I disturbed it, in the act of devouring a female widgeon. In the same place I shot a
short-eared owl. Reed-buntings abounded. I took a nest
containing four eggs; it was built inside an old fieldfare's
nest, and was nine feet from the ground, in a willow-tree.
This is another example of the manner in which birds
accommodate themselves to the circumstances of a flooded
country. We found the little bunting very common, and

---

* The goshawk (*Astur palumbarius*, Linn.) is only found in the British Islands as a rare straggler. It breeds in most of the hilly and wooded districts of Europe, and winters on both shores of the basin of the Mediterranean. Eastwards it breeds as far south as the Himalayas and North China, occasionally straggling into Central India and South China during winter. In the valley of the Petchora we did not meet with it north of the Arctic Circle.

just beginning to build. Once or twice a white-tailed eagle hovered overhead. In long grass covering the raised bank of the island, we discovered a black-cock's * nest containing five eggs; also a widgeon's nest with seven eggs, and a teal's with six.

The next afternoon we left the Yorsa river; the day was fine, but the wind contrary. We stopped for an hour at Churvinski Ostroff, and had a short stroll on shore armed with walking-stick guns. My companion shot a tree-sparrow, and I a small spotted woodpecker. We also started a three-toed woodpecker out of its hole in a tree; I shot it, when immediately the female came up, and I secured her also. We whistled for our boatmen, who, by our orders, cut down the tree. The bird's hole was about fifteen feet from the ground, descending nine inches perpendicularly; there was no lining in it, except plenty of saw- or rather beak-dust. It contained two newly-hatched birds and one egg. On our way back we shot a pair of yellow-headed wagtails; the female had dry grass in her beak, which she was evidently carrying to build her nest. The male was not fully mature, having the nape brown, and dark feathers amongst the yellow of the crown. The yellow of the hen bird was much less brilliant than that of her mate; and the head and cheeks were greenish brown, with the exception of a pale yellow streak over each eye, meeting across the forehead. A few miles

---

* The black grouse (*Tetrao tetrix*, Linn.), the well-known "black game" of the British sportsman, appears to be found throughout the pine and birch regions of Europe and Asia, extending eastwards as far as North China, where, however, it is said to be a rare bird.

lower we brought down two little buntings and an oyster-catcher; we also took a brambling's nest and a duck's, both containing eggs. That evening we saw our first Arctic tern.* We spied them from a distance, and brought them within range by imitating their notes. We suspected this species by the ash-grey colour of the lower parts. Later in the night we had the opportunity of procuring both birds and eggs, and verifying our previous recognition. We had pulled up at one of the islands to boil the kettle for *tchai* and cook some fish; after this meal we began to explore. We shot three terns, and found three nests, securing five eggs in all. As I was in the act of taking up one of these nests, a hare ran up, stood in mute amazement, gazing at me for a second or two, and then turned and bolted. On this island we shot an oyster-catcher; it was evident the nest was there, but we could not find it.

Rain and contrary winds accompanied us all the next day; and at night we stopped at Abramoff. We got from the peasants there eggs of the common gull, and some of the white wagtail, and also eggs of the widgeon, the golden-eye, the fieldfare, and redpole. We also saw a couple of young ravens. We shot a ringed plover, a Temminck's stint, and a pair of yellow-headed wagtails. We were now leaving the more hilly country and the forests of pine, and were entering

---

* The Arctic tern (*Sterna macrura*, Naum.) is a circumpolar bird, though its breeding range extends into the temperate regions. It is common in various parts of the British Islands. This species frequents the rivers and lakes, as well as the sea-shore. It appears to winter south of the Mediterranean, ranging as far as the Cape, and the northern shores of South America.

a waste of willows. Far as the eye could reach, on all sides of us, stretched this never-ending, almost impenetrable willow-swamp, with winding *kourias* and lakes. The only break in the monotony was here and there a straggling bit of pasture land, on which stood a house or two, where a cow fed and the peasants fished, and where, in the autumn, they would make hay. Terns, gulls, and oyster-catchers were now not unfrequently seen, in addition to the almost numberless ducks that were breeding everywhere. On the shores could occasionally be seen a Terek sandpiper, a Temminck's stint, or a dotterel. In the thickets the blue-throat was giving way to the sedge-warbler, but the willow-wren remained the commonest bird. The notes of the redpole, the brambling, and the redwing still sounded. The fieldfare and the reed-bunting, as well as the yellow-headed, green, and white wagtails were still to be often met with, the little bunting being especially plentiful. That day I took my first nest of the Terek sandpiper. I was walking in a wood of tall willows, when the bird rose at my feet, and silently fluttered away. There were four eggs laid in a slight hollow, lined with broad grass. We also found the nest of an oyster-catcher, containing four eggs.

We were now a little to the north of the Arctic Circle; and at three in the morning moored our boat on the shores of an island, among whose willows grew an occasional birch or alder. I spent five hours upon it. Sedge-warblers were singing lustily, and sometimes so melodiously that we almost took them to be blue-throats. Soon, however, my attention was arrested by a song with which I was

not familiar. It came from a bird singing high in the air,
like a lark. I spent an hour watching it. Once it remained
up in the sky nearly half-an-hour. The first part of the
song was like the trill of a Temminck's stint; or like the
concluding notes of the wood-warbler's song. This was succeeded by a low guttural warble, resembling that which the
blue-throat sometimes makes. The bird sang while hovering; it afterwards alighted on a tree, and then descended
to the ground, still continuing to sing. I shot one, and
my companion, an hour after, shot another. Both birds
proved to be males, and quite distinct from any species
with which either of us was previously acquainted. The
long hind claw was like that of the meadow-pipit, and
the general character of the bird resembled a large and
brilliantly-coloured tree-pipit. It was very aquatic in its
habits, frequenting the most marshy ground amongst the
willows.

On our return home five skins of this bird were submitted
to our friend Mr. Dresser, who pronounced it to be a new
species, and described and figured it in a work which he was
then publishing on the Birds of Europe. In honour of my
having been the first to disover it, he named it after me,
Anthus seebohmi,* but, alas for the vanity of human wishes!

---

* The Siberian pipit (*Anthus gustavi*, Swinhoe) was perhaps the most in- teresting discovery which we made during our journey. It was first de- scribed by Swinhoe in 1863, from specimens obtained at Amoy, in South China, on migration. It is seldom that the history of an obscure bird is so suddenly and completely worked out as has been the case with this species. In 1869 G. R. Gray, of the British Museum, redescribed the species as *Anthus batchianensis*, from skins col- lected by Wallace on the island of

I afterwards discovered that the bird was not new, but had been described some years before from examples obtained on the coast of China. I had subsequently the pleasure of working out its geographical distribution, as the reader who cares to peruse the accompanying foot-note may learn. The honour of having added a new bird to the European list still remains to us, and is one of the discoveries made upon our journey on which we pride ourselves.

In the evening we reached Viski, a small town with a church built upon a flat piece of pasture land. It was the first village containing more than half-a-dozen houses, and the first church, that we had seen since leaving Ust-Zylma. It is reputed to be the residence of several rich peasants, one of whom is the owner of 10,000 reindeer, valued at a sovereign each. Without exception it is the dirtiest place I have ever been in. The peasants keep cows, but as they have no arable ground the manure is valueless, and is

---

Batchian. In 1871 Swinhoe announced the identity of Gray's birds with the species which he had previously described from South China. Three years later he rediscovered the species in North China on migration, and also obtained a skin from Lake Baikal. The year after our visit to the Petchora, Drs. Finsch and Brehm found it in the valley of the Obb, a little to the north of the Arctic Circle, and I afterwards found skins in the British Museum from Borneo and Negros, and also obtained information that it had been procured in winter at Manilla and Celebes. In 1877 I found it breeding in considerable numbers in the valley of the Yenesay in latitude $70\frac{1}{2}°$, and on my journey home I identified skins in the Museum at St. Petersburg, collected by Baron Maydell in the Tschuski Land, north of Kamtschatka, and on Baring Island to the east of that peninsula, collected by Wossnessensky. We may therefore conclude that the Siberian pipit breeds on the tundras beyond the limit of forest growth, from the valley of the Petchora eastwards to Behring's Straits, that it passes through South-Eastern Siberia and East China on migration, and winters in the islands of the Malay Archipelago.

thrown outside the house to be trodden under foot. There was an excellent shop in the place, where we laid in a store of tobacco, white flour, &c. In the village we saw a sand-martin and a magpie, but no sparrows.

On leaving Viski we entered upon the true delta, a labyrinth of water and islands, one almost as dead a flat as the other. The islands were almost all alike; but a little while ago they had lain three or four feet deep under the overflow of the great river; they were monotonous willow-swamps, with here and there narrow strips of sandy land appearing thickly covered with grass, and sparingly sprinkled with willows and alders; everywhere were the winding *kourias* and chains of lakelets. On the dry places ducks of various sorts were breeding. We identified a shoveller. There were widgeons, scoters, and teal. On one island we found two pintails' nests with eggs, and I shot our first tufted duck,* a species which we found very rare in the Petchora. As soon as I fired there rose between me and it a flock of red-necked phalaropes,† which alighted between me and the floating

---

* The tufted duck (*Fuligula cristata*, Leach) appears to be confined to the eastern hemisphere, occasionally breeding both in England and Scotland, though it must be considered principally as a winter visitant to the British Islands. This duck has a wide range, both during the breeding season and in winter, being found in summer as far north as the limit of forest growth, and also throughout the basin of the Baltic. In winter it is very common in the basin of the Mediterranean, ranging eastwards through Scinde, Central and Southern India, China and Japan. In the valley of the Petchora it appeared to be rather scarce, and we did not see it further north than latitude 67½°.

† The red-necked phalarope (*Phalaropus hyperboreus*, Linn.) is a circumpolar bird, and breeds in the north of Scotland, being only a spring and autumn visitor on migration to the rest of the British Islands. It frequents in summer the tundras above

body. I shot five; they were the first we had yet secured; and later in the day we brought down four more. My companion meanwhile was exploring another island, where he fell in with a flock of ruffs at their "lecking" place. He shot two. Geese were becoming more and more plentiful; in one instance we marked a flock of fifty at least. Swans often passed us by twos and threes. The sandpipers, the Terek, and Temminck's were as common as ever. We watched one of the latter to its nest, shot it, and secured the four eggs. Early next morning I brought down a skylark; the second only that we had seen; I also shot a blue-throat, which had by this time grown very rare. The commonest warbler, abounding in some places, was the sedge-warbler; next to it was the willow-warbler. Now and then also we heard the redwing, and generally where we stopped there would greet us the song of the new pipit pouring down from the sky. The bird would remain up in the air for a long time, then fly down and alight in the middle of a dense willow swamp, rendering it impossible for us to secure another specimen. A red-throated pipit that my companion shot out of a tree, furnished us with the best possible evidence that this species is much more arboreal in its habits than the meadow pipit. The yellow-headed wagtail had now entirely

---

the limit of forest growth, being rarely found south of the Arctic Circle at that season except at high elevations. In winter it is found in various parts of Southern Europe, and occasionally in North Africa. Eastwards it winters in Persia, Southern Turkestan, occasionally wandering into India, and being more abundant in South China and the islands of the Malay Archipelago. In the western hemisphere its winter range extends as far south as Central America.

replaced the green wagtail, and had become quite a common bird. Occasionally we still saw the white wagtail. At one island we shot a pair of small spotted woodpeckers, which must have found the alder and willow trunks very small for their nests. I found also two fieldfares' nests, one with four, the other with six eggs. Late in the evening we came upon a large flock of great snipe, and in the course of half an hour we had shot ten. They were flying about in companies of about six, continually alighting on the ground, where the sound of their feeding was often heard. One or two common snipe were also hovering overhead and frequently drumming. On one island we saw signs that the breaking up of the Petchora did not take place so silently in the delta as it had done at Ust-Zylma. On the flat shore we discovered a small range of miniature mountains, some eighteen to twenty feet high. We took them at first, from a distance, to be low sandhills, but on nearer approach found them to be a pile of dirty blocks of ice.

We arrived at Pustazursk at midnight on June 18th, and spent the night shooting. The country was a sort of rolling prairie, rising here and there, into dry moorland, on which grew birches, junipers, and a few pines. The lower land remained a willow swamp. Among the sandhills we found a couple of terns' nests, and a nest of the Terek sandpiper. Plenty of Temminck's stints were about, but we failed to find any nests. We shot a couple of sand-martins preparing to build. In a walk that I took on the dry moorland, I stalked a couple of willow-grouse, sitting upon a birch-tree, very conspicuous objects for a mile around. I also rose a shore-lark from its nest, in which I found four young birds; and secured a golden plover, one of whose axillary feathers was blotched with brown. In this part of the moor, the yellow-headed wagtails abounded. Down in the marshy ground I shot a ruff, and saw several others, besides a number of red-necked phalaropes; but of all the birds the most interesting were the pipits. Our new pipit was here by no means uncommon; two or three would sometimes be singing together. We secured two more specimens, one of which must have been trilling its roundelay up in the air for nearly an hour before we were able to shoot it. These pipits poured their song indifferently from the sky, or perching on a bough, or down upon the ground. The red-throated pipit also we found settling freely in trees. In the swampy ground we saw many sedge-warblers, fieldfares, and red-wings, and one or two blue-throats. The next night we again spent shooting, in a willow-covered island, just opposite Kuya. We had grown very weary of those islands, and somewhat disappointed in the result of our ornithological experience of the delta. We had indeed secured some interesting species of birds, but each island had proved almost a repetition of the others; the same landscape, the same conditions, the same bird-life. We were nearing Alexievka, however, and on the eastern side of the river we could almost distinguish the low outline of the skirts of the great Zemelskaya Tundra, stretching away, we knew, on the east to the Ural Mountains, on the north-east to the gates of the Kara Sea; and the Tundra was the unexplored land, the land of promise.

On this island we took the nest, containing seven eggs, of

a pintail, shooting the bird as she was flying off. We found also those of the red-necked phalarope, the great snipe, and the reed-bunting. Our most exciting nest-discovery was that of a swan. It was a large nest, containing three eggs, made of coarse grass, lined with a little down and a few feathers. It was placed upon a bank between two marshes, half concealed by willow-scrub. The most interesting birds we shot were a black scoter, a herring-gull, and a long-tailed duck,* the first we had yet seen on our travels. Its cry was not unlike the word "colguief." Of all species of ducks, it is the tamest and yet one of the most difficult to shoot, for it is an expert at diving, and eludes the sportsman's aim by its rapid and repeated plunges under the surface of the water.

Just before reaching Alexievka, we anchored for an hour at another island, about which seven swans were sailing. The graceful birds, however, did not give us the chance of a shot. Upon this island we had an excellent view of our first great black-backed gulls,† and also of Buffon's

---

* The long-tailed duck (*Harelda glacialis*, Linn.) is a circumpolar bird, breeding north of the Arctic circle, principally on the tundras above the limit of forest growth. In the British Islands it is only a winter visitant, being found also in various parts of Central Europe, rarely, if ever, straying as far as the basin of the Mediterranean. The Siberian birds appear to winter in Japan and in America; it wanders down to the great central lakes and to similar latitudes on both coasts. In the valley of the Petchora we found it as far north as latitude 68½°, but it was one of the few birds we met with which escaped our notice at Ust-Zylma during the period of migration. These birds probably do not fly across country, but follow the coast line.

† The great black-backed gull (*Larus marinus*, Linn.) is also a circumpolar bird, breeding in a more southern latitude than its congeners, the glaucous gull and the Siberian herring-

skua.* The former were sitting amidst several Siberian herring-gulls, but their superior size allowed us to identify them at a glance. The Arctic tern was breeding on this island; ruffs, phalaropes, and Temminck's stint abounded upon it. On one part, covered with dwarf willows, interspersed with taller trees, to my astonishment I heard the warble of the Siberian chiff-chaff, two specimens of which

---

gull, rarely, if ever, ranging north of the Arctic circle. It nests in various parts of the British Islands, Northern Europe, Japan, the great lakes of North America, Labrador, and Greenland. In winter it is found as far south as the Mediterranean, and has been recorded from Florida. Although we identified several individuals in company with small parties of the Siberian herring-gull—their superior size being evident at a glance—we did not succeed in obtaining any examples, nor did we meet with their eggs or young.

* The Buffon's skua (*Stercorarius parasiticus*, Linn.) is a circumpolar bird, being found upon the moorland districts beyond the limit of forest growth of Europe, Asia, and America. It winters on the sea-coasts of Europe, and in about the same latitudes in Asia and America. In the British Islands it must be considered as a somewhat rare winter visitant, though it has been said to breed in Scotland. On several occasions we observed the peculiar kestrel- or tern-like hover of the Buffon's skua, and also saw these birds pick up from the ground, or seize upon the wing, dunlins and stints, in the one case acting like a hen-harrier, in the other seizing their prey like a falcon. We had cause, also, to suspect their depredations amongst the eggs; and grey plovers and other birds often joined in driving them away from their domains. Sometimes in the evenings or mornings we saw long straggling flocks of these skuas passing over the island of Alexievka, and crossing and recrossing the branch of the Petchora which separates that island from the mainland. We found them common all over the tundra as far north-east as we penetrated. In the specimens of the two species which we obtained we found a marked difference in the coloration of the legs and toes, those of the Richardson's skua being uniform dark brown, while those of Buffon's skua were blotched with bluish-grey. In one specimen of the latter there is a single feather of the under-tail coverts white with dark brown bars; in all the other specimens procured the under-tail coverts are of a uniform smoky brown. This single feather is doubtless a last trace of immaturity. We saw many specimens of the Pomatorhine skua outside the Golaievskai banks on our journey home by sea, but saw nothing of this species during our stay in Russia.

I secured. The red-throated pipits were there perching, as usual, in the boughs; and I noticed also one or two of our new pipits, and a number of reed-buntings.

This bird-haunted island was our last stoppage before reaching Alexievka. We arrived at our destination on the evening of the 19th June, after ten days' voyage down the great river and through the intricacies of the monotonous delta.

PLOUGHING AT UST-ZYLMA.

ALEXIEVKA FROM THE TUNDRA.

CHAPTER XV.

Alexievka—The timber rafts—The island—Nest and eggs—Buffon's Skua—Sailing for the Tundra—Description of the Tundra—Its vegetation—Nests of Lapland bunting and red-throated pipit—First sight of the grey plover—Its nest—Watching by the nest—Shot at last—Omelette of grey plover's eggs—Birds seen on the Tundra—Eggs collected during the day—Blowing eggs—Nest of the Petchora pipit.

ALEXIEVKA is the shipping-port of the Petchora Timber-trading Company. It is a group of houses built upon an island in the delta of the great river, where the ships are laden with larch for Cronstadt. The larch is felled in the forests five or six hundred miles up the river, and roughly squared into logs varying from two to three feet in diameter. It is floated down in enormous rafts, the logs being bound together with willows and hazel boughs. These rafts are manned by a large crew, some of whom help to steer it down the current with oars and poles, and others are hired for the season to assist in loading the ships at Alexievka. Many of the men bring their wives with them to cook for the party; sleeping-huts are erected on the raft, and it becomes to all intents and purposes a little floating village, which is frequently three months in making the voyage down the river. Marriages have been known to take place on these rafts; occasionally a funeral has to be performed; and sometimes all hands are engaged in helping to keep the raft from running ashore or grounding on a sandbank. Sometimes in stormy weather it is necessary to moor the raft under the lee of an island or a promontory, to avoid the danger of having it broken up by the violence of the waves. With the greatest care in the world, this will sometimes happen. The Russian has a good deal of the fatal facility to blunder which characterises the Englishman, and shiploads of stranded logs of larch are strewed on the islands of the delta, and on the shores of the lagoon of this great river.

When we landed on the island of Alexievka it was a rapidly drying-up willow swamp of perhaps half-a-dozen square miles, some six feet above the level of the Petchora, which swept past it with a rapid current. In some places the willow swamp was impenetrable, in others bare grassy oases varied the flat landscape, and there were one or two larger lakes on the island. During the floods which accompanied the breaking-up of the ice, the whole of the island was under water, and the men were busily clearing away the mud which had deposited itself on the floors of the houses. An extensive series of wooden fortifications protected the houses from being carried away by the ice. For four months of the year the village was a busy scene, full of life and activity, but for the remaining eight months a solitary man and a dog kept watch over the property of the Company, and even they had to desert their charge and escape to the shore during the breaking-up of the ice.

Three rooms were generously placed at our disposal, and we proceeded to make ourselves as comfortable as the circumstances would permit. Our first care was to buy a brace of willow-grouse and a bean-goose for the pot; our next to purchase eggs of the yellow-headed wagtail, bean goose, willow grouse, and long-tailed duck. A nest of the white wagtail, which we found, contained remarkably brown eggs; it was made chiefly of roots, and a little stalky grass lined with reindeer hair. The next day, peasants brought us two nests of the yellow-headed wagtail; these also were composed of fine roots and dry leafy grass, the inside lined with reindeer hair; one had, besides, two small feathers and a piece of duck-down.

The mosquitoes, that of late had tried us severely, were now giving us a respite, driven back by the cold north wind and occasional snowstorms. All day I kept indoors, going out but for half an hour, when I bagged a Siberian chiff-chaff and a red-throated pipit, perched in a tree. The nests came in plentifully. The first day of our stay were brought in to us those of the blue-throat, the redpole, the reed-bunting, the willow-warbler, two of the bean-goose, with the goose snared upon it, and one of the pintail duck. With these were brought two widgeon's eggs. The weather continued very cold; the Petchora looked sullen and tempestuous under the dark sky and bleak wind. The next day we again kept indoors, profiting by our enforced captivity in having a general overhauling of our skins. We found the Siberian chiff-chaff the commonest warbler amongst the willows of Alexievka. Its note is a "ching-chevy" repeated three or four times in rapid succession, the accent laid on the "ching," and the warble generally, but not always, ending with a final "ching." Probably owing to the coldness of the weather we did not then hear it in full song, as we had at Ust-Zylma and Habariki. We found Buffon's skuas numerous in Alexievka; they were usually in flocks of five or six. There seemed to be only one common sparrow in the place, and this I shot.

The 22nd of June was inscribed in our journal as a red-letter day. We were dead tired when we turned into our hammocks at half-past ten the night before, and slept the clock round and an hour over, rising at half-past eleven. When we woke we found it was a bright warm day, the wind had dropped, and the great river looked no longer like an angry sea. We decided to cross it, ordered our men to get the boat ready, made a hasty breakfast, and set sail at last for the land of promise, the mysterious Tundra, the Aarka Ya of the Samoyedes, the Bolshya Zemlia of the Russians. We pictured this great land to ourselves as a sort of ornithological Cathay, where all sorts of rare and possibly unknown birds might be found. So far we were just a little disappointed with the results of our trip. July would soon be upon us, and we had not solved yet one of the six problems that we had proposed to ourselves as the main objects of our journey. We had not seen the least trace of the knot, the curlew sandpiper, the sanderling, or the grey plover. Some birds that we had at first fancied might be little stints in full breeding plumage, we were now thoroughly convinced were nothing but Temminck's stints, and as we had hitherto met with but one species of swan, we had reluctantly come to the conclusion that we had not yet seen Bewick's swan. We congratulated ourselves that our observations on the arrival of migratory birds at Ust-Zylma were not without interest. We were much pleased that we had shot one specimen of the Arctic willow-warbler. The abundance of yellow-headed wagtails, and the prospect of bringing home many of the eggs of this rare bird, was a source of considerable satisfaction to us. Our two best things were undoubtedly the new pipit and the Siberian chiff-chaff. We hoped both these birds might be new, but our acquaintance with the various Indian species that might possibly migrate into this region was not sufficient to warrant us in entertaining more than a hope. We therefore looked forward to our first day on the tundra with more than usual anxiety and interest.

The tundra forms the east bank of the Petchora, and we anchored our boat under a steep cliff, perhaps sixty feet high, a crumbling slope of clay, earth, sand, gravel, turf, but no rock. We looked over a gently rolling prairie country, stretching away to a flat plain, beyond which was a range of low rounded hills, some eight or ten miles off. It was in fact a moor, with here and there a large flat bog, and everywhere abundance of lakes. For seven or eight months in the year it is covered with from two to three feet of snow. Snow was still lying in large patches in the more sheltered recesses of the steep river-banks; and on one of the lakes a large floe of ice, six inches thick, was still unmelted. The vegetation on the dry parts of the tundra was chiefly *carices*, moss, and lichen, of which the familiar reindeer-moss was especially abundant. In some places there were abundance of cranberries with last year's fruit still eatable, preserved by the frost and snow of winter. Here and there we met with a dwarf shrub, not unlike a rhododendron, with a white flower and aromatic-scented leaves (*Ledum palustre*), a heath-like plant with a pale red flower (*Andromeda polifolia*), and dwarf birch (*Betula nana*) running on the ground almost like ivy. The flat boggy places had evidently been shallow lakes a few weeks ago after the sudden thaw, and were now black swamps, water in the middle, grown over with yellow-green moss, and *carices* towards the edge. They were separated from each other by tussocky ridges of moor, which intersected the plain like the veins on the rind of a melon. We found no difficulty in going where we liked; our indiarubber waterproofs were all-sufficient. We crossed the wettest bogs with impunity, seldom sinking more than a foot before reaching a good foundation, a solid pavement of ice. Birds were but thinly scattered over the ground; but there were sufficient to keep our curiosity on the *qui vive*. The commonest bird was the Lapland bunting; and we took two of their nests in the tussocky ridges between the little bogs. The next commonest bird was the red-throated pipit; and we took two of their nests in similar positions. As we marched across the tundra we fell in with some dunlins,* and took a couple of their nests. This was encouraging. The dunlin was a bird we had not seen at Ust-Zylma, and one possibly that migrated direct across country from Ust-Ussa. We had not walked more than a couple of miles inland before we came upon a small party of plovers. They were very wild, and we found it impossible to get within shot of them; but a distant view through our binocular almost convinced us that we had met with the grey plover † at last. We had not walked very far

---

* The dunlin (*Tringa alpina*, Linn.) is a circumpolar bird visiting the British Islands in winter, and breeding in considerable numbers in Scotland, being most numerous in the autumn migration. Its principal breeding-ground is on the tundras beyond the limit of forest growth, but it is also found nesting in considerable numbers south of the Arctic circle. It winters in the basin of the Mediterranean and in Africa as far south as Abyssinia. Eastwards it winters in Beloochistan, India, China, and Japan. On the American continent it migrates as far south as the Southern States and Cuba. This was another of the species which we did not see on migration at Ust-Zylma, the bulk of the migration probably taking place along the coast. We met with it on the tundra as far north as we went.

† The grey plover (*Squatarola helvetica*, Linn.) was one of the birds which we failed to observe at Ust-Zylma during migration, the main flocks probably migrating along the coast. To obtain the eggs of this species was one of the principal objects of our journey, the only authentic specimens known to exist being those collected by Middendorff near the north-east cape in Siberia. The grey plover is a cosmopolitan bird, being found more or less abundantly in every portion of the globe. In the British Islands it is only known as a spring and autumn migrant, being much more numerous in the latter season than in the former. Its breeding grounds are the tundras above the limit of forest growth, where, however, it appears to be extremely local. It passes through Central and Southern Europe on migration, wintering in

before other plovers rose; and we determined to commence
a diligent search for the nest, and offered half a rouble to
any of our men who should find one. Our interpreter
laughed at us, and marched away into the tundra with a
"C'est impossible, monsieur." We appealed to our Samoyede, who stroked his beardless chin, and cautiously
replied, "Mozhna." The other men wandered aimlessly up
and down; but the Samoyede tramped the ground systematically, and after more than an hour's search found a
nest on one of the dry tussocky ridges intersecting the bog,
containing four eggs about the size and shape of those of the
golden plover, but more like those of the lapwing in colour.
The nest was a hollow, evidently scratched, perfectly round,
somewhat deep, and containing a handful of broken slender
twigs and reindeer-moss. Harvie-Brown concealed himself
as well as he could behind a ridge, to lie in wait for the bird
returning to the nest, and after half an hour's watching shot
a veritable grey plover. Soon afterwards another of our
men found a second nest, also containing four eggs, in
exactly a similar situation. Harvie-Brown took this nest
also in hand, and in about an hour succeeded in shooting
the female. The third nest was found by the Samoyede.
This time I lay down behind a ridge some thirty yards from
the nest, and after waiting a quarter of an hour caught sight
of the bird on the top of a distant tussock. Presently she
ran nearer to another ridge, looked round, and then ran on

South Africa, India, South China, the islands of the Malay Archipelago, and Australia. In the western hemisphere its range has not been so accurately recorded, but it is known to winter in Cuba and some parts of South America.

to the next, until she finally came within fifty yards of where I was lying. I had just made up my mind to risk a shot when she must have caught sight of me, and flew right away. In a quarter of an hour I caught sight of her again, approaching by short stages as before, but from an opposite direction. I must have been in full sight of her. When she had approached within fifty yards of me, as near as I could guess, I fired at her with No. 4 shot and missed. I remained reclining where I was, with little hope that she would try a third time to approach the nest, and whiled away the time with watching a Buffon's skua through my glass as it cautiously approached in my direction. Turning my head round suddenly I caught sight of the grey plover running towards the nest within fifty yards of me. I lifted my gun and fired again, but was so nervous that I missed her a second time. I was so vexed that I got up and walked towards the skua, which still remained *in statu quo*. I missed a shot at it too, spent some time in a vain search for its nest, and returned to my old quarters. In ten minutes I saw the grey plover flying up. It took a wheel in my direction, coming almost within shot, and evidently took stock of me, and satisfied itself that I was a harmless animal practising with blank cartridge, and having no evil design upon its eggs. It alighted about fifty yards beyond the nest, and approached less timidly than before. When it came within fifty yards of me I fired, this time with No. 6 shot, and laid the poor bird upon its back. As we returned to our boat Harvie-Brown found a fourth nest, and, after watching as before, secured the bird. We accidentally broke two of the eggs belonging to the third nest, but reached Alexievka at midnight with fourteen identified grey plover eggs. Two sittings were quite fresh, and made us an excellent omelette for breakfast the next morning. The other two were very slightly incubated.

On the tundra we saw several Buffon's skuas, and shot two. I also shot a willow grouse on a piece of swampy ground near a lake, where a few dwarf willows were growing. On the lakes we saw many pairs of long-tailed ducks. A few pairs of yellow-headed wagtails, which evidently had nests, a redwing, a Temminck's stint, a few pairs of bean-geese, a redpole, and a hawk, which, as far as I could make out with my glass, was a male peregrine—this completed the list of birds we saw on the tundra.

On our return to head-quarters we found that the price we had paid for the eggs to the workmen had induced many of them to go out bird-nesting, and at night our bag for the day stood as under, as far as eggs were concerned:

Grey plover	11
Dunlin	7
Great snipe	4
Lapland bunting	25
Red-throated pipit	39
Yellow-headed wagtail	10
Mealy redpole	16
Reed bunting	12
Redwing	3
Bean goose	11
Widgeon (with down)	17
Temminck's stint	1
	162

This was a grand haul. Any little lingering feeling of

disappointment which we still experienced, was now completely gone. The grey plover eggs alone would have made our trip a success. They were unquestionably the first that had ever been taken in Europe. We spent the next two days in blowing our eggs and writing up our journals, occasionally strolling out among the willows on the island, to bag a few yellow-headed wagtails and other birds to keep Piottuch employed. We found that the swans' eggs that we had brought from Kuya were perfectly fresh. The eggs of the bean-goose, on the contrary, some of them more than a week old, were mostly considerably incubated. The ducks' eggs were all fresh, or nearly so. Most of these were widgeon's, pale cream-coloured eggs; the down large, dark brown, very distinctly tipped with white and with pale whitish centres. The red-throated pipits' and Lapland buntings' eggs were, many of them, too much sat upon to be easily blown, as were also the dunlins' eggs. The eggs of Temminck's stint, red-necked phalarope, yellow-headed wagtail, and most of the redpoles were all fresh or very slightly sat upon. The eggs of the gulls, both those of the common species and of the Arctic herring-gull, were quite fresh, whilst those of the Arctic tern were, some fresh, and some considerably incubated. During these two days we found several nests of the fieldfare on the island, a nest of the willow-warbler and one of the yellow-headed wagtail. The latter was on the ground, concealed amongst the old tangled grass, which the floods had twisted round a stake. It was principally composed of dry herbage, with one or two feathers in the lining. Our two *raræ aves*, which we christened the Petchora pipit and the Siberian chiff-chaff, were by no means uncommon, but we failed to find either of their nests. Amongst the nests, however, which our excellent coadjutants the Zyriani brought us was one which we at once concluded could belong only to the Petchora pipit. It contained five perfectly fresh eggs, larger than those of the red-throated pipit, and similar in colour to those of the meadow pipit. The nest was somewhat larger than that of the red-throated pipit, composed of more aquatic-looking flat-leaved grass, and contained fragments of *Equiseta* in the lining. Our collection of eggs increased rapidly. We had now 145 sittings, numbering 681 eggs.

OLD RUSSIAN SILVER CROSS.

STANAVIALACHTA.

CHAPTER XVI.

The tundra near the Yooshina river—Golden plover's eggs—Various nests—Lapland bunting—Various birds—Richardson's skua—Various means of propelling our boat—The tundra near Stanavialachta—Eyrie of a peregrine falcon—Various nests—Abundance of willow-grouse—Nest of the willow-grouse—Visit to two islands in the delta.

The next day we left Alexievka in the morning to spend a few days exploring the tundra in the neighbourhood of Stanavialachta, the old loading-place of the Petchora Timber-trading Company, about forty versts down the river, where, we learnt, there were several wooden houses that we could occupy. We sailed about twenty versts down to the mouth of a small tributary called the Yooshina. The tundra here was less marshy, the ground more hilly, and upon it were more willows. The country looked so inviting that we cast anchor and went on shore for a stroll. We soon saw some plovers, and were in hopes of a second haul of grey plovers eggs. After a time our Samoyede discovered a nest, but the eggs in it were of a much lighter ground colour than those we had found before. We waited and shot the bird, but to our disappointment it turned out to be a golden plover. We afterwards saw several more. We could not detect any difference in the habits of the two species at the nest. We secured a bean-goose off its nest with seven eggs, and were very successful in finding nests of small birds. We took eggs of reeve, ringed plover, willow-warbler, Lapland bunting, red-throated pipit, blue-throated warbler, redwing, Temminck's stint, and willow grouse. The redwing's nest contained six eggs. It was in a willow about four feet from the ground. Redpoles were common, and oftener to be met with on the ground than in the willow and birch bushes. The Lapland bunting we constantly saw both running and hopping on the ground. These charming birds were very tame and very numerous. They perched freely in the bushes. They were busily employed in the duties of incubation, and we rarely, if ever, heard them sing. In Finmark I used to hear their song constantly; but then they were only just beginning to breed. We saw many red-throated pipits, carrying flies in their mouths, evidently destined to feed their young, and if we came inconveniently near their nests, they would fly uneasily from bush to bush. Near a couple of deserted turf huts we noticed the white wagtail and the wheatear. Yellow-headed wagtail was also frequently met with on the tundra, but not in anything like the numbers in which we found it on the islands of the delta. On the banks of the great river numerous Siberian herring-gulls were slowly sailing past, and we shot four. I shot a Richardson's skua,* which heedlessly flew within range of my gun. This was the first example of this species which we had yet seen. It was as white underneath as the Buffon's skuas, but the centre tail-feathers were much shorter. Curiously enough we never met with the dark-bellied variety of Richardson's skua in the Petchora. It must be the western form. I found it by far the commonest variety in Finmark. We saw a few Arctic terns, and got one egg. On the lakes the long-tailed duck was common, and I shot two males. These birds are very quarrelsome, and by no means so shy as the other ducks. My companion identified a red-breasted merganser,† but did not succeed in

---

* Richardson's skua (*Stercorarius crepidatus*, Gmel.) we found upon the tundra mingling with the large flocks of Buffon's skuas, or scattered in pairs over their breeding haunts. Nowhere did we find them so abundant as the latter species, of which we obtained no eggs, though we found several nests of the former. Richardson's skua is a circumpolar bird, breeding upon most of the islands of the Arctic Ocean. In winter it distributes itself along the coasts of Europe and Africa, extending eastwards as far as Scinde. It has not been recorded from the western shores of the Pacific, but it appears to be found on both coasts of the American continent, occasionally wandering south of the equator.

† The red-breasted merganser (*Mergus serrator*, Linn.) is also a circumpolar bird, breeding throughout the Arctic regions and in the northern portion of the temperate zone. In the British Islands it breeds in Scotland, and is frequently met with in winter in most parts of England. The European birds winter in the south, rarely, if ever, crossing the Mediterranean. The Siberian birds winter in China and Japan, and the North American examples retire to the Southern States. The first bird of this species was seen by Harvie-Brown at the lakes on the tundra to the south of the Yooshina

shooting it. I saw a great snipe, a large flock of red-necked phalaropes, a few pairs of fieldfares, and several black-throated divers. Every day the tundra became gayer with flowers, and we continually regretted that we were not botanists. I noticed *Equisetum variegatum* for the first time. The evening, or what ought to have been the evening, turned out so cold, with a strong contrary wind, against which our stupid keelless boat could make little headway, that finding the tide was also against us, we cast anchor in a creek for a night's rest. In the morning, by dint of hard rowing for some time, then of thrusting with a pole, as is done in the flat-bottomed boats on the Grecian lagoons, then turning out two of our men, and making them drag us along, canal-boat fashion, we at length arrived at Stanavialachta. We spent the day in making the Company's deserted houses sufficiently weatherproof to afford us good shelter for a few days. In the evening we turned out for a stroll; the tundra in this locality was much more hilly, and was diversified with more lakes than in the neighbourhood of Alexievka. The high ground was very dry, and we seldom came upon any impassable bog. The vegetation also was more abundant, the flowers more varied, and the willows and dwarf birch-trees more numerous. The weather was very unfavourable: a strong gale was blowing from the west; it was very

---

river. He fired at it and wounded it severely. They were afterwards seen by him on six different occasions, and perfectly identified, viz. at Alexievka, Bougrai, and on the river Dvoinik, and on the small river flowing into the inland sea. They always declined capture, diving rapidly at the flash, swimming a long way up or down stream, and reappearing out of range. We failed to discover the nest.

cold, with occasional attempts at rain; yet we saw many birds. The red-throated pipit was by far the commonest. My companion shot a meadow-pipit from a tree, and caught another sitting on its nest. We saw several golden plover, a flock of seven or eight Buffon's skuas, a pair of dotterel,* one or two shore-larks, besides securing the nest of a bean-goose containing two eggs. On the grassy top of a mound, halfway down the mud cliffs overlooking the great river, and within sight of the Arctic Ocean, I came upon the eyrie of a peregrine falcon. It contained four eggs, one of which was much lighter in colour than the others. This mound had probably been used for some years as a nesting-place by the falcons, since the grass was much greener upon it than upon the surrounding places. A little way off there rose another mound, just similar to it, and this was apparently the falcons' dining-table, for scattered all about it were feathers of grouse, of long-tailed duck, and of divers small birds.

While I remained near the nest, the two falcons hovered around, uttering sharp cries; when I approached nearer still, they redoubled their screams, hovered over me, closed their wings, and descended perpendicularly till within a few yards of my head. Their movements were so rapid that I wasted

---

* The dotterel (*Eudromias morinellus*, Linn.) is one of those birds which are not found east of the Himalayas and the watershed between the Yenesay and the Lena. In the British Islands it is principally known as a spring and autumn migrant, a few only remaining to breed on the Cumberland and Scotch mountains. Its great breeding-grounds are on the grassy hills on the tundras, beyond the limit of forest growth. In the rest of Europe, South-Western Siberia, and Turkestan it passes through on migration, wintering in Persia and Africa north of the equator.

half-a-dozen cartridges in trying to secure them, and had at last to leave them baffled in the attempt. My companion and I returned to the charge on the following day; but again we were defeated. A mile up the river, however, we found a second eyrie upon an exactly similar green-topped mound. The nest contained three eggs, and the behaviour of the birds, as we neared it, was the same as had been that of the falcons of the day before. My companion succeeded in shooting the male. We found many nests of other birds. Our Samoyede in the morning brought us one of the black-throated diver, containing two eggs, and in the course of the day we found a second. We also secured nests of the golden plover, long-tailed duck, wheatear, Temminck's stint, blue-throat, and Lapland bunting; in the latter were young birds. Our most interesting find, however, was the nest, with two eggs, of Richardson's skua, placed on a tussock of mossy ground. It was lined with some reindeer moss and leaves of the surrounding plants. The devices of the birds to deceive us, as we came near it, attracted our attention and revealed its vicinity. They often alighted within fifteen yards of us, shammed lameness and sickness, reeled from side to side as if mortally wounded, then when we persisted in our onward course they flew boldly at us, and stopped repeatedly.

We again saw the dotterels, but apparently not yet nesting. Willow-grouse were as plentiful on this part of the tundra as red grouse on the Bradfield moors on the 12th. Their white wings, their almost entirely white bodies, made them very conspicuous objects. They usually rose within shot from a patch of willow cover. Sometimes we would see a pair knocking about the tundra, like two big white butterflies, with a peculiar up-and-down flight, then they would go tumbling into a willow-grown knoll on the hillside. It might be owing to their extreme conspicuousness that their flight always seemed so much more clumsy than that of the red grouse. One of their nests, which we found on the ground, contained a baker's dozen of eggs. It was a mere hollow scraped in the turf, lined with a leaf or two, a little dry grass, and a few feathers. The next day we succeeded in shooting the female peregrine, on the first eyrie we had discovered, then, after taking a sketch of the place, we set out for Alexievka, visiting on our way a couple of islands on the delta. The first on which we disembarked was very marshy, and covered with small willows. On this island the willow-warblers were rare, but we occasionally heard the Siberian chiff-chaff, and we noticed one almost incessantly repeating "chi-vit'-che-vet'." The yellow-headed wagtail was common, the shore-lark disappeared altogether, the Lapland bunting was represented by a solitary bird. Red-throated pipits were still numerous; but we did not see the meadow pipit. The sedge warbler abounded. We also saw several Temminck's stints, phalaropes, a flock of eight Buffon's skuas, and ducks of various sorts. The other island was almost entirely a grassy marsh, interspersed with spaces of open water. A flock of Siberian herring-gulls hovered about a party of fishermen, who were catching with a seine net a small fish exactly resembling the herring. Temminck's stints congregated in great numbers on the dry or drying mud, but we could find no trace of their nests. Phalaropes single and in flocks were common; we took three of their nests, also one of a tern. Ducks as usual abounded; we noticed among them a pair of shovellers, and carried off a nest containing three eggs and a little down, which belonged to this bird. On the river we continually passed flocks of scaup and black scoter.

The sketch of Stanavialachta at the head of this chapter was taken from the eyrie of one of the peregrines; the second eyrie was half-way down the point to the extreme left. To the right in the distance is the eastern boundary of the Bolvankaya Bucht; to the left, the outer islands of the Delta.

OLD RUSSIAN SILVER CROSS.

GREY PLOVER'S NEST AND YOUNG.

CHAPTER XVII.

Examination of nests—Excursion to Wasilkova—Search for breeding haunts of Bewick's swan—News from England—Grey plover's eggs—Flock of Buffon's skuas—Black scoter's nest—Watching for skuas' nests—Another nest of grey plover—Scaup's eggs—The Zyriani.

On the 29th of June the weather was very wet. We spent the day in blowing eggs and examining our nests. We had now five nests, which we were pretty sure were those of our new pipit; they were entirely distinct from that of the red-throated pipit. Instead of being composed of fine round grasses they were made of flat-leaved grass, knotted water-plants and small leaves; in two of these were *Equisetæ*. The eggs in them were larger, more lark-like, a dark ring circled the larger end, and they were all more or less mottled, especially those of the lighter variety.

Buffon's skua, we found, had been feeding upon beetles and cranberries; another fact worth noticing was that the ten great snipes which we shot near Pustazursk were all males.

The following morning proving fine we set off on an excursion to Lake Wasilkova, which at high tide was but a bay of the Petchora. The tundra inland was the usual stretch of rolling moorland, swamp and bog, interspersed with lakes and ranges of low sandy hills. On the swamps we found dunlins, on the moors golden plover, and once we saw a grey plover. In both localities we met the Lapland bunting and the red-throated pipit, and the dry grassy hills were haunted by shore-larks. On one of the lakes and along the coast, we came upon Siberian herring-gulls; long-tailed ducks abounded on the stretches of open water, but we failed to find a nest. We came to a spot on the shore where a pair of peregrines had built their eyrie, but the peasants had taken the eggs away for food. Under a low willow bush we shot a black scoter as she sat on her nest. Once we saw a hen-harrier beating up the hillsides, and caught sight of a white-tailed eagle, as it flew overhead. Among the willows in the low swampy ground we shot a pair of wood sandpipers, and caught three of their young, apparently a couple of days old. We also saw a raven and many Buffon's skuas. During the day the mosquitoes were very troublesome in the sheltered parts of the tundra, but a cold north wind kept the hilltops clear.

Hitherto, we had been unable to identify the swans that during our voyage had flown overhead, or settled on the ice in the river. We were convinced in our minds that there were two different sizes, but had been unable to establish the fact. On one island, near Kuya, we had found one nest containing four large eggs, but we had failed to secure the bird. To determine the breeding haunts of Bewick's swan was the hope and one of the principal objects of our journey; as yet the offer of five roubles reward for any swan's eggs accompanied by the parent bird, had resulted only in two or three nests being brought to us, but in no case had the swan been snared. Our Samoyede now brought us two swan's eggs that he had found thrown out of a nest, and advised us of a second nest containing four eggs. We despatched him at once with a trap to the nest to try and catch the swan. That day we also bought two very small swan's eggs, smaller than those of the ordinary wild swan, from a fisherman. He told us that his mate had the skin of the parent bird, which he had caught at the nest. The fishing encampment from which he came was lower down the river, on an island opposite the hamlet of Stanavialachta. We could not think this was a made-up story, for the man could not have heard of the reward we had offered for eggs accompanied with the captured parent bird, as we were the first to speak to him on his arrival. We therefore at once determined that if we did not discover Bewick's swan in the neighbourhood of Alexievka, we would make an excursion to Stanavia-lachta for the express purpose of obtaining the head and skin of the bird whose eggs we had just bought.

The following day our Samoyede returned from his futile excursion in quest of the swan. He had failed to secure her.

A SWAN'S NEST.

From the appearance of the trap it seemed as if the swan had shuffled up to her nest on her belly, after the manner of a diver, for the trap had gone off and only secured a few breast feathers. Simeon set off on a second expedition. The first time the nest had been discovered the eggs were exposed to view, this time they were carefully covered with down. Simeon now reset the trap, this time laying it over the eggs, and carefully concealing it with the down. His hope was that the bird would remove the down with her beak and be snared by the neck. On the morrow he came back to us, however, with the four eggs and no swan; she had never returned, having apparently forsaken her nest, as we had feared she would. Simeon brought with him four ducks' nests, but the down was all mixed and the find was therefore valueless. These are some of the disappointments caused by the clumsy mismanagement of untrained men. A cold east wind that blew all day, prevented us doing much; we went out for an hour only, and shot a few yellow-headed wagtails, and a phalarope. We had plenty to interest us however, in reading the letters and papers that had reached us from England. The steamer had arrived from Ust-Zylma the day before, bringing us tidings of home from April 4th to May 13th, inclusive. The post had reached Ust-Zylma on the 26th; the last letters had therefore been five weeks *en route*, and so far as we know they had not been delayed in Archangel. From Ust-Zylma to Alexievka they would have taken more than another week to travel, had it not been for the steamer. On the 13th of May the Consul at Archangel wrote that the ice on the Dvina was expected to break up in seven days. A letter dated the 26th described the Dvina as quite free from ice for some days past, showing that it and the Petchora broke up within a day or two of each other.

The cold north-east wind that continued blowing kept us near home, but as it also kept the mosquitoes at bay we did not complain very bitterly of it. In the face of the cutting gale we crossed over to the tundra on the following day, in search once more of the grey plovers. On the way we visited an island and took a nest of the ringed plover. Soon after landing at our destination we soon heard the note of the birds we were in search of, and saw two or three, but could not discover any signs of their having a nest. After our previous experience we decided to vary our tactics. Hitherto we had found the nests by sheer perseverance in searching, and had afterwards watched the female to the nest and shot her. We now decided to watch the female on to the nest in the first instance, and, having by this means found it, to secure the female afterwards as a further and more complete identification of the eggs. It was also perfectly obvious that the extreme care we had taken not to alarm the bird was unnecessary. Our little manœuvre of walking away from the nest in a body, leaving one behind lying flat on the ground to watch, under the impression that the bird could not count beyond three, and would think that we had all gone, was clearly so much artifice wasted. The birds were evidently determined to come back to their nests in spite of our presence; nor was there any cover to hide us if the contrary had been the case. Our care not to handle the eggs until we had secured the bird was also of no use, as we often proved afterwards. On a marshy piece of ground I shot a reeve; and then we struck across a very likely piece of land, little flat pieces of bog with mossy ridges between. Presently Harvie-Brown, who was in front, whistled; and as I was coming up to him I saw a grey plover to my left. He called out to me that he had put up a pair near where he was standing. I soon caught sight of another bird, on the ground, lifting its wings as if to attract me from its nest. It then quietly ran off, and I went to the spot—but finding nothing, lay down to watch. Harvie-Brown did the same about eighty yards off. It was not long before I caught sight of both birds at some distance. One, which I at once concluded must be the male, remained in one spot, the other was running towards me, stopping on some elevation every few yards to look round. By-and-by it flew between Harvie-Brown and me, and alighted on the other side of me. The other bird soon followed, and remained as before, apparently watching the movements of the restless bird, which I now felt sure must be the female. To this latter bird I now confined my attention, and kept it within the field of my telescope for more than half an hour. It was never still for more than a minute together; it kept running along the ground for a few yards, then ascending one of the ridges looking round and uttering its somewhat melancholy cry. It crossed and recrossed the same ridges over and over again, and finally disappeared behind a knoll about forty yards ahead of me, and was silent. I carefully adjusted my telescope on a knoll to bear upon the place in case I lost it, and was just making up my mind to walk to the spot when I again heard its cry, and saw it running as before. The male was still *in statu quo*. The crossing and recrossing the ridge upon which my telescope was pointed then continued for another quarter of an hour, and at last the bird disappeared behind the same ridge as before. I gave her a quarter of an hour's grace, during which she was perfectly silent, and then sat up to see if Harvie-Brown was satisfied that she was on the nest. His point of sight was not so favourable as mine; and thinking I had given up the watch as hopeless, he fired off his gun as a last resource, and came up to me. As soon as he fired, both birds rose almost exactly in front of the knoll upon which my telescope pointed. Upon his arrival to learn what I had made out, I told him the nest was forty or fifty yards in front of my telescope. We fixed one of our guns pointing in the same direction, so that we could easily see it. We then skirted the intervening bog, got our exact bearings from the gun, and commenced a search. In less than a minute we found the nest with four eggs. As before, it was in a depression on a ridge between two little lakes of black bog. In returning to our boat we crossed a higher part of the tundra near the river bank, and saw some golden plovers. The eggs in this, our fifth nest, were considerably incubated, which was probably the reason why the birds showed more anxiety to lure us away.

On our way back towards the river we crossed a marsh where we saw some dunlins, and secured one young in down. On the higher part of the tundra, nearer the water's edge, were several golden plovers: we shot one, and noticed a pair of grey plovers amongst them. The two species were quite easy to distinguish even at a good distance, without the help of a glass. On a piece of low tundra, near the Petchora, we came upon a large flock of Buffon's skuas. My companion stopped to watch the grey plovers, and I marched after the skuas. We had usually seen these birds hawking like terns over the tundra, in parties of seven or eight; now and then we had met a pair alone, on the ground. They were always wild, difficult to approach, and hitherto we had succeeded in shooting a few only. As I neared the spot where the large flock was assembled, I watched them alighting on the banks near the great river. I walked towards them, and soon caught sight of a score of herring-gulls, on the shore to the right. Before I had got within a hundred yards of the latter, they all rose and flew towards me; the skuas also rose and followed them. I let the gulls go by and aimed at the nearest skua, as soon as it came within range. Fortunately I brought it down; that moment I was surrounded by about a hundred or a hundred and fifty skuas, flying about in all directions, generally about ten remaining within shot. They were very noisy, uttering a cry like "hack, hack" as they darted towards me, or screaming wildly as they flew about. This lasted about twenty minutes, during which I finished what remaining cartridges I had, some of which were dust. I missed several birds, but left seven killed and wounded on the field. My companion now joined me; he brought down four more and a Richardson's skua; the birds then all retired except one, that kept flying from one to the other of us, every now and then making a downward swoop, like a tern, over our heads. We soon discovered the cause of its anxiety; a young skua in down, a day or two old, lay on the ground at our feet. Our search for nest or eggs was vain. As it was getting late, after shooting a pair of dunlins on a space of marshy ground, and a willow-grouse among some dwarf willows, we returned to our boat, resolving to renew our search for eggs of Buffon's skua and grey plover on the morrow. We turned to look towards the spot of our encounter with the former: the whole flock had returned to it; they looked like great black terns on the wing as they hovered over it, with their peculiar kestrel- or tern-like flight. On several occasions after, we observed that the skuas have many habits in common with the tern.

The north-east wind continued blowing the next day, but the sunshine was bright and warm. When evening came on and the sun got low down in the horizon, for of course it never set, the wind increased and we felt it very cold. We spent our morning blowing eggs. In the afternoon we sent Cocksure on another expedition after a swan, whose nest with four eggs had been found and brought to us by one of our men. Towards four we crossed the river to the tundra. Our crazy old flat-bottomed boat could only sail with the wind dead on her stern, so we had to row with the stream for about a mile down the river, and then sail up again with the wind. By the appearance of the surrounding landscape we calculated that since we had last been on that part of the Petchora, the water must have fallen four feet at least. Some of the islands had doubled in size, and sandbanks lay bare, that before we had sailed over unsuspecting. We chose for our disembarkation a spot near a deserted house called Boogree, and soon after landing we shot a black scoter off her nest. It contained six eggs and an abundance of down; it lay in a little hollow sloping towards the river, and was entirely concealed amongst dwarf birch. The scoter does not breed apparently on the islands, but prefers a drier situation on the tundra, upon some sloping bank, overlooking a river or a lake, and sheltered by dwarf birch or willows. We first paid a visit to the marshy ground and saw there many dunlins, Lapland buntings, and red-throated pipits; one of the latter was carrying in its bill a caterpillar at least an inch long. Our next resort was to the river's sandy banks, where we found a ring dotterel's nest. We then visited the Buffon's skua ground. The large flock had left, but about a dozen remained behind. We watched them for an hour, and shot one. They were mostly hawking up and down the moor, occasionally resting on the ground. Suddenly, a skua uttered its alarm note; it sounded as if we had approached too near its nest. I whistled for my companion to come, and we lay down, about 120 yards apart, for an hour. The skua did not run about on the ground, but kept uneasily flying from one spot to the other, seldom remaining long in one place. One spot, however, it visited four times, and rested longer in it than in the others. The third time it visited it I made up my mind the nest was there, and carefully adjusted my gun on a hillock to cover the spot in case I lost it. The fourth time the bird visited it, Harvie-Brown and I got up together, each followed our bearings, and in about a minute we crossed each other at the nest, in which were two eggs. The bird was near at hand, shamming lameness to attract our attention. My companion walked up to it and shot—to our disappointment and disgust, not a Buffon's skua, but a Richardson's skua. After this we turned our attention to the grey plover ground. We found one of our men trying to watch one of these birds on to the nest. We lay down, one fifty yards to his right, and the other as much to his left. The birds behaved exactly as those we watched the day before. After the female had crossed and recrossed one hillock many times, and finally disappeared behind it, I made up my mind that the nest was there, and rose. My sudden appearance alarmed the male, who flew up, showing his black axillaries very distinctly in the evening sunshine as he skimmed over my head. We then all three rose, and in less than a minute met at the nest, which contained three eggs. I sat down to pack the eggs; and Harvie-Brown followed the male, who came up as we found the nest. Whilst I was packing the eggs and warming my hands, and talking "pigeon-Russ" with the man, the female came within range, and I took up my gun and shot her, thereby completing the identification of the eggs. On our return home we found that Cocksure had sent word to us that the swan had not revisited her nest as yet, and begged one of us to go to relieve guard. My companion accordingly, after a substantial meal, set off at midnight; meanwhile the men we paid to help us brought in the results of their day's work : a red-throated diver, trapped on the nest, with two eggs; half-a-dozen phalaropes' eggs, a duck's nest, containing seven large olive-grey eggs, and down, almost black. These, they assured us, were the eggs of the *bolshaya tchornaya ootka* (the great black duck). We recognised them, however, to be the same as those our Samoyede had brought home on the 2nd, and on which he had shot a female scaup. The down tallied exactly with that he had then brought home, as well as with some taken later from the breast of a female scaup. This convinced us that the eggs now brought in were those of the scaup. The next take was a long-tailed duck's nest, with five eggs, Then a man came in bringing us four small nests of *malenkya petëëtza* (small birds), a sedge-warbler's, a red-throated pipit's and two willow-warblers'.

The men who had collected these spoils for us were in the employment of the Company, to whom belong the steamers, the yacht or cutter, everything upon the island of Alexievka, and even the island itself. The Company derives a large and profitable trade in timber, which is shipped principally to Cronstadt for the Russian Government. Whether the company be Mr. Sideroff or Mr. Iconikoff, or both, or neither, remains one of those commercial secrets so common in Russia, and which nobody can ever get at the bottom of. These *employés* in Alexievka were all Zyriani from Ishma, a race of people said to be of Finnish origin. Some were reported to be very rich, the proprietors of large herds of reindeer. Like the people of Ust-Zylma, they are peasants, but were described to us as being more luxurious in their living and in the furniture of their houses. They were also said not to get drunk so often as the Ust-Zylma folk, but when inebriated, not to be good-natured and obtrusively affectionate as these are prone to be, but quarrelsome and given to fighting. They have the reputation of being better workmen, and certainly beat the Ust-Zylmians hollow at bird-nesting. In feature or size the two do not differ much; perhaps the Zyrians' eyes are more sunken and their cheekbones a little more prominent;

and there may be a greater number of red- and yellow-haired men among them. There were several fishing encampments of these peasants in different places down the river, and we found that it was customary in the wealthier families for one son to go in summer on the tundra, with the reindeer and the Samoyede servants. A Samoyede servant, we were told, gets per annum 15 copecks; a sum which probably represents his cost for the year. The language of the Zyriani is totally different from Russ, and belongs to the agglutinative family of languages. The tribe belongs to the Orthodox Greek Church, and not to that of the Old Believers.

OLD RUSSIAN SILVER CROSS.

KUYA.

CHAPTER XVIII.

Second visit to Stanavialachta—Peregrine falcons—Plague of mosquitoes—Midnight on the tundra—Nest of the velvet scoter—Little Feodor sent in quest of the swan's skin—A Russian bath—Feodor's return—Identification of eggs of Bewick's swan—Mosquito veils—Our eighth nest of grey plovers—Our servants—Our ninth nest of grey plovers—The tenth nest.

On the following morning when my companion returned from his watch at the swan's nest, which had turned out a complete failure, we consulted with Piottuch what was to be done. The swan had evidently forsaken her nest. Time was rapidly flying, and we feared the breeding season would be over before we had obtained identified eggs of the smaller species. It did not appear as if we could do anything at Alexievka; we had evidently yet to learn how swans were trapped at their nests on the Petchora; and we came to the conclusion that our wisest course was to go in search of the peasant who owned the skin of the swan belonging to the two small eggs we had bought some days ago. When we last heard of him he was fishing at one of the islands in the delta which we had visited not far from Stanavialachta, and we determined to make a second expedition to this locality. Fortunately for us, an opportunity occurred on the following day to run over to this place in the steamer belonging to the company. Outside the bar in the lagoon the cutter was cruising about with pilots to bring any ship which arrived up the river to Alexievka. The steamer had to visit this cutter to take the men a fresh stock of provisions, and we were delighted to make arrangements with Capt. Engel to take us with him, to drop us at Stanavialachta, and pick us up on his return.

We left Alexievka on the 6th of July and landed at our old quarters, and learnt to our disappointment that the peasant we were in quest of had found the fishing so bad that he had given it up in disgust and returned to his native village of Mekitza, some miles north of Alexievka. We were determined to settle the question if possible: we ascertained that he had not sold the swan-skin, but had taken it with him; so we decided to send one of our men to Mekitza as soon as we returned to Alexievka. In the meantime we started for the tundra to revisit our previous shooting-grounds. We stopped a few minutes on the shore to watch a family of Samoyedes fishing with a seine-net. They seemed to be catching nothing but a small fish resembling a herring, and even these did not appear to be at all plentiful. Leaving the shore, our curiosity led us first to visit the eyries of the two pairs of peregrine falcons, at each of which we had shot one of the birds. We found that the male of the first had paired with the female of the second; a fresh lining of feathers had been put into the latter's nest, and doubtless there would soon be eggs. The dotterels still haunted the hillsides. We shot some near each of the deserted houses—two by one, three by the other. Doubtless the right thing to have done would have been to lie down and watch the birds on to their nests and to have taken the eggs. But, in the first place, a dotterel is very difficult to see through a mosquito-veil; the next, to lie down and become the nucleus of a vast nebula of mosquitoes is so tormenting to the nerves, that we soon chose to adopt the consolatory conclusion that the grapes were sour and not worth the trouble of reaching after; or, in plain words, that the birds had not begun to breed, and it was no use martyrising ourselves to find their eggs. The mosquitoes were simply a plague. Our hats were covered with them; they swarmed upon our veils; they lined with a fringe the branches of the dwarf birches and willows; they covered the tundra with a mist. I was fortunate in the arrangement of my veil, and by dint of indiarubber boots and cavalry gauntlets, I escaped many wounds; but my companion was not so lucky. His net was perpetually transformed into a little mosquito-cage; his leggings and knickerbockers were by no means mosquito-proof; he had twisted a handkerchief round each hand, but this proved utterly insufficient protection: had it not grown cooler on the hills, as the sun got low, he would certainly have fallen into a regular mosquito-fever. We were told that this pest of mosquitoes was nothing as yet to what it would become later. "Wait a while," said our Job's comforter, "and you will not be able to see each other at twenty paces distance; you will not be able to aim with your gun, for the moment you raise your barrel

WATCHING GREY PLOVERS THROUGH A CLOUD OF MOSQUITOS.

half-a-dozen regiments of mosquitoes will rise between you and the sight." When the coolness of evening set in we had pretty good shooting for an hour or two; but after nine or ten o'clock we found nothing. There is very little to be met on the tundra or anywhere else at midnight, for in spite of brilliant sunshine, the birds retire to roost at the proper time and all is hushed. Our best find was the nest of a velvet scoter.* We shot the female as she rose from it; there

---

* The velvet scoter (*Œdemia fusca*, Linn.) appears to be confined to the eastern hemisphere, though it is replaced in North America by a form so

were eight eggs in it and a good supply of down. It was placed under a dwarf birch, far from any lake or water. We shot three willow-grouse and caught three young birds in down. While we were seeking for them the male frequently flew past within easy shot, and the female ran about with head depressed and wings drooping, coming sometimes within two or three yards of us. We saw two pairs of wood sandpipers, who had established themselves in a small space of marshy ground. They evidently had young, for they were continually flying round and alighting upon the willows. To search for young in down, through long grass, wearing mosquito-veils, must prove a vain quest, and we did not long pursue it. We caught the young of the Lapland bunting, and shot one of this year's shore-larks, a very pretty bird. We saw a few divers, a large harrier or eagle, and on the shore of the Petchora we watched a flock of Siberian herring-gulls stealing fish from the nets of the Samoyedes, and as we went down river we came on another flock similarly employed. We saw no swans on the tundra, but they were common on the islands in the river; one or two pairs were frequently in sight, and still there continued to fly overhead flocks of migratory ducks, always going north.

---

very closely allied as to be only just specifically separable. In the British Islands it is a winter visitant, possibly occasionally breeding in Scotland. Its breeding range extends north of the Arctic circle, as far as the limit of forest growth. In winter it is found in various parts of Central and Southern Europe, occasionally crossing the Mediterranean. Eastwards it winters in China and in Japan, in which latter country the American form (*Œdemia velvetena*, Cass.) is also found. In the valley of the Petchora we did not observe it farther north than latitude 68°.

All the day it had been a dead calm, but for the slight south breeze that had risen towards evening. The next morning a long-unfelt pleasant breath of wind was blowing down the river; it was not enough, however, to drive back the visitation of mosquitoes that was almost making us wish for the blustering north gale back again.

Despatching Little Feodor, our most intelligent man, by the steamer to Kuya, we bade him walk over to Mekitza, then ferret out the peasant and the swan's skin, and bring us home the latter. Meanwhile we spent the day blowing eggs. In the evening we took a Russian bath—an experience worth describing. We lay down upon a platform in a wooden house; a primitive stove was in it, built of stones loosely piled one upon the other; a hole in the side of the house with a sliding door let out the smoke. A wood-fire was kindled in the stove; it was allowed to go out when the stones were thoroughly heated; the steam resulting from the pouring of a glass of cold water upon them soon cleared the room of all foul air and smoke. As we lay stretched on the platform we occasionally threw water upon the hot stones, and flogged ourselves with a small broom composed of birch-twigs, still clothed with leaves; after which we rubbed ourselves down with matting, sponged all over with cold water, then went into another apartment to cool ourselves, smoke a few *papyros*, and dress. The peasants frequent these bath-houses, and often walk out of the hot steam naked, the colour of boiled crabs, to plunge into the Petchora.

The next day was one of our red-letter days. Little

Feodor, our boatman, returned, bearing with him the longed-for trophy—the swan's skin. He told us he had gone to Mekitza, only to learn there that the peasant whom he sought had departed to another island to fish. Going to his house he found, however, that the man had left the skin with his wife, and she, good soul, had cut off the beak and given it to her children for a plaything. Feodor paid her a rouble for the skin, with the feet still attached to it, and got the beak into the bargain. There was no other swan's skin in the house, nor, as far as we could ascertain, was there another in the village; this one was still soft and greasy, showing the bird had been but recently killed. This, undoubtedly, was the skin of a Bewick's swan;* the beak also was equally indisputable. The eggs in our possession were exactly the size one would expect a swan so much smaller than the wild swan would lay. We had every reason to believe and none to doubt that this was, indeed, the skin of the bird caught upon the nest containing the two eggs we had purchased. The chain of evidence connecting them was in all reason complete, and the identification of the eggs satisfactory. Let us recapitulate and go over the links of the narrative, the more fully to establish the conclusion we had arrived at. Two peasants are fishing together at Pyon'ni, an island near the mouth of the delta of the great river, twelve versts north

---

* Bewick's swan (*Cygnus minor*, Pall.) is occasionally found in winter in the British Islands. It breeds on the tundras above the limit of forest growth from the valley of the Petchora eastwards probably to the Pacific. In winter it is found in various parts of Europe and Asia as far south as China. In the valley of the Petchora we found it as far north as we went.

of Stanavialachta. They find there a swan's nest, containing two eggs, and they set a trap for the bird, which they succeed in catching. In the division of spoil, one takes the eggs, the other the swan. One peasant, wearied out by the pertinacity of the cold north-east wind, goes up stream to fish in smoother waters. On his way he stops at Alexievka, where we are, and we buy from him a number of ducks' and gulls' eggs, also two swan's eggs unusually small. As we purchase these we tell him that we shall be glad to pay the price of any swan's skin he can get us. He replies that the skin of the swan whose eggs he has just sold to us is in the possession of his partner, that the bird was trapped at the nest before they were taken out of it, adding that he has left his mate fishing on an island opposite Stanavialachta. On inquiry we find that two of our boatmen know this man, that we have seen him ourselves on the island where we found the two shoveller's eggs; we remember that he made a haul with a seine net of a small basketful of fish resembling herrings, which he presented to one of our men. We now take the first opportunity to go down to Stanavialachta and learn there that this peasant, disgusted as his comrade was by the prevalence of the cold north-east wind, has returned home to Mekitza. We send our most intelligent man to his house and get the skin.

The relative size of the two birds is very different, as may be appreciated at a glance, without the help of measurements. The bill of Bewick's swan is more than half an inch shorter than that of the larger species; the lengths of the wing, measuring from the carpal joint, are respectively $20\frac{1}{4}$ inches and $23\frac{1}{2}$; the lengths of the middle toes 5·15 and 6·1. Our eggs of Bewick's swan were about $3\frac{9}{10}$ inches long. We have eggs of other swans, doubtless of the large species, which measure $4\frac{1}{10}$, $4\frac{1}{10}$, $4\frac{1}{10}$, and $4\frac{1}{10}$ inches; these measurements make it seem probable that exceptionally large eggs of Bewick's swan might be of the same size as exceptionally small eggs of the common wild swan. The eggs appear to vary very little in shape.

That afternoon I took a walk on the island, armed with my stick gun. The birds were extremely tame. The yellow-headed wagtail seemed more abundant than ever. Reed buntings also were common. I got a shot at a swan, but the distance was a trifle too great. The weather was very hot, and the mosquitoes were swarming. Our home-made mosquito veils proved a great success; they and our cavalry gauntlets just made life bearable in these Arctic regions; still we longed for the cold winds back again to expel the plague of blood-sucking insects. Veils are necessary evils, but they interfere sadly with work, and increase much the difficulty of finding the shot birds through the long grass.

The next morning a swan's egg made us an excellent omelette for breakfast, after which I turned out for half an hour amongst the willows to shoot a few yellow-headed wagtails. They abounded on the marshy ground. I also secured two or three redpoles, some reed buntings, and a phalarope.

We set sail at noon, with a north-east wind, to visit the tundra eight or ten versts higher up the great river. For some distance before we landed the coast was very flat, with willows down to the water's edge. Amongst these dwarf trees we repeatedly heard our two especial favourites the Petchora pipit and the Siberian chiff-chaff. As soon as we got beyond the willows we landed on the tundra, and started in pursuit of a large flock of Buffon's skuas, but were soon stopped by a pair of grey plovers, which showed by their actions that we were near the nest. We lay down as before, forty or fifty yards apart, and watched the birds. They ran about, up and down, and all round us; and at the end of half an hour we were no wiser than at first. There was evidently something wrong. Harvie-Brown then shouted to me, "Have you marked the nest?" I replied by walking up to him and comparing notes. We then watched together for another half-hour with exactly the same result. I suggested that we must be so near the nest that the bird dare not come on, and advised that we should retreat to the next ridge, which we accordingly did. We had not done so many minutes before the female made her way on to the ridge where we had been lying. She then ran along the top of the ridge, passed the place where we had been stationed, and came down the ridge on to the flat bog towards where we then were. I whispered, "She is actually crossing over to us." Suddenly she stopped, lifted her wings and settled down on the ground. We both whispered, almost in the same breath, "She is on the nest." I added, "I saw her lift her wings as she settled on to the eggs." Harvie-Brown replied, "So did I," and added, "I can't hold out any longer against the mosquitoes." I replied, "I am perfectly satisfied; she is within range, take her." He lifted his gun to his shoulder. She ran off the nest to the top of the ridge and stood there until my companion shot her. We then walked up to the nest, the first we had seen on the flat. The eggs were quite fresh, or nearly so; and the nest must have been made nearly a fortnight later than those we had previously taken. During that time the bogs had become much drier, so that we could cross them without much difficulty; and this would probably be the reason why this nest was placed lower down. The eggs had all the appearance of a second laying, being less blotched than usual, one of them remarkably so. It is worth noticing that whilst we were watching in our first position, very near the nest, the birds were almost quite silent, and did not call to each other as they usually do.

After carefully packing the eggs, we walked on, and speedily started another pair. This time we lay down together, as nearly as we could tell, on the spot from which the birds rose, which seems to be generally from forty to fifty yards from the nest. The clouds of mosquitoes formed such a mist on the tundra that we had some difficulty in marking our birds; but by raking the horizon with a binocular, and getting well stung through our veils in the process, we soon found the female, and watched her on to a ridge just opposite to us. She soon settled down; and within a quarter of an hour after we had lain down we were both perfectly satisfied that she was on the nest. We gave her a few minutes' grace, and then walked up to the nest, without making any effort to shoot the bird, having perfectly identified her, and being almost tired out by the mosquitoes. The eggs in this nest were considerably incubated. The nest was placed, as before, in a hollow on a ridge. The ground on this ridge was not so mossy as usual, and there was much bare brown turf to be seen. Whether this had anything to do with the colour of the eggs it is difficult to say; but the fact is that these eggs are quite brown in ground-colour.

It was very late, or rather very early morning, when we returned to our quarters, and had to spend an hour slaughtering mosquitoes before we could make the room habitable; then we had our dinners to cook and our pipes to smoke before we could retire to rest. At noon I turned out of my hammock and spent the day indoors. The wind was north-west, and there were continual hints of rain. Our men were tired after the long row the day before. They were not in good condition, nor could it be expected they should be. They had now reached the last day of a four weeks' fast, during which they were supposed to eat nothing but bread and water, with fish if they could get it. During the period of probation it was intensely ludicrous to watch the expression on our steersman's face when he held up as many fingers as there still remained days of fasting to be gone through, opening his mouth wide the while, then grinning all over as he said, "Moi skaffum." "Skaffum" is pigeon-English for "eat," derived, we were told, from the Swedish (*skaffa*, to provide). This fellow's name was Feodor; he was a good-natured simpleton, indescribably lazy and always thinking of his stomach—we had nicknamed him "Moi skaffum." Gavriel, our other Russian, was not very much sharper, but was by no means lazy when directed in his work, but he had not the sense to discover for himself what wanted doing. Our half-bred Samoyede, also called Feodor,—Malenki Feodor we dubbed him—was a sharp, active lad, always finding out something to do; with a little training Malenki Feodor would have made an excellent servant. He learnt, when with us, to skin birds well, and was by this time a fair nester. Simeon, our thorough-bred Samoyede, was a philosopher, stolid, phlegmatic, and a good worker. He was our bird-nester *par excellence*. He knew the tundra well and the birds upon it; for three years he had lived in Varandai, and in his palmier days had reindeer of his own. Nothing moved Simeon; success did not elate him, nor failure depress him. He would take the extra rouble we always gave him when he brought us a rare bird's nest as a matter of course, without a "thank you." And when, as we witnessed once, he steadied the boat for a drunken German captain, who brutally trod upon his hand, evidently thinking it a fine thing to show his contempt for the poor Samoyede, Simeon equally took the insult as a matter of course, did not offer to withdraw his hand nor move a muscle of his face. If Simeon had any hot blood in him, the veins of it must have run very deep under his sallow skin.

The next day I did not do much either, but Cocksure being out of birds, I turned out amongst the mosquitoes and got him a few. I shot several yellow-headed wagtails, which were as abundant as ever, and also three Terek sandpipers, the first we had secured, although we had occasionally heard their notes on the island. A nest of shovellers' eggs, quite fresh, was brought to us during the day.

Our ninth nest of the grey plover we took on the 12th of July. A stiff warm gale from the east, with occasionally a smart shower of rain, kept the air clear of mosquitoes in the morning. In the afternoon the wind fell, and the mosquitoes were as bad as ever; but we were too busy to heed them much. At eleven we crossed to the tundra. We soon came upon a pair of grey plovers, which rose a couple of hundred yards ahead of us, their wings glittering in a gleam of sunshine after a smart shower. These birds have frequently a very curious flight as they rise from the nest, tossing their wings up in the air, reminding one somewhat of the actions of a tumbler pigeon. We lay down, as near as we could tell, to the spot from which they rose, and were somewhat puzzled at their behaviour. The male seemed equally, if not more anxious than the female, running about as much as she did, continually crying, and often coming very near us, and trying to attract our attention by pretending to be lame. The female rarely uttered a note. We suppose this must have been because one of us was too near the nest. Harvie-Brown moved his post of observation after we had spent some time without being able to discover anything; and then the female behaved as usual, and I soon marked the position of the nest. We walked straight up to it, and found the four eggs chipped ready for hatching. We had no difficulty in shooting both birds, and afterwards hatched out two of the eggs, obtaining a couple of good specimens of young in down. With a little practice this mode of finding birds' nests becomes almost a certainty. One has first to be quite sure which is the male and which is the female. When the birds are near enough, and one can compare them together, the greater blackness of the breast of the male is sufficient to distinguish him; but we found that the females varied considerably in this respect, and that it was better to notice the habits of the birds. The female generally comes first to the nest, but she comes less conspicuously. She generally makes her appearance at a considerable distance, on some ridge of mossy land. When she has looked round, she runs quickly to the next ridge, and looks round again, generally calling to the male with a single note. The male seldom replies; but when he does so it is generally with a double note. When the female has stopped and looked round many times, then the male thinks it worth while to move; but more often than not he joins the female by flying up to her. The female very seldom takes wing. She is very cautious, and, if she is not satisfied that all is safe, will pass and repass the nest several times before she finally settles upon it. The female rarely remains upon one post of observation long; but the male often remains for ten minutes or more upon one tussock of a ridge, watching the movements of the female.

We walked some distance before we came upon a second pair; but at length we heard the well-known cry, and got into position. We spent nearly two hours over this nest, and were quite at sea at the end of the time. We changed our position several times, but to no purpose. The female went here and there and everywhere, as much as to say, "I'm not going on to the nest as long as you are so near." By and by the mosquitoes fairly tired us out, and we gave up the watching game and commenced a search. At last we found out the secret of the bird's behaviour. We picked up some broken egg-shells, and concluded at once that the bird had young. We tried to find them, but in vain. These two hours however were not wasted. The birds came nearer to me than they had ever done before. I often watched them at a distance of not more than ten yards, and was able to hear their notes more distinctly. The note most frequently used is a single plaintive whistle, *köp*, long drawn out, the *ö* pronounced as in German, and the consonants scarcely sounded. This I am almost sure is the alarm-note. It is principally uttered by the female when she stops and looks round and sees something that she disapproves of. If the male shows any anxiety about the nest, which he seems to do more and more as incubation progresses, he also utters the same note. The double note, *kl-ee* or *kleep*, the *kl* dwelt upon so as to give it the value of a separate syllable, is also uttered by both birds. It is evidently their call-note. I have seen the female, when she has been running away from the male, turn sharp round and look towards him when he has uttered this note, exactly as any one might do who heard his name called. Whilst we were watching this pair of birds a couple of other grey plovers came up, and called as they flew past. The male answered the call and flew towards them. On the wing this whistle is lengthened out to three notes. I had some difficulty in catching this note exactly. It is not so often uttered as the two others I have mentioned, and is generally heard when you least expect it; but I am almost sure it is a combination of the alarm-note with the call-note—*kl-ee-köp*. If I wanted to make a free translation from Ploverski into English I should say that *kl-ee* means "Hallo! old fellow," and *köp* means "Mind what you are about!"

We procured our tenth nest of the grey plover the same afternoon. It was found by our Samoyede, who brought us three eggs and male and female shot at the nest. He accidentally broke the fourth egg. As it contained a live young bird, we placed these three eggs in our hatching-basket, where we had made a snug nest of bean-goose-down.

By this time we were pretty well tired with tramping the tundra. The ceaseless persecution of the mosquitoes, and the stifling feeling caused by having to wear a veil with the thermometer above summer heat, had taxed our powers of endurance almost to the utmost; and we turned our faces resolutely towards our boat; but a most anxious pair of grey plovers were too great an attraction to us to be resisted. We watched them for some time, during which a pair of ringed plovers persisted in obtruding themselves impertinently between us and the objects of our attention. This pair of grey plovers also puzzled us, and we concluded that they possibly had young, and consequently we gave up the search. We had each marked a place where we thought the nest might be; and we each of us went to satisfy ourselves that it was not there. The two places were about fifty yards apart. The birds first went up to Harvie-Brown and tried to attract him away by flying about and feigning lameness. Then they came to me and did the same. They were so demonstrative that I felt perfectly certain of finding the nest, and shot at the female. She dropped in the middle of a wet bog. I then shot the male, walked up to him, and left him with my basket and gun to struggle through the bog to pick up the female. Before I got up to her, I saw her lying on the turf on her breast with her wings slightly expanded. I was just preparing to stoop to pick her up, when she rose and flew away, apparently unhurt. I must have missed her altogether, as she was evidently only shamming to draw me away. I returned to search for the nest, and was unable to find it. Whilst I was looking for it Harvie-Brown came up, and I gave up the search, and we again turned towards the boat. When we had got about halfway towards the spot where Harvie-Brown had been looking, I caught sight of a young grey plover in down, almost at my feet. Stooping down to pick it up, I saw the nest with three eggs not a yard from me. This was the last and eleventh nest of these rare birds which we found. The young in down are very yellow, speckled with black, and are admirably adapted for concealment upon the yellow-green moss on the edges of the little bogs close to which the grey plover seems always to choose a place for its nest.

Our attempt to hatch the highly incubated eggs, and thus obtain specimens of young in down, was successful. We soon had five young grey plovers well and hearty, and secured three or four more afterwards.

MOSQUITO VEIL.

LITTLE STINT'S NEST, EGGS AND YOUNG.

CHAPTER XIX.

Trip to the Golievski Islands—Shoal of white whales—Glaucous gull—Dunlins and sanderlings—Black scoter—Dvoinik—Little stint—Curlew sandpiper—Snow-bunting—Overhauling our plunder—The Company's manager—Discussions concerning the stints—Probable line of migration followed by birds.

ON the 13th of July an opportunity presented itself of visiting the Golievski Islands at the entrance of the lagoon.

These islands are little more than sandbanks, and the beacons erected upon them for the guidance of vessels entering the river are washed away every spring by the ice. To re-erect these beacons and to inspect others on various promontories on the shores of the lagoon, the steamer makes a trip every July. Capt. Engel asked us to accompany him, and we gladly accepted the invitation.

Passing Stanavialachta and Cape Bolvanski, we sailed almost due north to the bar, where the lead announced scarcely thirteen feet of water. We then steered nearly east to within three miles of the shore, whence we afterwards kept in a north-easterly direction; a few miles after passing Cape Constantinovka we altered our course to north, and made Island No. 4 about midnight. Off Cape Constantinovka we came upon a shoal of white whales or beluga, which played like porpoises round the steamer.

We stayed a couple of hours on Island No. 4, erecting the beacon upon it. The night was foggy at intervals, but the midnight sun shone bright. The island is a flat desert of sand, unrelieved by a blade of grass. It may be a couple of square miles in extent in the summer time, and is not much affected by the tide that rises only four or six inches. We found a large flock of glaucous gulls upon it;* we could only discover two nests. They were heaps of sand,

---

* The glaucous gull (Larus glaucus, Linn.) breeds on the shores of the Arctic Ocean of both hemispheres, migrating southwards on the approach of winter, in Europe as far south as the Mediterranean, in Asia as far as Japan, and in America as far as Long Island on the Atlantic coast. It visits the shores of Great Britain during autumn and winter, but has not been known to breed so far south.

hollowed slightly at the apex and lined with some irregularly disposed tufts of seaweed. The young in down were running about on the flat sandbank. We secured half-a-dozen and shot four old birds. The young were less spotted than those of most gulls usually are: the old birds were pure white, with delicate, dove-coloured mantles, paler than those of our herring-gull. The legs and feet were pale flesh-tinted pink; the beak and the line round the eye were straw-yellow. The point of the beak was horn-colour, with the usual dark vermilion spot on the angle of the lower mandible. The pupils of the eye were blue-black, and the irides very pale straw-yellow. The interior of the mouth was the colour of the feet. The birds to whom the two nests belonged were easily shot; they made repeated downward darts upon us, like terns. The rest of the flock kept well out of range, soon settling down at a point on the extreme end of the island, and, on being fired at there, flew right away. Among these glaucous gulls were two immature birds and one or two Siberian herring-gulls. After the dispersion of the flock that had engaged all our attention, we began to notice the presence of small parties of sandpipers feeding about the island. They were very wild, running about on the low, wet sandbanks, rising hardly a couple of feet above high-tide level, and about the margins of the little pools in the lower parts of the island. Among them were some dunlins; we succeeded in shooting a couple of these, and one or two sanderlings.* These birds were

---

* The sanderling (*Calidris arenaria*, Linn.) is a common bird on the coasts of Great Britain and Ireland during winter, and still more so in spring

peculiarly interesting to us. We had scarcely hoped to come across them. We saw no evidences, however, of their breeding upon the island; they seem to have settled upon it

and autumn, when great numbers pass along our shores on their passage to and from their breeding-grounds. They usually arrive during August and leave us again towards the end of May. This interesting wader breeds so far north that its eggs are almost unknown in collections. When we visited the Petchora, properly authenticated eggs of this species were absolutely unknown. Eggs, said to be those of the sanderling, had been obtained in Iceland and in Arctic America, but it was not until 1876 that all doubt upon the subject was removed. In the Appendix to Nares' 'Voyage to the Polar Sea' (vol. ii. p. 210) Captain Fielden, the naturalist to the expedition, gives the following account of the breeding of the sanderling, which is illustrated by an excellent chromo-lithograph of the eggs of that bird. "I first observed the sanderling in Grinnell Land on June 5th, 1876, flying in company with knots and turnstones; at this date it was feeding like the other waders on the buds of *Saxifraga oppositifolia*. This bird was by no means abundant along the coasts of Grinnell Land; but I observed several pairs in the aggregate, and found a nest of this species containing two eggs, in lat. 82° 33' N. on June 24th, 1876. This nest, from which I killed the male bird, was placed on a gravel ridge, at an altitude of several hundred feet above the sea; and the eggs were deposited in a slight depression in the centre of a recumbent plant of willow, the lining of the nest consisting of a few withered leaves, and some of the last year's catkins. August 8th, 1876, along the shores of Robeson Channel, I saw several parties of young ones, three to four in number, following their parents, and, led by the old birds, searching most diligently for insects. At this date they were in a very interesting stage of plumage, being just able to fly, but retaining some of the down on their feathers." The eggs of the sanderling, as figured by Captain Fielding, are miniature eggs of the less strongly marked varieties of the curlew, and are of the same size as the eggs of the lesser tern. This discovery of a breeding-place of the sanderling at the extreme northern limit of animal life on the shores of the polar basin, a little to the west of Cape Union, is one of the most interesting additions to the history of British birds which has recently been made. There can be little doubt that the distribution of this bird during the breeding season is circumpolar, since in winter the sanderling is found on both coasts of the American continent as far south as Chili and Brazil. It is very common in Africa in winter down to the Cape, and in Asia it has been found during the cold season on the coasts of India and China.

merely to feed. The only trace of nests we found was that of the two of the glaucous gull. The shores of the island were devoid of all material for nest-building, except sand and a very slight quantity of seaweed. A few whelks, some broken mussels, and other bivalves lay sparingly scattered about; here and there a few pieces of drift-wood, and near the south shore the stranded decaying body of a seal, probably the harp seal.

At two o'clock we returned on board, and after a couple of hours' sleep, we woke to find ourselves lying at anchor in a thick fog that completely hid Island No. 3 from us. The sun, however, was shining brilliantly overhead. After an early breakfast we watched the fog lifting, and gradually we caught sight of the island, over which a flock of ten thousand black ducks was whirling and circling. This island we computed to be some eight or ten miles in length. It appeared to be exactly the same sandy desert as Island No. 4, but we were told that some persons who had visited it declare that grass grows upon it. Unluckily for us, its beacon had not been carried off, only laid upon its side by the ice, so that in an hour's time it was repaired and set up on its legs again, and all hands ordered back on board. Near it lay another dead seal, apparently the common one, in a condition described by Cocksure as having "beaucoup d'aroma." A few herring and glaucous gulls were upon the island, and we found two empty nests; but what interested us most was the presence of large parties of dunlins and small flocks of sanderlings. Numbers of black ducks continually passed like clouds overhead. The large flocks did not come near enough for identification, but we made out among smaller ones the long-tailed duck and the black scoter, and were inclined to think that the large flocks were composed of the latter species.

At eight o'clock we had a more substantial breakfast than that partaken of in the earlier hours; then we went to lie down on sofas in the cabin. All day we drifted down a sea almost as smooth as a mirror; not a breath of wind stirred during the night or day. We had also left the mosquitoes behind, and only saw one or two after leaving the delta of the Petchora. The steamer returned to No. 4 Island as we slept, to get into the right course and deposit a "carabas" on the William Bank, and a long pole (with a besom on the top and a stone at the foot) upon the Alexander Bank.

We commenced our next day at 4 P.M. It was a very short one, but it proved a very eventful one. After a refreshing wash and a promenade on deck for half an hour, we dined and smoked a pipe. By that time the boats were ready, and we went on shore a couple of versts south of the river Dvoinik, there to erect another beacon, which we were afterwards told the Samoyedes had pulled down.

Harvie-Brown and I struck off at once for the tundra in the direction of the Pytkoff Mountains (580 feet high), about fifteen miles distant. The tundra was very flat, and we soon came upon ground exactly similar in character to that tenanted by the grey plovers near Alexievka. We had not walked far when we heard the well-known cry, and there rose four grey plovers. My companion soon after met with another pair and lay down to watch them. We parted company here, and I heard later that feeling ill, the effects probably of irregular meals and sleep, he soon after returned to the ship, having met with nothing of interest, except the grey plovers, and a few Buffon's and Richardson's skuas, and also picking up the feathers of a snowy owl.

After leaving him I went on for about a quarter of an hour, then finding the tundra "flat, stale, and unprofitable," I turned sharp to the north, towards what I took to be a large lake, but which in the maps is set down to be a bay of the sea. *En route* I saw nothing but an occasional Lapland bunting or red-throated pipit. Arrived at the water's edge, however, I spent an interesting hour. A large flock of sandpipers were flying up and down the banks. They looked very small and very red; and, in order to watch them, I hid amongst some dwarf willows, teeming with mosquitoes. I did not heed their bites, for my hopes and doubts and fears made me for the time mosquito-proof. Presently some birds swirled past, and I gave them a charge of No. 8. Three fell—three little stints*—the real Simon Pure at last. I now waited a

---

* The little stint (*Tringa minuta*, Leisl.) was one of those few birds which we did not meet with at Ust-Zylma on migration, and one whose eggs we looked upon as one of the great prizes which might possibly be within our reach on this trip; authentic specimens being unknown in any collection; the only examples known to have been obtained having been procured by Middendorff on the Taimyr River in Siberia in latitude 74°. This species breeds only on the tundras beyond the limit of forest growth, probably from the North Cape in Norway to the valley of the Yenesay. It passes the shores of Great Britain in both seasons on migration, but is much more numerous in autumn than in spring. It winters in North and South Africa and India. In Eastern Siberia its place is taken by a nearly allied species—*Tringa albescens* (Temm.)—which differs in summer in being much more chestnut on the throat, and may be recognized at all seasons by its longer tarsus.

few minutes, and soon heard their notes again. This time a small flock passed me over the water, and I dropped a couple into it. I endeavoured to wade in after them, but the mud was too much for me; a smart north wind was blowing also, so I turned back and waited on the shore; there I spent the time examining every dunlin that came within the range of my glass, in the hopes of discovering one without the black belly. After a while I walked on, not caring to shoot more, but desirous of finding some evidence of the little stint's breeding haunts. At a short distance before me rose sandhills sprinkled over with esparto-grass; towards these I now bent my steps. The intervening ground was covered with thick, short, coarse grass, and was studded with little pools of water. I had not gone far before I came upon some sandpipers feeding on the edge of a small island in the bay. There was no kind of cover near, so, approaching as close as I dared, I fired. There must have been six or seven birds; all rose but one, who tried to follow the rest, but was wounded, and he dropped into the water, fluttering feebly on, till he reached another island. The mud on the banks was so deep and sticky that it was with difficulty I again got within range, and with a second shot laid him upon his back. When I managed to reach him my pleasure was great on picking him up to find a curlew sandpiper.* This

---

* The curlew sandpiper (*Tringa subarquata*, Güld.) is a regular spring and autumn migrant on the shores of Great Britain and Ireland. It rarely if ever remains the winter with us, but passes through in September and October in considerable numbers, and again, but in much smaller flocks, in May. It is not known that eggs of this bird, common as it is, have ever been taken. Even its breeding-grounds have yet to be discovered. The ill-

was the single specimen of the species that we obtained on our journey. I now hastened on to the sandhills. The mosquitoes had by this time forced me to wear my veil, but when on reaching the hills I saw a number of small waders running hither and thither, I threw it back; still I could detect nothing but ringed plovers. I shot one, to be certain of my identification, and hoping also that the report would rouse rarer game. A shore-lark in first plumage was the only variety of bird that rose at the sound. I secured it. Wandering on farther, I was still disappointed. Beds of wild onion and large patches of purple vetch had replaced the coarse grass. I returned on my footsteps to the edge of the bay, and missed a shot at a swan; a snowy owl also flew past out of range.. The curlew sandpipers had disap-

considered statement made by Dr. Finsch that he had found the young in down on the Yalmal peninsula was afterwards contradicted by himself. There can be little doubt that the curlew sandpiper breeds in Arctic Siberia, but the precise locality remains a mystery. It occasionally winters on the shores of the Mediterranean, and is exceedingly common in South Africa, from October to April. It is also found at the same season of the year on the coast of India, China, and the islands of the Malay Archipelago. In America it appears to be only an accidental straggler to the west coast. It was a great disappointment to us to obtain no definite clue to its breeding haunts; but from the accounts we heard, conflicting and untrustworthy as these often were, we gathered that marshy plains and swamps of great extent lie along the courses of the numerous rivers and small streams which flow from the Pytkoff Mountains to the sea to the north-eastward of Dvoinik. Of this fair land of promise we were only permitted to obtain a very distant and unsatisfactory view, as on the only occasion when we might have seen it, had the air been clear, from a height upon the tundra to the north of the inlet, a white mist lay along the distant hollows, completely concealing the features of the landscape. The curlew-sandpiper does not always follow the coast-line in its migrations. Bogdanoff records that it is seen on the Volga and on the Kama both in spring and autumn.

peared. The flock of little stints were still there, but I left them to follow a snow-bunting, the first I had seen since leaving Ust-Zylma. I shot it. Then, to my consternation, I discovered through my glass that the last man had left the beacon, and I must return; a pair of black-throated divers were sailing about the bay, one or two herring-gulls were flying about, but my time was up. I was a good mile from the ship, so, turning by the sandhills, I made my way to the beacon, bagging a fine male grey plover as I went. As soon as I got on board, we started for Alexievka.

My wonderful success at the last moment determined us that by some means we would return to this land teeming with rare birds. We marked, as we steamed along, that the sandhills continued on the north side of the river Dvoinik as far as Cape Constantinovka. It was probable that the breeding-ground of the "little stints" might be found on these coasts or on the mountains. Those I had seen might be last year's birds, not breeding this year, but haunting the neighbourhood of the older ones, as is the case with the flocks of dunlins. It was tantalising to have to hurry away from what seemed an Eldorado; and as we looked at the old washing-tub that usually carried us on our trips to the tundra, and knew that for its life it could not dare cross the Bolvanski Bucht, we felt inclined to parody on Richard III.'s cry, and exclaim aloud, " A boat! a boat! my kingdom for a boat!"

Our young grey plovers in down, when we visited them, we found thriving. There were five small birds, in excellent condition.

The five sanderlings that we had shot on the islands were three males and two females. The testicles of the former were small, the latter had eggs about the size of a pin's head. Both males and females showed signs of moult; they had some bare places almost like sitting-spots, but no recent ones.

The curlew sandpiper turned out to be a female, with very small eggs, and showed no signs of having been breeding this year.

The next day we were too wearied, after the excitement and fatigues of the previous one, to do more than turn out for a few minutes to shoot a couple of Temminck's stints. We wished to compare them with the little stints secured the day before. Side by side the birds are perfectly distinct. The little stint is a shade the smaller, but the measurements are the same, as its bill is a trifle the longer. There is not much difference in the extent of wing, the measurements being respectively 11·8 and 11·9 inches. The length of wing from the carpal joint is:—

   Temminck's stint .. .. 4·05 in.
   Little stint .. .. 3·6 in.

A more important measurement may be the length of the tarsus. The smaller bird has decidedly the longer tarsus. ·85 against ·75 inch. The colours of the legs and feet are very different. The little stint's are almost black; those of the Temminck's stint brown, or perhaps grey. The bill of the little stint is also much darker than that of the other species. The easiest distinction lies in the colour of the back and wings. In this respect the little stint is a small dunlin, and the Temminck's stint a small Terek or common sandpiper. The little stint is dark brown, almost black, each feather edged with pale chestnut, or rich umber-brown. The other species is grey, with something like a touch of green, and the feathers have pale tips, rich enough sometimes to be called a grey yellow-ochre; those on the bastard wing appoach a grey umber-brown. The colour of the shaft of the first primary, and the comparative distinctness of the white edges of the secondaries, supposed in the Temminck's stint to form a second white bar in flight, appear exactly the same in both species.

The five little stints in our possession proved to be all males. Temminck's stints were very common at Alexievka. They were breeding abundantly: sometimes we found them in single pairs; sometimes almost in colonies; but we had never met with flocks of these birds since leaving the neighbourhood of Habariki. Those that we had come upon afterwards had never failed to show us by their ways that we were intruding upon their breeding quarters. When Harvie-Brown visited Archangel, in 1872, he found Temminck's stints breeding on one of the islands of the delta of the Dvina. This was probably not far from the southern limit of their migration. He also continually observed this species in other localities, congregating in small flocks together, and evidently not breeding. These might have been the birds of the preceding year. If, as it is pretty well established, few sandpipers breed until the second year, and the young birds flock, during their first summer, somewhere near the southern limit of the breeding-stations, it might also be augured that the little stints I had seen were probably breeding at no great distance from the spot I had visited the previous day. The thought of the probable vicinity of the nests, the discovery of which had been one of the strong motives of our journey, excited us so much that we did not go to bed, but spent the night plotting and planning the possibilities of getting to Dvoinik again. There were difficulties in the way. Unluckily for us, the Company's manager was a very impracticable man. It was his first year in office; he was young, inexperienced, and comparatively uneducated. For the nonce, he was absolute monarch of Alexievka, and the absoluteness of his power was "too many" for him. A German (from Revel), he had yet so much of the Russian in him, that when scratched the Tartar would out. He was very unpopular, and one glimpse behind the scenes revealed to us rebellion "looming in the distance." There were allowances to be made for the man. No gentlemen would come to such a place as Alexievka, or face the existing muddle, for the sake of the miserable pay "la pauvre compagnie," as Cocksure calls it, gives. The Provalychik had a plentiful crop of cares under his crown. So far as we could see, he was plotting and being plotted against. He was not backed up by the Bureau at St. Petersburg. His domestic affairs looked ugly; and amongst his subordinates he had scarcely one reliable man he could trust. The whole situation was a specimen of what the Germans call "Russische Wirthschaft." We knew the man could render us an invaluable service without exposing the Company to the slightest loss, but as yet we had not been able to make him see with our eyes. We longed for the arrival of Sideroff, fearing, however, he would come too late. Meanwhile we tried to work the oracle, and had not yet given up the task in despair.

Whether the birds that I had seen in flocks on the tundra were those of the year before, or not, continued a matter of discussion between my companion and myself. He considered that maritime birds that feed principally when the tide falls, have consequently a periodical dining-hour, and a special dining-room, and therefore get into the habit of flocking together at dinner-time. I remained still of the opinion that birds of the same species were breeding not far off, probably on the coast between the Bolvanski Bucht and Varandai; or it might be on the Pytkoff Mountains. We had also many debates concerning the probable line of migration followed by "*les rares oiseaux*," as we called the grey plover, the little stint, the curlew sandpiper, and the sanderling; and in this we began to question the usually received theory, that these birds migrate up the Baltic and along the coast of Norway to their breeding haunts. My own notion had long been that birds migrate *against* the prevailing winds; that they migrate *to* their breeding-ground in a narrow stream, returning from them in a broad one. If these birds therefore winter on the shores of the Mediterranean, they probably leave by way of the Black Sea, cross by the Sea of Azov to the Volga, near Sarepta, follow the Volga to Kazan, thence along the Kama to Perm; then over the low hills of the Ural to the Obb, and so on to the Arctic Ocean. Some breed near the mouth of the Obb, others on the eastern or the western coast. The stragglers who wander off as far as Archangel and the North Cape, may be barren birds, with nothing else to do.

After starting this hypothesis, we bethought ourselves that we had with us a list of the birds of Kasan, in a book lent to us by M. Znamin-ki. These chapters are headed "Materials for making a Biography of the Birds of the Volga," and the work itself is entitled, 'Descriptive Catalogues of the High School of the Imperial University at Kasan,' edited by MM. Kovalevski, Levakovski, Golovinski, and Bogdanoff; published at Kasan in 1871. From this book, Cocksure drew for us the following information:—

"*Little and Temminck's stints* are seen in flocks during the first fortnight in May on the Volga, from Simbirsk to Kasan, and on the Kama as far as Ufla. They are not seen during the summer, but are found again at Simbirsk in the middle of August.

"*Curlew sandpipers* are seen in Kasan in spring and autumn only, both on the Volga and Kama.

"*Sanderlings* are seen in autumn at Kasan, and have been seen in spring on the Sarpa.

"*Grey plovers* are seen in small flocks in May and September, near Kasan, but are not to be met with every year.

"*Yellow-headed wagtails* arrive at Kasan, with the common species (viz. middle of April): a few pairs are seen until the beginning of June."

These extracts prove that part of the migration of these species takes place across country; but probably the main stream follows the coast, especially in autumn, as I was myself an eye-witness, the year after my return from the Petchora, on the island of Heligoland.

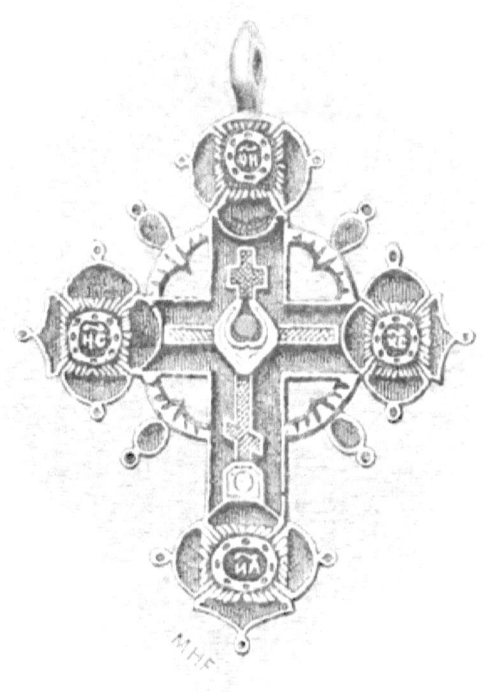

OLD RUSSIAN SILVER CROSS.

THE LIGHTHOUSE AT
HELIGOLAND ON
A MIGRATION NIGHT.

CHAPTER XX.

Hybernation of birds—Migration of birds—Reed-warblers—Origin of migration—Transvaal warblers—The Mammoth age—Insect life—Lines of migration—Heligoland—Its ornithologists—Variety of birds—Wind and weather—The throstle-bushes—Migration by sight—Order of migration—Stray migrants—The yellow-browed warbler—Migration on Heligoland—Skylarks—Migratory instincts—Other facts of migration.

It is very difficult to realise the fact that not longer ago than towards the close of the last century the belief in the hybernation of swallows was held by many ornithologists. That certain species of mammals spend the winter in a torpid state is proved beyond all possibility of doubt; but there is no evidence of the hybernation of any species of birds. Never was theory founded on more flimsy substratum of supposed facts, or supported by weaker logical argument. Swallows made their appearance in spring, no one knew how or whence. During the summer they were remarkable for being almost constantly on the wing, but late in the autumn a noticeable change took place in their habits. They were observed more and more to congregate in large flocks, and towards evening to perch in numbers on houses, and frequently in trees. Finally they collected in thousands on the reeds and willows on the banks of the Thames, and disappeared during the night. In the morning not a swallow was to be seen, and ornithologists came to the startling conclusion that they had plunged into the dark waters of the river, and buried themselves in the mud at its bottom, to reappear the following spring, refreshed by their winter's sleep. And this theory was gravely accepted as one among many other unfathomable secrets of Nature! After a time it was, however, discovered that the disappearance of many of the summer resident birds from their breeding-grounds in this country was the signal for their appearance in some parts of Southern Europe or Northern Africa, and the theory of migration was accepted as resting upon a basis of indisputable fact when birds were seen in the act of migrating. At certain stations, such as Gibraltar and Malta, and notably on the island of Heligoland (all, curiously enough, under British rule), birds were seen passing over, not in small flocks only, but by thousands and tens of thousands, so that no possible doubt could remain as to the great fact of migration. The periodical disappearance of the swallow remained, however, almost as great a mystery as before. The impulse of migration was called an instinct; but did not the less remain an unfathomable secret of Nature, and the only cause that could be assigned for it was that it must have been originally implanted in certain species at their creation and denied to others.

The discoveries of Darwin and Wallace have placed the facts of migration in an entirely new light, and added a new interest to a subject which has always been one of the most fascinating departments of ornithology. The origin of the habit of migration is still involved in much mystery. It is probably a fact in the history of birds of comparatively modern date. It is not confined to any one geographical region, nor to any one family of birds, nor can we assume that it will be present or absent in every species of the same genus. The birds of the Nearctic region are as migratory as those of the Palæarctic. Many birds visit South America and Australia only during the breeding-season. If we include as birds of the tropical regions those species which visit them after having bred in the cooler regions, they will also contain a considerable proportion of migrants, even though no bird migrates there to breed. We may lay it down as a law, to which there is probably no exception, that every bird breeds in the coldest regions of its migrations. No bird migrates to the tropics to breed because there is no hotter region for it to migrate from. The well-authenticated stories of birds breeding a second time in the place of their winter migration probably have the same scientific value as the stories of swallows having been found hybernating in caves and hollow trees, or of toads having been found in the recesses of otherwise solid rocks.

Many birds, such as the robin, the blackbird, the song-thrush, &c., which are resident in England, are migratory in Germany. There is every probability that it is only within comparatively recent times that these birds have ceased to migrate in England, and we may fairly conjecture that should the English climate remain long enough favourable to the winter residence of these birds, they will develop into local races, which will eventually have rounder and shorter wings than their continental allies.

In some genera of birds it is comparatively easy to determine the geographical range from an examination of the shape of the wing. In the genus *Acrocephalus*, or reed-warblers, for example, *A. turdoides* has a very pointed wing. Its migrations extend from South Sweden to the Transvaal. *A. orientalis* is scarcely distinguishable except in having a slightly less pointed wing. Its migrations extend from Japan to Borneo. *A. stentorius* has a decidedly more rounded wing, and the limits of its migrations are from Turkestan to India; whilst *A. syrinx* has the roundest wing of all, and appears to have become a resident in the island of Ponape. In the smaller species of the genus the fact is equally striking. The sharp-winged *A. schœnobænus* ranges from the Arctic Circle to South Africa, whilst the more rounded-winged *A. dumetorum* and *A. bæticatus* have very limited ranges.

There is a considerable difference of opinion as to the

origin of migration, some ornithologists holding that the original home of a species was its winter quarters; others supposing that before the instinct of migration was formed the species was a resident in the district where it now breeds. Both views have their difficulties; but the preponderance of evidence seems to me to be largely on the side of the latter theory. In turning over a box of Transvaal skins, shot during the breeding season between September and March, it seems impossible to come to any other conclusion. Throwing aside the brilliant birds of the district, we shall find, especially if the box comes from Potchefstrom, a variety of reed-warblers and allied birds, which speak of swamps abounding with insects, where birds of this kind delight to breed and find unlimited food. As a matter of fact most of these birds do breed there, and, because the winter is so mild, remain there all the year round. But mixed up with these African types we shall find a fair sprinkling of our own reed-warblers, who have gone down there to avoid our cold winters. These birds are not breeding; they have migrated to the Transvaal to enjoy the mosquitoes of the Potchefstrom swamps, and when the Potchefstrom birds have finished breeding and begin their six months' rest from family cares, they will some of them migrate to the Arctic regions of North Europe to breed amongst the mosquitoes which swarm on the river-banks on the outskirts of the tundra. We can scarcely conceive it possible that these species were ever resident birds in the Transvaal. It seems much more rational to conclude that they were once resident birds in the subarctic regions of

Europe, and now by the change in the winter temperature of their original home have come to South Africa as migrants, apparently out of season in regard to their breeding habits, to mix amongst birds, many of whom are closely allied to, if not congeneric with, themselves. The cause of migration is want of *food*, not want of *warmth*. The feathers of a Siberian jay or a Lapp tit are proof against any cold.

Admitting that the various species of birds that breed in countless thousands in the Arctic regions were once residents there in the days when the climate was much warmer than it is now, we still find some difficulties to explain. In the first place, the Mammoth age does not appear to have been so very much warmer than the present climate. It is said that the remains of the foliage of conifers, such as now exist in Siberia, have been found in the stomachs of frozen mammoths. In the second place, the question may be fairly asked: How about the three months' night? Would that be no bar to the wintering of so many birds in the Arctic regions? But are we sure that there was three months' night? May it not be possible that the obliquity of the earth's axis to its orbit was much less in those ages, and that this was one cause of the comparative mildness of the winters, whilst the summers were for the same reason cool enough for the growth of conifers? An increase in the obliquity of the earth's axis would possibly account for the glacial period which destroyed the mammoths and compelled the birds to migrate.

It is alleged that many birds leave their winter quarters because in southern climates the heat dries up everything, and lessens the production of insect-life. Many of our European birds winter on both shores of the Mediterranean. In wandering through the valleys of Asia Minor, or the mountain-gorges of the Parnassus, or on the islands in the lagoon of Missolonghi, in May and June, I noticed no absence of insect-life. On the contrary, insect-life appeared to be superabundant. Vegetable-life appeared to be threatened by innumerable grasshoppers. One of the prominent features of the district was the countless thousands of beetles which swarmed on every plant, and, if we may judge from the number and size of their webs, the countries I have named must be a perfect paradise for spiders. That these districts are suitable for the maintenance of insectivorous birds during summer is proved by the fact that, soon after the *Phylloscopi*, which have wintered there, have left, their place is filled with birds belonging to the allied genus *Hypolais*, so that the olive-trees are well supplied with insect-eating birds both winter and summer. One species of swallow winters in Greece, one is found there all the year round, and three other species are summer migrants to that country. In some cases no doubt the weaker birds are turned out by the stronger. Swallows arrive in Düsseldorf early in April. For some weeks they circle over the town, like a swarm of bees. Early in May the swifts arrive, and soon become as abundant as the swallows were, whilst the latter birds are rarely seen during the summer.

Too much has probably been made of the great lines of migration, the highways which lead from the summer to the winter quarters. It has been asserted that there is a connection between these routes and the position of submerged continents across which the birds migrated in past ages. Probably there is some such connection, but in all probability an accidental one. To prove the case it would be necessary to show that migratory birds chose a longer route across a shallow sea in preference to a shorter route across a deep sea. It would be necessary also to prove that the habit of migration is older than the subsidence of the submerged land.

I venture to think that the *modus operandi* of migration has been to a large extent misunderstood. Few birds migrate by day. By far the greater number of species migrate by night. The number of places where nocturnal migrations can be systematically observed is very small. Two circumstances are requisite to make such observations successful. First, a sufficiently large population sufficiently interested in the event to permit no nocturnal migration to pass undiscovered. Second, a sufficiently intelligent naturalist to record the sum of many years' observation. Probably in no place in the world are these desiderata so exactly fulfilled as upon the island of Heligoland. Soon after my return from the valley of the Petchora, Mr. Gätke, the celebrated ornithologist and artist, who has resided for so many years on Heligoland, invited me to visit the island, to renew the acquaintance of the grey plover, the little stint, the blue-throat, the shore-lark, the little bunting, and others of my Petchora friends, and to see something of the wonderful stream of migration which sets in every autumn from the Arctic regions to the sunny South, and flows abundantly past the island. Heligoland is a very small place, probably not much more than a hundred acres in extent. It is an isolated triangular rock of red sandstone, with perpendicular cliffs two or three hundred feet in height, dropping into a sea so shallow, that at low water you can scramble round the island at the foot of the cliffs. Most of the surface of this rock is covered with rich soil and grass. About a mile from the island is a sandbank, the highest portion covered over with esparto grass, and the lower portions covered by the sea at high tide, reducing the island from perhaps fifty acres to twenty-five. The resident birds on Heligoland and Sandy Island probably do not exceed a dozen species; but in spring and autumn the number of birds that use these islands as a resting-place during migration is so large, that as many as 15,000 larks have been known to have been caught there in one night, and the number of species of birds obtained on these two small plots of land equals, if it does not exceed, that of any country of Europe. There are several species of Siberian and American birds which have never been obtained in any part of Europe except upon the island of Heligoland. The list of Heligoland birds is so varied, that many ornithologists have doubted its accuracy. No one can visit the island, however, without being convinced of the *bona fides* of all concerned. The authenticity of the Heligoland skins is beyond all possible question. During the time I spent on the island, from the 23rd of September to the 18th of October, I either shot or saw in the flesh such a variety of birds that I could almost agree with my friend Mr. Gätke when he stated that he would willingly exchange his collection of rare birds shot in Heligoland for those which had passed over the island without being obtained. It is probable, however, that the latter bear a much smaller proportion to the former in Heligoland than in any other place. The fact is that this little island is the only part of the world of which the ornithology has been properly worked. Every little boy on the island is a born and bred ornithologist. Every unfortunate bird which visits the island has to run the gauntlet of about forty guns, to say nothing of scores of blowpipes and catapults. The flight and note of every bird is familiar to every islander. Each bird has its own local name in the Heligoland language. A new bird is instantly detected. The fisherman steers with a gun by his side; the peasant digs his potatoes with a gun on the turf, and a heap of birds on his coat. On an island where there are no cows, and sheep are kept for their milk only, meat is of course very dear, especially as it has to be brought by steamer from Hamburg, one of the dearest cattle-markets on the continent of Europe. Birds therefore naturally form an important article of diet to the Heligolanders. Every bird which appears is whistled within range with marvellous skill. The common birds are eaten, the rare ones sold to the bird-stuffer, and the new ones taken to Gätke. Many of the Heligolanders are clever shots. Long before sunrise the island is bristling with guns; and after dark the netters are busy at their throstle-bushes; whilst at midnight the birds commit suicide against the lighthouse. When we consider that this has been going on for a quarter of a century, and that the results have been carefully chronicled for that length of time, the wonder is not that so many species of birds have occurred on Heligoland, but that so many have hitherto escaped detection. This must be accounted for on the theory that, after all, the appearance of birds on Heligoland is only accidental. Comparatively little migration is observed by the casual visitor who frequents the Restaurant to enjoy the oysters and the lobsters, or rows across to Sandy Island to bathe on the shore, and take a constitutional on the "dunes." Now and then a flock of waders may be detected hurrying past; flocks of pipits occasionally land on the island, feed for an hour or two, and then pass on; and sometimes a scattered and straggling stream of hooded crows, of heavy and laborious flight, will continue all day long. But by far the most important migration will be found to have taken place "while men slept." Every flock which passes over probably drops a few tired or hungry birds, and a walk through the potato-fields in the morning after a migration night, sometimes turns up the most curious and interesting variety of species which have sought the only cover on the island to feed, or rest, or hide. Perhaps the first bird you flush is a skylark; the report of your gun starts a golden plover, or a jack snipe; then you observe some small birds skulking in the potatoes, and you presently secure a little bunting, an aquatic warbler, and a shore-lark. Your next shot may be a corncrake, followed by a ring ousel or a Richard's pipit. Every night, however, is not a migration night. Sometimes for a week together you may diligently tramp the potatoes without finding a bird. Migration is a question of wind and weather. Acuckens, the bird-stuffer on Heligoland, told me that birds migrate northeast in spring, and south-west in autumn. Gatke, on the other hand, maintains that the directions are due east and west. Both agree that birds dislike an absolutely favourable or absolutely contrary wind. The former ruffles their feathers and chills them; the latter, if too strong, impedes their progress. They prefer a side wind, and probably alter their course slightly to accommodate themselves to it. It is even said that they will sometimes tack. Weather is perhaps as important as wind. Under ordinary circumstances a bird does not require to rest on Heligoland, and the arrivals for the most part are said not to be from any point of the compass, but perpendicularly from the sky. The islanders describe with great gusto the sudden arrival of thrushes in this manner. There are scarcely any trees on the island, so the peasants make artificial bushes with a net on one side into which the poor thrushes are driven with sticks and lanterns as soon as they alight. Some hundreds are thus frequently caught in one night. By long experience the Heligolanders know when to expect an arrival of birds. Aeuckens related to me how they would watch on favourable nights by the throstle-bushes, when on a sudden, without a moment's warning, a rush and whirl of wings would be heard, and the throstle-bush would swarm with thrushes, not dropped, but apparently shot like an arrow from a bow, perpendicularly down from the invisible heights of mid air. It is supposed that migration takes place for the most part at a high elevation, beyond the range of our vision; that the birds migrate by sight, and not, as has been assumed, by blind instinct; that they are guided by prominent landmarks with which they have gradually become familiar; and that many birds which are not gregarious at any other time of the year become so during the periods of migration, in order to avail themselves of the experience of the veteran travellers of their own or of other species. The desire to migrate is a hereditary instinct originally formed and continually kept up by the necessity to do so in order to maintain a struggle for existence against the changes of temperature, but the direction in which to migrate must be learned afresh by each individual. The theory that migration ordinarily takes place at high elevations is supported by the fact that it is only in dark or cloudy weather that migration on a large scale is observed. It is supposed that the landmarks being obscured by clouds, the birds are obliged to descend to see their way, for it is observed that as soon as the clouds begin to break, the migration apparently comes to an end. On dark nights the stream of migration suddenly stops when the moon rises. Each bird has its time of migration. Weather has, apparently, nothing to do with this date. Good weather does not seem to hasten the birds to their breeding haunts, nor bad weather retard their starting. If the suitable conjunction of circumstances occur during the season of a certain bird's migration, that bird visits the island. If the season goes by without such conjunction, the bird does not visit the island. The period of its migration is over. The migration of this species has taken place at high altitudes, it may be, or by other routes; and it is in vain to look for it until the next season of migration comes round, when, given the necessary wind and weather, the appearance of the bird may confidently be expected.

The period of migration of each species lasts about a month. In spring, during the first week, the flocks consist principally of adult males; during the second week, they principally consist of adult females; in the third week, follow the birds of the year; whilst finally, during the last week, arrive the cripples—birds which have lost their toes, birds with half a tail, birds with one mandible abnormally long, or birds with some other defect. In autumn the order of migration is somewhat different. For weeks before the regular period of migration is due stragglers in various stages of plumage arrive, loaf about in a desultory manner for a few days, and then disappear. Some of these birds are in summer plumage, some of them in their winter dress, whilst others are in a transition stage, moulting as they migrate. These *avant-courriers* are supposed to consist of barren birds, odd birds who have been unable to find a mate, or birds whose nests have been destroyed too late in the season to allow of a second nest to be made. Having nothing else to do, the hereditary instinct to migrate not being checked by the parental instinct, they yield to its first impulses, and drift southwards before the general body of their species. When the period of migration sets in in earnest, astounding as the fact is, it is nevertheless true that the birds of the year are the first to migrate, birds which of course have never migrated before. This circumstance, which all the

Heligolanders with whom I conversed agreed in corroborating, may to a large extent account for the fact that the rare stragglers recorded as visiting Heligoland and other countries are for the most part birds of the year on their first autumn migration. It is not to be wondered at that on their first journey they should frequently stray from the direct course. Probably the mortality amongst birds of the year is very great, especially amongst those who take the wrong road on their first migration. The yellow-browed warbler (*Phylloscopus superciliosus*, Gmel.) breeds in immense numbers on the Arctic Circle in Siberia. The main line of migration of this as well as of several other species of birds breeding in the same district is eastwards, passing through North China and conducting them to South China, Burmah, and the eastern portion of India, where they winter in abundance. Several birds, some nearly allied, and one congeneric, migrate west instead of east from the same breeding-grounds, and with these a few yellow-browed warblers appear annually to mix and find their way to Europe, passing Heligoland in small numbers nearly every autumn. Probably most of these wanderers perish during the winter, as they have been observed in spring on Heligoland only once every few years. This charming little bird has once been recorded from the British Islands. I saw one or two during my short stay on Heligoland, and was fortunate enough to shoot one. For nearly a week, whilst I was visiting this interesting locality, the weather was unfavourable. There were scarcely half-a-dozen birds on the island. I used to take a constitutional with my gun

twice or thrice a day, spending most of the rest of the time
in Mr. Gätke's studio, chatting about his birds, visiting
regularly Aeuckens, the bird-stuffer, to inquire if anyone
else had had better luck. On the 11th of October I shot
three shore-larks. Aeuckens told me that the appearance of
this Arctic species was a very good sign, that he had often
noticed that a few birds always preceded the favourable weather,
and that we might soon expect a change and plenty of birds.
The next day the west winds which had prevailed for a week
slackened a little. In the afternoon it was a calm, with a rising
barometer; in the evening a breeze was already springing
up from the south-east. I called upon Gätke, who advised
me to go to bed, and be up before sunrise in the morning,
as in all probability I should find the island swarming with
birds. Accordingly I turned in soon after ten. At half-
past twelve I was awoke with the news that the migration
had already begun. Hastily dressing myself, I at once made
for the lighthouse. The night was almost pitch dark, but
the town was all astir. In every street men with large
lanterns and a sort of angler's landing-net were making for
the lighthouse. As I crossed the potato-fields birds were
continually getting up at my feet. Arrived at the lighthouse, an intensely interesting sight presented itself. The
whole of the zone of light within range of the mirrors
was alive with birds coming and going. Nothing else was
visible in the darkness of the night but the lantern of the
lighthouse vignetted in a drifting sea of birds. From the
darkness in the east, clouds of birds were continually emerg-
ing in an uninterrupted stream; a few swerved from their

course, fluttered for a moment as if dazzled by the light, and then gradually vanished with the rest in the western gloom. Occasionally a bird wheeled round the lighthouse and then passed on, and occasionally one fluttered against the glass like a moth against a lamp, tried to perch on the wire netting and was caught by the lighthouse man. I should be afraid to hazard a guess as to the hundreds of thousands that must have passed in a couple of hours; but the stray birds which the lighthouse man succeeded in securing amounted to nearly 300. The scene from the balcony of the lighthouse was equally interesting; in every direction birds were flying like a swarm of bees, and every few seconds one flew against the glass. All the birds seemed to be flying up wind, and it was only on the lee side of the light that any birds were caught. They were nearly all skylarks. In the heap captured was one redstart and one reed-bunting. The air was filled with the warbling cry of the larks; now and then a thrush was heard; and once a heron screamed as it passed by. The night was starless and the town was invisible; but the island looked like the outskirts of a gas-lighted city, being sprinkled over with brilliant lanterns. Many of the larks alighted on the ground to rest, and allowed the Heligolanders to pass their nets over them. About three o'clock A.M. a heavy thunderstorm came on, with deluges of rain; a few breaks in the clouds revealed the stars; and the migration came to an end or continued above the range of our vision.

The conclusion I came to after my Heligoland experience was that the desire to migrate was an hereditary impulse, to which the descendants of migratory birds were subject in spring and autumn, which has during the lapse of ages acquired a force almost, if not quite, as irresistible as the instinct to breed in spring. On the other hand, the direction in which to migrate appears to be absolutely unknown to the young birds in their first autumn,

VIEW OF HELIGOLAND.

and has to be learnt by experience. The idea that the knowledge of where to migrate is a mysterious gift of Nature, the miraculous quality of which is attempted to be concealed under the semi-scientific term of instinct, appears to be without any foundation in fact. It appears that each individual bird has to find out its proper winter quarters for itself, and learn the way thither as best it may. That birds have keen organs of sight is a fact well known to all who have watched them obtaining their food or eluding their enemies. That they must have wonderful memories for place is shown by the distance they roam from their nests, and the concealed spots in which they seem to have no difficulty in finding them again. Amongst true migratory birds, that is amongst birds which have a winter as well as a summer home, as distinguished from gipsy migrants who perpetually loaf about on the outskirts of the frost during winter, continually changing their latitude with the temperature, it appears to be a general rule that the farther north a species goes to breed the farther south it goes to winter. It is not known if this applies to individuals as well as to species. The various times of arrival of many species of birds in most latitudes of Europe are well known and carefully recorded, but of the dates of departure from the various latitudes of Africa where they winter we know little or nothing, otherwise this question might easily be settled. It is obviously much easier to record the date of arrival of a bird than of its departure. In the one case a single entry is sufficient; in the other, memoranda may have to be daily recorded for weeks. At Valkenswaad, in Holland, I noticed that the earliest migrants were those with the widest range. Birds whose breeding-range extended to or beyond Britain were the earliest to breed, whilst those whose eggs I was most anxious to obtain, those whose breeding-range did not extend to our islands, were very late in arriving. It seems to be a curious fact that, as a general rule, though subject, no doubt, to many exceptions, the birds who have come from the longest distance arrive the earliest. The facts of migration are, however, so many, and the theories which they suggest are so various, that we must bring this rambling, if not irrelevant, chapter to an end, and return to the narrative of our doings in the valley of the Petchora.

OLD RUSSIAN SILVER CROSS.

DOING ROBINSON CRUSOE AT DVOINIK.

CHAPTER XXI.

Trip to Kuya—The prahms—Travelling in a rosposki—The birds we saw—Arrival of the *Triad* at Alexievka—We win over the manager—The *Ino*—Doing Robinson Crusoe in a wrecked ship—Nest of the long-tailed duck—Our first little stint's nest—The tundra—Sunset and sunrise—Little stint's eggs—The tundra near Bolvanski Bucht—Phalaropes—Interior of the tundra—Change of plumage in phalaropes—An early morning start—Confusion of time—The snowy owl—Two more nests of little stint—A march of geese on the tundra—An old grave.

A DAY or two after our return from the Golievski islands, a chance suddenly turned up of making a trip up stream to Kuya. The rafts, which ought by this time to have reached Alexievka, had not arrived, and ill-natured rumours of their having run aground were brought down by some fishermen. The manager of the company had also run out of various *articles de luxe*, which his soul lusted after; so the steamer was ordered to Kuya, and we gladly accepted berths in her. On the way we met one of the rafts coming down from Kuya. We drove on to Mekitza to visit the prahms; queer-looking vessels, something like canal boats, carrying a gigantic mast in the centre, and an arched roof above. They come down every summer from Cherdin, near Perm. Each vessel is a shop, where miscellaneous merchandise is sold or bartered, and the owners are sometimes very wealthy men. The goods fetch high prices on board. We paid elevenpence for sugar per pound, and six shillings for tea. The merchant from whom we bought our provisions was reputed to be worth a million sterling. Nor was it extraordinary, considering the amount of traffic he managed to secure. He had come down to Mekitza with three prahms, had cleared the cargo of two, and sold the vessels; very few goods now remained in the one in which he intended to make his journey homeward. In the villages the prices were much lower than those asked on the prahms. Thus we paid only 1¾d. per lb. for excellent fresh beef.

At Kuya several timber-rafts passed us, proceeding to Alexievka; these we waylaid. They were carrying a batch of letters for us, up to June 7th. Having secured this welcome trophy, we set our faces towards our head-quarters

The five versts between Kuya to Mekitza and back we travelled in a "rosposki," a machine composed of four wheels, about two feet in diameter, the axle-trees of which are connected by three parallel poles, upon which we sat. This vehicle is, without exception, the most uncomfortable carriage it has ever been my ill-luck to travel in. There is no support for the back, nothing to hold on by the sides; only three bare poles to sit on, and not height enough from the ground to swing one's legs about in peace. On the way we saw sand-martins, hooded crows, arctic terns, common gulls, ringed plover, and Temminck's stints. We got young in down of the ringed plover and arctic tern, and shot a long-tailed duck with her brood of ducklings. At Kuya we saw both the common and the tree sparrow.

The morning had been intensely hot; in the afternoon the wind rose, veered round to the north, and the night was stormy and cold. The next day the chill continued, and for the time being the plague of mosquitoes was stayed. It was a pleasant surprise, on reaching Alexievka, to find anchored in the river an English schooner, the *Triad*, Captain Taylor. She had come over from Iceland, where she had carried coal, and was now chartered for larch to Cronstadt. We at once planned to secure berths in her to carry us to Copenhagen, which she intended sailing for in ten days. She was likely to make Elsinore in a month.

The cold weather continued the next day. We spent two hours at Wassilkova, but saw little of interest. The red-throated pipits were in the moult, and not worth shooting. We brought home some of their young, also those of the yellow-headed wagtail and dunlins, and a pintail duck and its half-grown ducklings. The next day my companion secured another specimen of our new pipit, which we had been looking for in the neighbourhood. The day was memorable for having brought successfully to a conclusion our negotiations with Captain Arendt, the manager of the Company. A watch, a revolver, a musical box, and a ten-pound note had brought him round, and on the morrow the steamer was to be placed at our disposal. We were in high spirits, shouting, "Hurrah! for Dvoinik and the Little Stint!" The next morning we were fairly off by ten A.M. It was cold and numbing, with a light breeze blowing from the north-west. As we neared the bar, we sighted a brig under full sail. We hoisted a *rendez-vous* flag, and went on board. Though flying Danish colours, we found she was an English vessel—the *Ino*, from Newhaven. The captain told us he had been some days trying to get into the Petchora, but he was unable to reach it by steering between islands Nos. 3 and 4, owing to the ice, and that he had come round the east passage between islands 7 and 8 and Varandai. This accounted for the extraordinarily cold weather we had been having since the previous Sunday.

About four we landed at Dvoinik, and took possession of a stranded vessel that was lying high and dry upon the beach. It was settled that the Company's steamer should call for us on the following Tuesday, Wednesday, or Thursday, according to the final arrangements for the starting of our schooner, the *Triad*, in which we were to make part of our homeward passage. Meanwhile we were to live at Dvoinik, in regular Robinson Crusoe fashion. The deserted vessel looked very comfortable, and we anticipated a jolly time.

Leaving the men to sweep up the hold, we started off in high glee for a raid upon the little stints. We hastened over the tundra, making for the marshy ground upon which I had seen the dunlins, but not one was there. Doubtless the young could fly by this time, and had joined their parents on their favourite feeding ground. On the brackish lake close by we shot a brood of long-tailed ducks, and afterwards found an empty nest in the short, coarse grass, placed exactly at high-tide water-mark. It contained down enough to identify the species. There was no cover to the nest, except a margin of thin turf, that looked as if it had been turned up by a spade. Possibly it had been pulled up thus by the bill of the bird. On the lake there were, as before, a couple of black-throated divers. I waited for a short while, hiding in the cleft of the bank, as I had done on the previous occasion, when I had shot the little stints, but none were to be seen. I then skirted the margin of the bay to its narrow entrance, having spied a grey plover or two, a pair of Arctic terns, and a few herring-gulls. When there, a small number of dunlins passed rapidly overhead, and I repeatedly saw flocks of little stints. However, these might have been the same flock passing and repassing. They were very wild, and I could not get a shot. Some time before, my companion and I had parted company. We now met at one of the capes at the southern extremity of the high promontory. Cocksure was with him. On comparing notes I found their experience had been much the same as mine, only Cocksure had shot a Temminck's stint, near the sandhills. In returning we separated again to cover more ground; and again when we met, and compared notes, we found that to each the sandhills, the lakes, and the shores had proved a blank, destitute of bird-life.

We then separated for a stroll on the tundra. I had not gone far before I heard our interpreter Piottuch shouting in a state of great excitement. Harvie-Brown was the first to come up; and I joined them shortly afterwards. I found them sitting on the ground, with a couple of little stints in down. I sat down beside them, and we watched the parent bird as she was fluttering and flying and running all round us, sometimes coming within a foot of one of us. After securing the old bird we went on a short distance, and Piottuch again made loud demonstrations of delight. This time it was nest and eggs. The nest was like that of most sandpipers, a mere depression in the ground, with such dead *maroshka* (cloudberry) leaves and other dry material as was within easy reach, scraped together to serve as lining. The position was on a comparatively dry extent of tundra, sloping from the top of the little turf cliffs that rise from the lagoon down to the sandhills at the twin capes, between which the tide runs in and out of a little inland sea. These sandhills are flanked on the side next the sea with piles of drift-wood of all sizes and shapes—lofty trees which have been mown down by the ice when the great river broke up and in many places overflowed its banks, squared balks of timber washed away by the floods from the stores of the Petchora Timber-trading Company, and spars of luckless ships that have been wrecked on these inhospitable shores. They are sparingly sprinkled over with esparto grass, and soon run into an irregular strip of sand and gravel. This part of the coast, however, does not seem to have any attraction for the little stints. There were plenty of ringed plover upon it, and a few Temminck's stints; and we saw a pair of snow-buntings with five young, which had probably been bred amongst the drift-wood. At Dvoinik, however, for perhaps a verst from each twin cape, between the sand and the mouth of the little inland sea, is an extent of dead flat land, covered over with thick short grass, and full of little lakes, mostly very shallow and filled with black or coffee-coloured mud with an inch or two of brackish water upon it. Some of these pools are covered with aquatic plants; and others are open water. These lakes and pools seem to be the real point of attraction; and on their edges the little stints feed, in small flocks of from half-a-dozen birds to a score, as they happen to meet from the tundra. The large flock of perhaps a hundred or more birds, which was occasionally seen, might possibly have been last year's birds and not breeding; but more probably it consisted entirely of males, which, so far as we had an opportunity of observing, do not take any part in incubation. The ground where the nests were placed was full of tussocks or hummocks, close together, the swampy ground between being almost hidden, or traceable only by rows of cotton-grass. The tussocks are covered with green moss, with now and then a little reindeer-moss; but this undergrowth is almost hidden with cloudberry, a few species of *juncus*, and sundry *carices*, with occasionally a few dwarf shrubs and flowers of the tundra. The nests were within a hundred yards of the place where I shot the five little stints on the 14th of July, on a comparatively dry extent of tundra gently sloping towards the north-east, lying between the lagoon and the inland sea—exactly the place that one would expect them to breed in, not too swampy, but probably the coolest place the birds could have chosen. The Pytkoff Mountains, though at a considerably greater elevation (513 feet above the level of the sea), are no doubt warmer, because more inland. The sandy shore, having little or no cover, would also be hotter from the sun. Facing the north-east, this part of the tundra catches the most of the prevailing winds at this season of the year, and the least sun; and no doubt the large bay or inland sea on one side, and the open water on the other, help to cool the air. The choice of a breeding-place bears only a secondary relation to latitude, longitude, or elevation. It is inaccurate to state that at the westerly or southerly limit of their distribution birds breed at the greatest elevation. This may or may not be the case, according to circumstances. The whole question is doubtless one of temperature; and the true statement of the case must be, that at the *warmest* limit of their distribution birds choose the *coolest* locality in which to breed— a statement which almost amounts to a platitude, but one, nevertheless, that cannot be too constantly remembered by field-naturalists in search of undiscovered breeding-grounds.

We had already given names to the different sorts of ground on the tundra. The dry, grassy hills were the shore-lark ground; the dead flat bog, intersected with tussocky ridges, was the grey plover ground; the swampy marsh, covered with long grass, was the reeve ground. Where the grass was shorter and more tangled and knotted it became dunlin ground; and where this short grassy swamp was sprinkled over with tussocks of dryer earth, covered over with moss and flowers, then it was the Lapland bunting or red-throated pipit ground. Where the tussocks lay so close together that they reminded one of the hundred vaults or rather domes of the Stamboul bazaar seen from the minaret of Santa Sophia, and the swampy ground was almost hidden, or traceable only by rows of cotton-grass, we agreed to call for the future "little stint" ground. The hummocks were covered with green moss, mingled here and there with a little hoary reindeer moss. This undergrowth was concealed by the *maroshka* (the cloudberry), a species of *juncus*, *carices*, the dwarf sweet-smelling rhododendron, and other shrubs and flowers of the tundra.

The following day the wintry chill of the last few days had disappeared, and it was summer-time abroad. The wind had dropped, the clouds had gone from the sky: this was the bright side of the change; the reverse was the clouds of mosquitoes that hung over the tundra. Brown and I visited the little stint ground, on the principle of "stick to your covey;" but not a bird or a nest could we see upon it. We shot a wheatear on the shore, saw a pair of sanderlings, dropped a fine glaucous gull, a reeve, and some other birds, then returned to our quarters. Our Samoyede brought us a couple of nests of long-tailed ducks, one containing three eggs, the other five. We were tired out, so having cooked a duck for dinner, we went to bed at 4 A.M., to rise at 11 A.M. We began our day (let the reader forgive the Irishism, it is only a Petchorski bull), by watching the sun set and rise again in the space of an hour or so; then we set off, hoping to get the start of the mosquitoes. It was a dead calm, and taking the boat, we crossed over to the north twin cape. We found the sand barren of special interest, as it had been on the other side, only the intrusive ringed plover made as much hubbub as a hundred little stints or grey plovers would have done, evidently considering its eggs were the only ones we could possibly be in search of. The lakes and pools were very similar in shape and appearance to those on the south cape. Temminck's stint were somewhat more abundant, and we fell in with one small party of little stints. Before leaving this ground we devoted an hour to duck-shooting for the pot, and bagged three longtailed ducks, and one pintail duck with two young in down. We then turned our attention to the tundra, which rapidly rose some forty feet or so, afterwards sloping gradually down apparently to the Pytkoff hills, distant some fifteen miles. In many places a white mist lay over the landscape, resembling far away lakes. There were abundance of small pools of water, but we could not distinguish them until within a short distance. In suitable ground the grey plover abounded, and we shot young Lapland buntings; yet on the whole the tundra did not look inviting—grey plovers and their eggs were not sufficient attraction to lure us to face the mosquitoes; so turning away from it we began to explore the shores of a river winding inland. On its high steep grassy banks we found shore-larks, old and young, and what was even more to the purpose and acceptable in our present Robinson Crusoe situation, was an abundance of leeks or eschalots, of which we laid in a plentiful supply. We recognised soaring overhead an eagle, we saw some skuas, ringed plovers, Temminck's stints, redpoles, but nothing of special interest. It was now about 8 o'clock, so we rowed back to the entrance of the inland sea, intending to cross over to our quarters on the south cape, when suddenly a dense white mist, coming from the Arctic ice, fell upon us. We hastened to run our boat ashore, stopping to shoot a sanderling on a sandbank, and soon after an arctic tern.

Our next nest of the little stint was taken on the 24th of July. Harvie-Brown and I had been up all night, shooting by the light of the midnight sun, hoping to avoid the mosquitoes, and were returning home to our wrecked ship in a thick white morning mist. I stopped behind to refresh myself with a bath, and afterwards turned towards the little stint ground. Just as I reached it I was glad to see Piottuch emerge from the white mist, with the intelligence that he had found another nest of the little stint, containing four eggs, about three versts off, and had shot the bird, leaving the nest and eggs for us to take. We walked on together a short distance, when I heard the now familiar cry of a little stint behind me, a sharp *wick*, almost exactly the same as the cry of the red-necked phalarope, or that of the sanderling. Turning quickly round, I saw the bird flying past as if coming up from its feeding-grounds. It wheeled round us at some distance and alighted on the ground about eighty yards ahead. We walked slowly up towards it, and stood for some time watching it busily employed in preening its feathers. By-and-by we sat down. It presently began to run towards

us, stopping now and then to preen a feather or two; then
it turned back a few paces, and lifting its wings settled
down, evidently on its nest. We gave it three minutes'
grace, to be quite sure, and then quietly walked up to the
place, and sat down, one on each side of the eggs. The bird
as quietly slipped off the nest, and began to walk about all
round us, now and then pecking on the ground as if feeding,
seldom going more than six feet from us, and often approaching within eighteen inches. It was a most interesting
and beautiful sight. The tameness of the bird was almost
ludicrous. We chatted and talked; but the bird remained
perfectly silent, and did not betray the slightest symptom
of fear or concern, *until I touched the eggs*. She then gave
a flutter towards me, apparently to attract my attention. I
turned towards her, and she resumed her former unconcern.
I stretched my hand towards her. She quietly retreated,
keeping about two feet from my hand. She seemed so
extremely tame that I almost thought for the moment that
I could catch her, and getting on to all fours I crept quietly
towards her. As soon as I began to move from the nest, her
manner entirely changed. She kept about the same distance ahead of me; but instead of retreating, with the utmost
apparent nonchalance, she did everything in her power to
attract me still farther. She shuffled along the ground as
if lame. She dropped her wings as if unable to fly, and
occasionally rested on her breast, quivering her drooping
wings and spread tail, as if dying. I threw one of my
gauntlets at her, thinking to secure her without damage,
but she was too quick for me. Piottuch then fired at her,

T

and missed. He followed her for some distance; but she kept just out of range, and finally flew away. We waited about a quarter of an hour at the nest, talking and making no effort to conceal ourselves, when she flew straight up and alighted within easy shot, and I secured her. The little stint seems to be a very quiet bird at the nest, quite different from Temminck's stint. When you invade a colony of the latter birds, especially if they have young, the parents almost chase you from the spot—flying wildly round and round, and crying vociferously, often perching upon a stake or a tree, or hovering in the air and trilling. We observed none of these habits in the little stint. So far as we saw, only the female takes part in incubation, and only the female is seen near the nest. On our way back to the wreck we met with a party of sanderlings on the shore, and shot two of them. No doubt these birds were breeding somewhere in the district. After a good dinner of willow-grouse and a siesta of three hours, we started to take the nest that Piottuch had marked. Whilst we had slept the weather had changed. The mosquitoes had all gone. A smart gale was blowing from the north, and a heavy sea was breaking on the shore. It was cloudy, and dark, and cold, with an attempt now and then at rain. The nest was a couple of miles off, very near the shore of the inland sea, but on somewhat similar ground—moss, cloudberry, grass, &c. The eggs were intermediate in colour between those of the other two nests. On our return to our quarters we found that our Samoyede servant had caught a young little stint, half-grown, a very interesting bird. Like the young of the dunlin, the first feathers are those of summer plumage. On comparing the young in down and half-grown birds of the dunlin with those of the little stint, we noted that the legs of young dunlin in down were pale brown, whilst those of the half-grown and mature birds were nearly black; the little stint, on the other hand, seems to have nearly black legs and feet at all ages.

The little stint is evidently much more nearly allied to the dunlin than to Temminck's stint, and ought to be called the little dunlin. The birds are very similar in colour. The eggs of the little stint can hardly be mistaken for those of Temminck's stint, but are in every respect miniature dunlins' eggs. The young in down of Temminck's stint are quite grey compared with the reddish-brown of the young of the dunlin. The young in down of the little stint are still redder, especially on the sides and the back of the neck.

The average size of the twenty eggs we obtained of the little stint is about $1\frac{1}{10} \times \frac{3}{4}$ inch, a trifle smaller than the eggs of Temminck's stint usually are. The ground-colour varies from pale greenish-grey to pale brown. The spots and blotches are rich brown, generally large, and sometimes confluent at the large end. They probably go through every variety to which dunlins' eggs are subject. All the little stints' eggs which we found, with one exception, which would probably be a barren one, were very much incubated.

The following morning the gale from the north continued. It was a mosquitoless day, but very cold; a heavy sea still broke against the shore; ever and anon the sun shone, but masses of cloud kept drifting over the sky. We spent the day in exploring the tundra in the direction of the Bolvanski Bucht. Far as the eye could reach, the country stretched before us, a gently undulating moor, an Arctic prairie, a Siberian tundra; no hills were on the horizon, save the short range of the Pytkoff Kamin. Plenty of lakes, large and small, gleamed upon the expanse, the banks of most of which were steep and of peat; others were flat, and covered with rushy grass; rarely were they sandy. Here and there the pools were almost dried up; some were so choked up by coarse grasses, rushes, and *carices*, as to become swamps, holding a little space of open water in the centre. These morasses were quite accessible, however, for our waterproof boots; we would sink some twelve to eighteen inches through water and mud, and reach a safe bottom, hard and level as a stone floor, a solid pavement of ice. We spent an hour or two wading round one of these open spaces of water, forming the centre of a choked-up lakelet. Upon a little island of firm ground, that raised its summit above the reeds, was the empty nest of some bird, probably a gull, and close to the open water was the nest of a black-throated diver, with one egg. The latter was placed upon a foundation of roots and dead grass, half turned to peat, raked up from the bottom of the swamp, and upon this was laid a lining of fresh green flaggy grass. The egg was very small; but both parent birds were flying overhead, often coming near enough for their species to be identified. On the open water phalaropes were swimming, and we frequently rose them from the grasses at our feet. Their behaviour plainly showed that they were breeding; they circled round us wildly, uttering their usual cry. We secured three young in down, only recently hatched.

We spent another hour on the banks of a large lake, upon which swam two pairs of long-tailed ducks, each with its brood. After waiting and watching and stalking, we got hold of two old birds, two of the young in down of one brood, and six more grown-up young of the other. On the sandy margin of another lake, white with the seeds of the cotton-grass, we saw several ringed plover, and shot one little stint. We came upon a few Buffon's skuas, and on their ground we found the grey plover abundant as usual. Returning home, I chose the lee shore for my route, and watched as I came along several glaucous and herring gulls, saw a pair of wheatears, and shot a shore-lark.

Meanwhile our Samoyede and our half-bred had made a long excursion into the tundra by the banks of the rivers Erisvanka and Eevka. They described the country as exactly the same as that which we already knew—moor, swamp, and bog, with plenty of lakes, large and small. They had met nothing of interest, except ducks, geese, and swans. These birds were now evidently leaving their breeding haunts and retiring into the tundra to moult. During that period of comparative helplessness and inability to fly, they are attacked by the Samoyedes on their way back from Varandai and the Bolshai Tundra. These Samoyedes will have grand battues amongst the geese, and will return to the Petchora laden with feathers and down, which they will sell at the

Pinega fair. Our men brought back with them but one bird. This was perhaps the most interesting of all to us; shot on the banks of a great lake in company with four others—a Bewick's swan.

On the morrow the storm of the preceding day continued, and rain fell during the morning; so we spent the hours inside our wreck, writing up our journals and examining the phalaropes. We found that the bill of some of them, though apparently not more slender, is much more flexible than that of the birds we had hitherto obtained. The rust-red on the neck of the latter is found on the crown of the head of the former; it is also present on the tail; it is more conspicuous on the back, and forms a broad edging to the longer feathers of the bastard wing. The wings are of a neutral tint, a soft bluish-grey, while those of our former birds are distinctly brown. The legs and feet differ also in colour. Those of the first-obtained birds are of a uniform dark lead colour, faintly tinged with yellow on the margin of the webs. In the birds last shot, the back of the legs and the under surface of the feet are pale yellow; the front of the legs and the upper surface of the feet are a grey flesh hue. The colour of the sides of the head and of the breast is notably darker in the former than it is in the latter.

The idle morning seemed a long one. After dinner we smoked a pipe, whiled away the time in chatting, and then retired, as I thought, very early to bed. I woke after some hours and got up, for I had had sleep enough, shouldered my gun, and went out, leaving all the others still deep in their slumbers. It was very windy, and ever and anon came gusts of rain, yet there were more birds than usual out feeding. "It's the early bird that catches the worm," I said to myself.

My first care was to seek out the little stint ground; I saw several birds upon it, but not the trace of a nest could I discover. Then I took a long stroll along the edge of the inland sea and by the banks of the river beyond; as I went along I constantly heard the clear, sharp, but not loud cry of the little stint and phalarope (*wick*), but I had not yet learned to distinguish the one from the other, nor could I then tell either from the cry of the sanderling. The spluttering note of the Temminck's stint is very distinct (*pt-r-r-r*); so is the dunlin's thick hoarse cry of *peezh*, or its grating call-note (*trr*), as well as the noisy *too-it* of the ringed plover.

I had been out some hours when I met my companion, and hailed him with "Good morning." He answered with "Good evening." We both agreed the hour was seven, but we differed as to its being A.M. or P.M. I was convinced it was the morning of the morrow, whereas Brown was persuaded it was yester-evening. A never-setting sun plays strange pranks with one's reckoning of time.

Harvie-Brown had worked the little stint ground, but had not seen a bird upon it. While with me, he shot a brace of grey plovers; then we parted, and I returned to the little stint feeding haunts. I secured a brace of them, a few dunlins, old and young, and a grey plover; also some young Temminck's stint half-way between feathers and down. As I was picking up the latter I discerned in the distance the form of a great white bird, which seemed to me to alight upon a distant lake. Taking it to be a Bewick's swan, I put a slug-cartridge into my gun and walked rapidly on in its direction. Before I got within shot of it the bird rose, and I saw a snowy owl drop behind the sandhills. I carefully stalked it, looked around, and after a time descried a white spot resting on the north twin cape, which, with the aid of my telescope, I discovered to be the owl. He, too, must have been watching me; perhaps he took my sealskin cap for some new species of lemming, for presently he rose and flew across the water directly towards me. By the time he had reached the other twin cape he evidently discovered his mistake, and alighted on the beach about sixty yards in front of me. I rose and walked towards him; he also rose, but before he had flown ten yards my shot reached him, broke one of his wings and dropped him into the sea. As he lay struggling in the water a score of glaucous and herring gulls came flying towards him, and sailed round and round him, making quite a small uproar with their cries. I was too anxious, however, to secure my first snowy owl to pay any heed to them, especially as my gun's extractor had got out of order; I therefore plunged into the water, and, as it was shallow, I soon landed my prize.

My gun's cartridge extractor was a complicated new-fangled patent invention, and already that day it had caused me to lose a pair of Buffon's skuas. I had shot a young dunlin, on the muddy margin of the inland sea, breaking with the same barrel the wing of an old dunlin; with the second barrel I had killed a little stint. The wounded bird lay a few yards off, when suddenly, down there flew upon it a couple of Buffon's skuas, who quarrelled over it, and carried it off before I could wade through the mud to the rescue.

After securing the owl, I carried my trophy home in triumph, overtaking my companion by the way. On reaching the wreck, we finally settled the question of evening or morning. We satisfactorily established that it was the former, so we dined and went to bed again.

The next day the gale continued, but there was some sunshine, and the cold kept the mosquitoes at bay. I spent my morning superintending the cooking of the swan our men had brought the preceding day. Meanwhile Harvie-Brown went out to the far end of the inland sea, and got a little distance from the spot where we had found the last nest of the little stint: he came upon two more. We had by this time twenty of these birds' eggs; all miniature dunlins' eggs, and like them, varying in colour. These two nests were not built on the tundra proper, but on the little stints' feeding-ground; a flat sandy strip of land on which grew short grass and bunches of a thick-leaved yellow flowering plant, sprinkled here and there with dried-up or drying pools, and upon which drift-wood lay scattered in all directions. The tundra stops at some 150 yards from the seashore, and this stretch of feeding-ground lies between it and the water's edge.

After lunching on the baked breast of the swan, I returned to the wreck, but by a different route to that which my companion had taken. I took the boat across to the north twin cape, and was an hour pulling half a verst against the heavy gale. I then skirted the margin of a long narrow inlet, exactly like the dried-up bed of a river, that runs some miles into the tundra, bending round almost behind the inland sea. I had not gone more than a mile when I heard the cackle of geese; a bend of the river's bed gave me an opportunity of stalking them, and when I came within sight I beheld an extraordinary and interesting scene. One hundred, at least, old geese, and quite as many young ones, perhaps even twice or thrice that number, were marching like a regiment of soldiers. The vanguard, consisting of old birds, was halfway across the stream; the rear, composed principally of goslings, was running down the steep bank towards the water's edge as fast as their young legs could carry them. Both banks of the river, where the geese had doubtless been feeding, were strewn with feathers, and in five minutes I picked up a handful of quills. The flock was evidently migrating to the interior of the tundra, moulting as it went along.

On the top of the high embankment, bordering the river, I came upon a wooden monument, about a foot in height and width, and from two to three feet in length. The wood was entirely rotten, and I easily broke or tore the lid that still covered it open. Inside I found bones like those of a dog, a broken vessel of glazed earthenware, the rusty remains of an iron vase, and an abundance of mould. Outside were fragments of bleached bone, like the remains of an infant's skull. This was doubtless a Samoyede's tomb; but we could not determine if it was that of an infant, whose remains had been buried in the box, or that of an adult interred below.

After loitering some time about this spot, I pushed on farther, crossing over a plateau of tundra, well covered in places with willows, some three feet high. Here I found willow-grouse, both old and young, well able to fly; many willow-warblers, a few redpoles, and one blue-throated warbler.

OLD RUSSIAN SILVER CROSS.

MIGRATION OF GEESE.

CHAPTER XXII.

On short commons—Bad weather—A foraging party—Russian superstitions—Return of the steamer—Beautiful flowers—Arrival at Alexievka—Departure for home—Thunder-storm—Water-spout—Sea-birds—Hard fare—Copenhagen—Summary of the trip.

MATTERS were beginning to look somewhat serious in our Robinson Crusoe encampment. The heavy gale continued to blow unabated, and it was very probable the steamer would not call for us until the sea grew quieter. Meanwhile our larder was nearly empty. We were reduced to half a loaf of bread, and to what birds we could secure. We breakfasted on a grey plover, a brace of dunlins, and three

duck's eggs, which, though somewhat incubated, yet made a
good omelette. There was nothing, however, for dinner; so
we all turned out to provide for the pot. Harvie-Brown
went south, and returned with only a few dunlins and a grey
plover; he had chased a bar-tailed godwit * for some distance
near the seashore, but had not got within shot. I had met
with no better luck, although I had brought down a dozen
dunlins and grey phalaropes as they fed on the margin of a
lake. I had been able, however, only to secure three. At
the first step I took in the direction of my prizes, I sank
lower than knee-deep into the black mud. My gun also
snapped at a willow-grouse within easy aim. We returned
to our quarters somewhat down-hearted; the gale was blowing
fiercer than ever, a thick mist covered the sea, gusts of
wind drove the rain into the wreck. We cooked ourselves
a supper of fried dunlins, allowed to each a weak basin of
Liebig's extract-of-meat soup, and half a slice of bread.
About midnight, as we smoked our pipes and listened to
the howling and spitting of the wind and rain outside, our
thoughts followed the forlorn-hope party we had sent out,
and we doubted whether it would meet with better luck than

---

* The bar-tailed godwit (*Limosa lapponica*, Linn.) is confined to the eastern hemisphere, ranging as far as Kamtchatka, the eastern form having been erroneously described as a new species under the names of *Limosa novæ-zelandiæ* (Gray) and *Limosa uropygialis* (Gould). In the British Islands it is only known as a spring and autumn migrant, being especially abundant in the latter season. But little is known of its breeding-grounds, the only authentic eggs having been obtained in Lapland near the Arctic circle. It winters on both shores of the Mediterranean, but has not been recorded from South Africa. Eastwards it winters in Scinde, Australia, New Zealand, the islands of the Malay Archipelago, China, and Japan. In the valley of the Petchora we only met with this single example, which we failed to secure.

we had. This party consisted of Cocksure, the Samoyede, and the half-bred. They had gone on what we firmly felt might be called, in a double sense, a wild-goose chase, in pursuit of the flock of geese I had seen the day before migrating across the water into the tundra. We went to bed hoping against hope, and were woke up towards four by the noisy arrival of our envoys, carrying back in triumph eleven old geese and five young ones. One of the party had taken the boat up the river upon which I had seen the flock. The other two followed, each keeping upon opposite banks. They came upon the geese a few versts higher up than the spot at which I had seen them, and falling upon them had made a grand haul of birds. The laying in of this stock of provisions lifted a burden off our minds. We now proceeded to administer, with better grace than we could have done before, a sound rating to our two lazy, good-for-nothing Russian servants. They were the only two who had grumbled during this time of perplexity; for ever muttering that if the storm did not abate, and the steamer come to our rescue, we should surely all be "*propal*" (lost). We had ordered one to join the forlorn-hope party, but he had soon returned, and all the night he had done little but kneel in a state of abject fear, trembling, crossing himself, and crying, "Hospodee, Hospodee, di kleb" (Lord, Lord, give us bread). These poor dupes of the miserable Greek Church have not learnt the wholesome doctrine Cromwell taught his soldiers, "To trust in the Lord and keep their powder dry." Like many other fanatics at home and abroad, they close their eyes to the truth that God *may* bless their work, but will *never* bless their idleness. As a just punishment for their sloth and cowardice, we condemned them to pluck the geese, on which we and the captors made a hearty meal; while we regaled ourselves they had to look on, and feast upon leeks.

The larger number of geese, being in full moult, had been unable to fly. Cocksure assured us that both old and young constantly hid themselves under the water, where some remained, just keeping their beaks above the surface, for ten minutes at a time. He added that he had often observed the same thing in Mezén during the moulting season.

The gale had exhausted its violence during the night, and gradually slackened and wore itself out during the day; when the following morning came, the weather was quite calm. With ten geese in our larder, we considered ourselves entitled to a lazy day; we wandered out in the tundra, making a small collection of the flowers that grow upon it, the bonnie bright Arctic blossoms that deck for a few weeks that region of ice. We shot an immature gull, and loafed about, feeling that we had exhausted the place, and hoping for the arrival of the steamer. A flock of what we took to be sandpipers, flying wildly overhead, uttering a note like that of the knot, roused our curiosity. When we at last succeeded in shooting one, the bird turned out to be a reeve. Another incident in this, our last day, was tracing the footprints of a swan in the mud, and identifying them as those of a Bewick's swan.

At two o'clock the following morning, I was on our wreck's deck, chatting with Cocksure, when on the horizon we caught sight of the steamer. All our companions were asleep, except

the half-bred; five minutes later, all were up and hard at
work packing. By five o'clock we were on board, steaming
over a sea smooth as glass towards Bolvanski Nos. At eight
we went on shore at Stanavialachta to visit the peregrine's
nest, where we expected to find a new lot of eggs. From a
distance we could see the male bird sitting on the spot. He
allowed us to approach to within ten or twelve yards, when
suddenly he took the alarm and rose. We fired and dropped
him on the beach below. There were no eggs in the nest.
Probably the female bird was sitting on the other eyrie; but
we were dead-beat with fatigue, and the hillsides swarmed
with mosquitoes, so we made our way back at once to the
steamer, shooting a willow-grouse as we went, a male in fine
summer plumage. The flowers on this part of the tundra
were very beautiful, vividly coloured, and abundant; especially lovely was a tall monkshood and a species of pink.
On board the steamer we stretched ourselves on the sofa in
the cabin, and fell asleep, only to awake when the steamer
stopped at Alexievka about noon.

The *Triad* was making ready to start on the morrow; her
cargo was to be about 8000 cubic feet of larch. Our stay
in these Arctic latitudes was now fast drawing to an end. I
spent the afternoon looking about the island, directing my
search especially for young of the yellow-headed wagtail.
Scarcely was a bird to be seen out of cover. Grass nearly
two feet high covered the ground, and the willows were in
full leaf. It was difficult enough to get a shot at a bird, and
almost impossible to find it when brought down. At last I
tried the coast, and found plenty of birds feeding amongst the

drift-wood and the prostrate willows that had fallen with the crumbling away of the banks. Yellow-headed wagtails, red-throated pipits, and reed buntings were here in abundance. I could not stay, however, for the sun was scorching hot, and the mosquitoes were swarming around.

I spent the night with Captain Taylor and Captain Arendt on board the *Triad*, giving a helping hand in superintending the loading of the schooner. The heat was so intense that I could scarcely bear the suffocation of my mosquito-veil, and seldom put it on. The consequence was I was more bitten in those few hours than I had been during the whole of my previous stay. I did not turn in till 6 A.M., and woke at 11, and spent my day making out our bills of lading for Captain Arendt. At 5 o'clock on Sunday, August 1st, we finally bade farewell to the tundra and to our wandering life, and began our journey towards Europe and civilisation. We left Alexievka in tow of the steamer, reaching the bar soon after midnight. The cutter signalled ten feet of water; as we were drawing so much, as was to be expected, we were soon aground. I sat up with the captain all night, as we tediously manœuvred through the shallow water. We had just lit the fire to cook some supper, when Engel suddenly heaving anchor, we got under weigh again. The captain took the helm, and I remained below cooking the steaks and making the coffee; but we were soon aground once more, and we ate our meal in the cabin. For some hours we went on, sometimes aground, sometimes scraping the bank, until at last we crossed the bar; then Engel towed us until we sighted the beacon at Dvoinik; all sails

U

were now set, and we steered N.E. by N. with a gentle breeze. All the following day and night we tacked from one bank of shoal water to another, with a head wind against us. The lead was kept constantly going, and as soon as the water under the keel was less than a foot, orders were immediately given to "'bout ship." By good luck or good management, we succeeded in getting out of the lagoon of the Petchora without running aground again, though Captain Taylor vowed that nothing should ever induce him a second time to risk a ship in such a dangerous and difficult river. We had scarcely cleared the banks more than half an hour before the wind dropped entirely; the sails flapped idly on the masts, and we sent the crew to bed. We were lounging on the after part of the ship, telling our adventures to the captain, when three curious clouds, like beehives, appeared to rise on the horizon. We were leaning over the bulwarks watching these unusual shapes in the sky, when our attention was caught by the sound of a distant rumbling. The sea was as smooth as glass, and we were debating whether the noise was not that of the Arctic ice, when the captain descried a distant ripple on the sea, and started up as if he had been shot. Hastily asking me to take the rudder, he ran to the hatchway and cried out, at the top of his voice, "All hands on deck!" Every possible exertion was made to haul down the canvas; but before this could be accomplished the gale came upon us, and the ship reeled as the squall struck her, first on the starboard and then on the port side. By the time the canvas had been taken in, the squall had become violent, the sea rose, peals of thunder followed each other rapidly, and rain came down in torrents. A still more extraordinary sight presented itself shortly afterwards—a waterspout. About half a mile from the ship the clouds came down in a funnel, and deluges of rain appeared to fall under it, the sea being lashed into foam as if ten thousand millstones had been suddenly hurled into it. It was some hours before the wind settled down again; but it proved to be a favourable one, and we made fair progress homewards through a Scotch mist from the Arctic ice.

For two days we had fog and fair wind, then came wind and sunshine. On the 3rd of August a few flocks of phalaropes passed overhead, and on the 4th a pair of snowy owls alighted on the ship. We saw also several kittiwake gulls and Pommerine skuas. Then from the 8th of August to the 29th came three dreary weeks, during which the ship wearily toiled on, against heavy gales and contrary winds; ever and anon would come a fair breeze, to prevent us despairing altogether of ever reaching Elsinore. It seemed hopeless often enough. Various were the tacks the captain tried on the way. One day we would lie-to with head to wind, and let the good ship drift back with the heavy gale towards Colguif; another we would tear along, blown forward by an equally fierce wind, which we welcomed, for it was bearing us homeward. Now we would lie motionless with sails idly flapping against the masts, and again we would be cutting the water with a favourable breeze impelling us on. As we approached the Cape the weather grew wilder, it seemed as if we could never round it; the bold promontory appeared to frighten away all fair winds. When we were within eighty miles of Cherie Isle, our search for it was vain; it lay shrouded in impenetrable fogs. At last we left the ill-starred land behind us. We passed the wild peaks of the Lofodens; we left the storm-tossed waves beating at their feet, and hailed the mountains behind Christiansand in genial weather. During those weeks we saw almost daily kittiwakes and Fulmar petrels; now and then there passed a skua or a puffin or two, but no bird on migration.

After another week of fair winds, head winds, calms, and gales, we reached Elsinore on the thirty-fifth day. All this time we had roughish fare on board. The *Triad* had no provision for passengers. The first week exhausted our stock of grog and fresh provisions, and the remainder of the journey we had to put up with hard captains' biscuits, Australian tinned meat, and coffee with no milk and short rations of sugar. When we landed at Elsinore, our first care was to order a good dinner, which we all agreed was the most superb entertainment we had ever sat down to. For the last fortnight we had dreamed of dining, but always woke before the happy moment arrived. Our dinner at Elsinore was enjoyed with an appetite which we never hope to experience again. Taking the night train to Copenhagen, we arrived there on the morning of Monday the 6th of September. We were disappointed in our efforts to find a steamer for England, so proceeded at once to Hamburg, where my companion found a boat for Leith; and I lost no time in putting myself and, not my "sieben Sachen," but my "siebzehn Sachen" on board a steamer for Hull.

I left Hamburg in the *Zebra* on Wednesday the 8th of September, and after a smooth passage landed in Hull on Saturday the 11th instant, having been away from home rather more than twenty-seven weeks. Of this time the journey out occupied about six weeks; another six weeks was spent in weary waiting for the arrival of spring; and the journey home took up a third period of six weeks, leaving only nine weeks in which the bulk of our ornithological work was done. Fortunately during this time we had twenty-four hours daylight, of which we frequently availed ourselves. By dint of hard work and long hours we succeeded in doing more in these nine weeks than we could possibly have expected. There can be no doubt that we were exceptionally fortunate in chancing upon the localities frequented by birds which appear to be extremely local during the breeding season.

OLD RUSSIAN SILVER CROSS.

FROM MEKITZA TO KUYA ON A BOSPOSKI.

CHAPTER XXIII.

Results of the trip—Summer in the Arctic regions—Circumpolar birds—Birds confined to the eastern hemisphere—Various ranges of birds—Migration of birds—Dates of arrival—Probable route—Conclusion.

THE results of our somewhat adventurous journey exceeded our most sanguine hopes.

Of the half-dozen British birds, the discovery of whose breeding-grounds had baffled the efforts of our ornithologists for so long, we succeeded in bringing home identified eggs of three—the grey plover, the little stint, and Bewick's swan. Of the remaining three, two, the sanderling and the knot, were found breeding by Captain Fielden, in lat. 82°, during the Nares Arctic expedition, but the breeding-grounds of

the curlew sandpiper still remain a mystery. We added
several birds to the European list, which had either never
been found in Europe before, or only doubtfully so; such as
the Siberian chiff-chaff, the Petchora pipit, the Siberian
herring-gull, the Arctic forms of the marsh-tit and the
lesser spotted woodpecker, the yellow-headed wagtail, and
the Asiatic stonechat. We brought home careful records
of the dates of arrival of the migratory birds which breed in
these northern latitudes, besides numerous observations on
the habits of little-known birds. Our list of skins brought
home exceeded a thousand, and of eggs rather more than six
hundred.

The number of species which we obtained was comparatively small, the whole of our collecting having been done
north of latitude 65°. The Arctic regions are frost-bound
for eight months out of the twelve, and buried under a
mantle of snow, varying in depth from three to six feet.
During this time they are practically barren of ornithological life; the small number of birds which remain within
the Arctic Circle forsake the tundras where they breed, to
find food in the pine forests at or near the limit of forest
growth, a few only remaining where the shelter of a deep
valley or watercourse gives cover to a few stunted willows,
birches, and hazel bushes. Practically it may be said that
there is no spring and autumn in the Arctic regions. Summer follows suddenly upon winter, and the forests and the
"tundra" as suddenly swarm with bird-life. Although the
number of species breeding within the Arctic Circle is comparatively small, the number of individuals is vast beyond

conception. Birds go to the Arctic regions to breed, not by thousands, but by millions. The cause of this migration is to be found in the lavish prodigality with which Nature has provided food. Seed- or fruit-eating birds find an immediate and abundant supply of cranberries, crowberries, and other ground fruit, which have remained frozen during the long winter, and are accessible the moment the snow has melted; whilst insect-eating birds have only to open their mouths to fill them with mosquitoes.

Of the 110 species which we obtained, the following are circumpolar birds breeding both in the eastern and western hemispheres, being nearly one-third of the total number:—

Osprey.	Dunlin.
Peregrine Falcon.	Sanderling.
Snowy Owl.	Shoveller Duck.
Short-eared Owl.	Pintail Duck.
Raven.	Scaup Duck.
Pine Grosbeak.	Golden-eyed Duck.
Mealy Redpole.	Long-tailed Duck.
Lapland Bunting.	Goosander.
Snow Bunting.	Red-breasted Merganser.
Shore-Lark.	Arctic Tern.
Bohemian Waxwing.	Great Black-backed Gull.
Sand Martin.	Glaucous Gull.
Willow-Grouse.	Richardson's Skua.
Grey Plover.	Buffon's Skua.
Red-necked Phalarope.	Red-throated Diver.
Curlew Sandpiper.	Black-throated Diver.

It will be observed that more than half of these species are water birds, showing that the communication between the Palæarctic and the Nearctic regions has been one of water rather than of land.

The following species are confined to the continents of

Europe and Asia, and range throughout the Arctic regions of the eastern hemisphere from the North Cape to Behring's Straits. A few of these are occasionally found in Greenland and in Alaska, but are not found in the intermediate or Nearctic regions, though many of them are there represented by very nearly allied species, showing that the communication across the Pole has been interrupted at a comparatively modern geological epoch :—

White-tailed Eagle.
Hobby.
Merlin.
Goshawk.
Sparrow-Hawk.
Hen-Harrier.
Eagle Owl.
Black Woodpecker.
Three-toed Woodpecker.
Cuckoo.
Magpie.
Siberian Jay.
Tree Sparrow.
Scarlet Bullfinch.
Brambling.
Reed-Bunting.
Ruff.
Temminck's Stint.
Common Snipe.
Great Snipe.
Whimbrel.
Common Crane.
Wild Swan.
Bean-Goose.

Skylark.
Red-throated Pipit.
Green Wagtail.
Blue-throated Warbler.
Wheatear.
Lapp Tit.
Common Swallow.
Black Grouse.
Hazel Grouse.
Little Ringed Plover.
Oystercatcher.
Greenshank.
Wood Sandpiper.
Spotted Redshank.
Common Sandpiper.
Bar-tailed Godwit.
Teal.
Widgeon.
Tufted Duck.
Velvet Scoter.
Black Scoter.
Smew.
Common Gull.

From the length of this list it might be reasonable to assume that ornithologists are right in separating the Nearctic region from the Palæarctic region, and that it would be an error, even as far as Arctic birds only are considered, to unite the two together into one circumpolar region. A more minute examination of the list may, however, lead us to a different conclusion. It is not correct to speak of a bird as an Arctic species, unless its breeding-grounds are principally within the Arctic Circle. We must, therefore, eliminate from our list those species whose breeding-grounds are principally south of the Arctic Circle, and only extend beyond it at the extreme northern limit of their range. This will dispose of thirty of the species we have enumerated, leaving only seventeen, of which at least two-thirds are represented in the Nearctic region by very closely allied species. Of the half-dozen species which may be said to belong especially to the eastern Polar region, every one is represented by a species in the western Polar region belonging to the same genus.

The following species range from Scandinavia eastwards as far as the watershed between the Yenesay and the Lena. The proportionate length of this list shows that this boundary is almost as important a one as Behring's Straits, especially when we consider that several of the species enumerated in the second list cross over into Alaska. On the other hand, we must not forget that our knowledge of the birds of the country east of the Yenesay and of China is very limited:—

Rough-legged Buzzard.	Redstart.
Hooded Crow.	Willow-Warbler.
Jackdaw.	Sedge-Warbler.
House Sparrow.	Capercailzie.
Northern Bullfinch.	Golden Plover.
Tree Pipit.	Dotterel.
White Wagtail.	Ringed Plover.
Fieldfare.	Little Stint.
Redwing.	

The dotterel and the little stint are the only species in this list of which it can be said that their principal breeding-grounds are north of the Arctic Circle. The nearest relations of the former species are undoubtedly to be found in the southern Palæarctic region, whilst the genus to which the latter belongs is well represented in the Polar regions of both continents.

Two species only appear to range from Scandinavia eastwards as far as the valley of the Obb, but do not cross the watershed into the valley of the Yenesay :—

> Rook.
> Yellowhammer.

The Ural Mountains, although they are the boundary between political Europe and Asia, are by no means so geographically or ornithologically. So far as we know, one species only of the Petchora birds recognises this chain as the eastern limit of its range, viz. :—

> Meadow Pipit.

Four species ranging westward from Kamtchatka throughout Arctic Siberia and across the Ural Mountains, do not appear to advance farther into Europe, during the breeding season, than the valley of the Petchora :—

| Siberian Pipit. | Siberian Stonechat. |
| Yellow-headed Wagtail. | Bewick's Swan. |

Six species, ranging westward from Kamtchatka throughout Arctic Siberia and across the Ural Mountains, appear to extend beyond the valley of the Petchora, as far as the White Sea, viz. :—

Siberian Lesser-spotted Woodpecker.
Little Bunting.
Arctic Willow-Warbler.

Marsh-Tit (eastern form).
Terek Sandpiper.
Siberian Herring-Gull.

One bird only appears to be so restricted in its geographical range as to be found only in the valleys of the Petchora, the Obb, and the Yenesay, viz. :—

Siberian Chiff-chaff.

Of the fourteen birds included in the last four lists, only four or five of them have their principal breeding-grounds within the Arctic Circle, and these all belong to genera which are represented in the Nearctic region, with the exception of the Arctic willow-warbler, which has been obtained in Alaska.

The final conclusion to which we must therefore arrive, from a study of the geographical distribution of the birds found in the valley of the Petchora, is that a circumpolar region ought to be recognised : that so far as the Polar regions are concerned the division into Nearctic and Palæarctic is a purely arbitrary one.

The migration of birds is a subject which interests all naturalists, and is a very attractive one to a great number of persons who do not pretend to any scientific knowledge of ornithology. The dates and order of arrival of migratory birds present so many points of interest that, for the sake of comparison, the following list has been made of all those birds which we had reason to believe to be migratory in the

Ust-Zylma district, leaving out those to which, from their rarity or localness, considerable doubt attaches as to their date of arrival:—

April	1.	Snow-Bunting.	May	18. Lapland Bunting.
,,	1.	Mealy Redpole.	,,	18. Whimbrel.
May	4.	Hen-Harrier.	,,	18. Teal.
,,	5.	Merlin.	,,	20. Willow-Warbler.
,,	10.	Bean-Goose.	,,	20. Wheatear.
,,	10.	Shore-Lark.	,,	21. Crane.
,,	10.	Snowy Owl.	,,	22. Siberian Chiff-chaff.
,,	11.	Wild Swan.	,,	22. Siberian Stonechat.
,,	11.	Bewick's Swan.	,,	23. Short-eared Owl.
,,	11.	Siberian Herring-Gull.	,,	23. Blue-throated Warbler.
,,	12.	White Wagtail.	,,	24. Brambling.
,,	12.	Redstart.	,,	24. Pine-Grosbeak.
,,	12.	Meadow-Pipit.	,,	26. Oyster-catcher.
,,	13.	Pintail and other Ducks.	,,	26. Ringed Plover.
,,	13.	Peregrine Falcon.	,,	26. Wood-Sandpiper.
,,	14.	Reed-Bunting.	,,	26. Temminck's Stint.
,,	15.	Common Gull.	,,	26. Common Swallow.
,,	17.	Golden Plover.	,,	31. Little Bunting.
,,	17.	Fieldfare.	June	3. Cuckoo.
,,	17.	Redwing.	,,	3. Double Snipe.
,,	17.	Red-throated Pipit.	,,	3. Terek Sandpiper.
,,	17.	Green Wagtail.	,,	3. Black-throated Diver.

This list is necessarily very imperfect. In addition to the difficulty of ascertaining the date of arrival of rare or local birds, we had a still greater difficulty to contend with. There can be no doubt that Ust-Zylma lies somewhat out of the line of migration, which is probably determined largely by the direction of the great valleys. Birds from the Mediterranean might fairly be supposed to reach the Volga *viâ* the Bosphorus, the Black Sea, the Sea of Azov, and the river Don to Sarepta. The natural course of birds from India and Persia would be to the Volga by way of the Caspian Sea. The line of migration would probably follow the Volga to Kasan, and thence along the Kama to Perm and Cherdin, close to the source of the Petchora. The course would then continue down the Petchora as far as its junction with the Ussa. It would then be reasonable to conclude that the hardy species, which migrate early, would have plenty of time to go round by Ust-Zylma; whilst the later arrivals would leave the Petchora at Ust-Ussa, and cross direct to the tundra. For example, the snow-bunting, hen-harrier, merlin, bean-goose, shore-lark, snowy owl, wild swan, Bewick's swan, and herring-gull are probably amongst the earliest breeders on the tundra, and pass through Ust-Zylma, whilst the later breeders on the tundra are not there at all. The following birds are all summer migrants to the tundra, but were not seen passing through Ust-Zylma during migration :—

Yellow-headed Wagtail.
Arctic Tern.
Siberian Pipit.
Red-necked Phalarope.
Long-tailed Duck.
Buffon's Skua.
Grey Plover.

Dunlin.
Richardson's Skua.
Dotterel.
Sanderling.
Curlew Sandpiper.
Little Stint.

Most of these are very late-breeding birds, but why they should breed late, or for what cause they seem to choose a different line of migration, seems at present inexplicable. Before a conclusion can be arrived at, many more facts must be collected. The field of ornithological research is one in which any amount of work may be advantageously done, and possibly the perusal of the present short narrative may help to arouse the enthusiasm of other adventurous ornithologists, and induce them to take up the running where we have left it off.

OUR HEADQUARTERS AT UST-ZYLMA.

INDEX.

A.

Age, the mammoth, 248.
Alexievka, arrival at, 173, 264.
——, description of, 174.
——, island of, 175.
——, arrival of *Triad* at, 264.
Angliski Russ, 11.
Archangel, arrival at, 14.
——, city of, 15.
——, prices at, 16.
——, weather at, 21.
——, birds at, 21.
Arctic willow-warbler, 159.
—— circle, 164.
—— tern, 163.
Arrival of mosquitoes, 134.

B.

Bad roads, 25, 58.
Bath, Russian, 216.
Bear, tracks of, 89.
——, saddle of, 89.
Bewick's swan, 2, 195, 214.
Bird, mocking-, the Swedish, 127.
Birds, 53, 58, 61, 67, 89, 90, 100, 115, 126, 138, 151, 155, 157, 168, 192, 264, 266, 271.
—— *en route*, 13.
——' eggs, 154, 156.
——, hybernation of, 242.
——, migration of, 243.
Birds, new, 117, 138.
—— resting on migration, 129.
——, Samoyede names for, 19.
——, scarcity of, 41, 49.
——, sea-, 292.
—— seen on the tundra, 180, 183.
Bird-life in the forest, 107.
Bird's-nest, our first, 61.
Black-cock, 9, 162.
Black scoters, 132, 230.
Boat, dragging across ice, 111.
——, our, 155.
——, various means of propelling, 189.
Bohemian waxwings, 9, 144.
Bolshanivagorskia, 32.
Brambling, 120.
Buffon's skua, flocks of, 201.
Bullfinch, northern, 37.
————, scarlet, 153.
Bullfinches, 14, 21.
Bunting, Lapland, 102.
——, little, 132.
——, reed, 96.
——, snow, 27, 28, 29, 50, 79.
Buzzard, rough-legged, 160.

C.

Cachets, 94.
Capercailzie, 9, 27, 59.
Captains Arendt and Engel, 48.
Castrén, 4.
Ceremony of blessing the steamer, 133.

X

Ceremony, marriage, 85.
Chiefs, election of, 20.
Chiff-chaff, the Siberian, 116.
Chooms, 72.
Circumpolar birds, 296.
Commerce, decline of, 16.
Commune, the, 86.
Copenhagen, 292.
Costumes of peasants, 113.
Crane, common, 120.
Crossbill, 14.
———, common, 27.
———, white-winged, 21.
Crosses, Greek, 35.
Crow, hooded, 9, 13, 14, 21, 27, 49.
Cuckoo, 140.
Curlew sandpiper, 2, 233.

D.

Dates of migration, 301.
Delta, the, 167.
———, visit to two islands in the, 192.
Departure for home, 288.
Diver, black-throated, 150.
———, red-throated, 160.
Dogs, 67.
Dotterel, 190.
Double snipe, 169.
Drunkenness, 60, 114.
Duck, golden-eyed, 106, 149.
———, long-tailed, 171, 266.
———, pin-tailed, 106.
———, scaup, 159.
———, shoveller, 106.
——— shooting, 104.
———, tufted, 167.
Ducks, 26.
Dunlin, 180, 228.
Dvoinik, 231, 265.

E.

Eagle, golden, 138.
———, white-tailed, 59.

Easter-eve, 60.
Eggs, 156, 183.
———, blowing, 184.
———, Bewick's swan's, 214.
———, grey plover's, 201, 205, 220, 223.
———, magpie's, 92.
———, omelette of grey plover's, 183.
———, scaup's, 205.
———, smew's, 157.
England, news from, 198.
Exile, Polish, 28.
Eyrie of peregrine falcon, 190.

F.

Falcon, peregrine, 93, 190, 210.
Feodor sent in quest of swan's skin, 213.
———, return of, 214.
Fieldfare, 102, 142.
Field-work, 115.
First rain, 90.
Flowers, beautiful, 288.
Foraging party, a, 285.
Forest, bird-life in the, 167.
——— scenery, 137.
———, the silent, 95.
Forests, 26.
Frost, cessation of, 89.
Funeral rites, 76.

G.

Game, 9, 16, 80.
Geese, a march of, on the tundra, 282.
Glaucous gull, 227.
Godwit, bar-tailed, 285.
Golden eagle, 138.
——— plover, eggs of the, 187.
Golden-eyes, 106.
Gulievski Islands, trip to, 226.
Goosander, 150.
Goose, bean, 96.
———, black, 19.

Goshawk, 161.
Grave, an old, 282.
Grey plover, 180, 181.
————, eggs of the, 201.
———————, nests, 201, 205, 220, 223.
Greek crosses, 35.
Greenshank, 107.
Grosbeak, pine, 14, 119.
Grouse, black, 9, 162.
————, hazel, 9, 80.
————, willow, 9, 14, 19, 154.
Gull, common, 99.
————, glaucous, 227.
————, great black-backed, 171.
————, Siberian herring-, 90.
Gulls, 98.
———— perching in trees, 108.
————, species new to Europe, 99.

H.

Habariki, trips to, 63, 136.
————, sail to, 155.
Hard fare, 292.
Hawfinch, 21.
Heligoland, 249.
——————, migration on, 257.
——————, ornithologists of, 249.
——————, throstle-bushes at, 253.
——————, variety of birds at, 250.
——————, wind and weather at, 253.
Hen-Harrier, 81.
Hobby, 139.
Hoffmansegg, 4.
Holidays, 114.
Home, departure for, 288.
Horses, modes of yoking, 12.
House-building, 115.

I.

Ice, dragging boats across, 111.
——, final break up of, 112.

Ice, Petchora free from, 131.
Ino, the, 265.
Inokentia, Father, 17.
Insect-life, 248.
Islands, visit to two, in the delta, 192.

J.

Jackdaws, 9, 13, 21, 29, 79.
Jay, Siberian, 27, 36, 138.
Journey from London to St. Petersburg, 7.

K.

Keyserling, 4.
Knot, 2.
Kotzoff, Peter, 17.
Kuloi river, 26.
Kuya, trip to, 262.

L.

Land, tenure of, 86.
Lapland, birds of, 3.
—————— bunting, 187.
—————————, nest of, 180.
Lark, shore, 89.
L'autre côté, 61.
Letters of introduction, 6.
Little stint, 2, 232, 239.
——————, our first nest of, 267.
Living, cheapness of, 16.
London to St. Petersburg, 7.
Long-tailed duck, nest of, 266.

M.

Magpie, 14, 21, 27, 67.
Mammoth age, 247.
Manager, the Company's, 258.
——————, we win over, 264.
Marriage ceremony, 85.

Martin, sand, 156.
May-day, 79.
Mealy redpole, 51.
Merganser, red-breasted, 188.
Merlin, 82.
Mézen, 29.
———, departure from, 29.
———, river, 30.
Midnight on the tundra, 211.
Migrants, stray, 256.
Migration of birds, 239.
————, birds resting on, 129.
———— by sight, 254.
————, lines of, 248.
————, order of, 254.
————, origin of, 245.
———— on Heligoland, 257.
————, other facts on, 258.
Migratory instincts, 258.
Mocking-bird, the Swedish, 127.
Moscow to Vologda, 9.
Mosquito-veils, 215.
Mosquitoes, 134, 210.

N.

Nest of grey plover, 181, 183.
——— Lapland bunting, 180.
——— little stint, 267, 281.
——— long-tailed duck, 266.
——— Petchora pipit, 185.
——— skuas, watching for, 204.
——— velvet scoter, 211.
Nests and eggs, 176.
———, examination of, 194.
———, various, 187, 191.
New birds, 117.
Nomad life, 55.
Northern bullfinches, 57.

O.

Officials, hospitality of, 47.
Old Believers, 45.

Old Believers, crosses of, 46.
————, prejudices of, 114.
————, superstitions of, 45.
Omelette of grey plovers' eggs, 183.
Ornaments, peasants' love for, 35.
Osprey, 138.
Our quarters, 44.
Our servants, 219.
Outfit, 5.
Overhauling our plunder, 236.
Owl, eagle, 84.
—, Lapp, 19.
—, short-eared, 118.
—, snowy, 19, 91, 280.
—, Ural, 19.
Oystercatcher, 123.

P.

Palæarctic birds, 297.
Party, a foraging, 285.
Peasants, costumes of, 113.
————, curiosity of, 34.
————, employments and amusements of, 35.
————' love for ornaments, 35.
Pelzam, 4.
Peregrine falcon, 93, 190, 210.
Petchora, banks of, 44, 95.
————, break up of ice on, 111.
———— free from ice, 131.
————, first view of, 38.
———— pipit, 165, 185.
————, sail down the, 158.
————, voyages to the, in seventeenth century, 4.
Phalaropes, 276.
————, change of plumage in, 278.
————, red-necked, 167.
Pigeons, 21.
Pinega river, 26.
Piottuch, 20.
————, his accident, 31.
Pipit, meadow, 101, 108.

Pipit, red-throated, 101.
———————, nests of, 180, 232.
———, Siberian, 165.
———, tree, 116.
Pizhma, river, 31.
Plover, golden, 100.
———————, eggs of, 187.
———, grey, 2, 201.
———————, nests of, 201, 205, 220, 223.
———, little ringed, 154.
———, ringed, 122.
Plunder, overhauling our, 256.
Polish exile, 28.
——— prejudices, 34.
Postal service in winter and summer, 24.
Post-houses, 11.
Prahms, the, 263.
Prejudices of Old Believers, 114.
Prey, birds of, 82.
Processions, religious, 113.
Provisions, prices of, 121.
'Purchas his Pilgrimes,' 3.
Pustazursk, arrival at, 169.
Pytkoff mountains, 231.

R.

Rae's 'Land of the North Wind,' 18.
Rafts, timber, 174.
Railway carriages, mode of heating, 8.
Rain, first, 90.
Raven, 14, 21, 27, 53.
Redpole, mealy, 21, 51.
Redshank, spotted, 147.
Redstart, 91.
Red-throated pipit, 180, 232.
Redwing, 102, 142.
Reindeer, 55.
———, diseases of, 56.
——— harness, 68.
———, lassoing, 65.
Results of the trip, 295.
Religion, 76.

Religious procession, 113.
Richardson's skua, 188.
River, wrong bank of the, 110.
Rivers Pinega and Kuloi, 26.
Roads, 12, 58.
Robinson Crusoe, doing, in a wrecked ship, 265.
Rook, 13, 103.
Rosposki, travelling in, 263.
Ruff, 131.
Russian bath, 213.
——— holiday, 113.
——— superstitions, 286.

S.

Samovar, the, 11.
Samoyede names, 19, 125.
——————— sledges, 68.
——————— songs, 19.
Samoyedes, 18, 27, 36, 54, 57, 64, 73, 74, 76.
———————, election of chiefs, 20.
———————, ignorance of doctors and medicinal plants, 20.
Sanderlings, 2, 228.
Sandpiper, 19.
———————, common, 158.
———————, curlew, 2, 253.
———————, Terek, 148.
———————, wood, 122, 148.
Scaup's eggs, 205.
Scenery, 13, 25, 30.
———, forest, 137.
Schrenck, 4.
Scoter, black, 132.
——— ———, nest of, 205.
———, velvet, 211.
Scoters, 231.
Sea-birds, 292.
Sedge-warbler, 169.
Servants, our, 219.
Shooting, 104.
——— parties, 47.
Short commons, on, 284.

Shoveller duck, 106.
Siberian chiff-chaff, 116.
——— jay, 36.
Skua, Buffon's, 172, 177, 201.
———, Richardson's, 188.
———, search for nest of, 204.
Skylark, 117, 258.
Sledging from Vologda to Archangel, 10.
Smew, 150.
———, eggs of, 157.
Snipe, common, 147.
———, great, 146, 169.
——— in trees, 157.
Snow, 60.
——— plains, 26.
——— shoes, 48.
Snow-bunting, 37, 50.
Snowy owl, 19, 91, 280.
Song, a new, 131.
Sparrow, common, 14, 20, 27, 104.
———, tree, 14, 20, 27, 104.
Sparrow-hawk, 129.
Stanavialachta, tundra near, 189.
———————, visit to, 208.
Steamer, ceremony of blessing the, 133.
———, return of the, 284.
Stint, little, 2, 232, 239, 267, 281.
———, eggs of the, 272.
———, Temminck's, 122, 130.
Stonechat, Siberian, 117.
St. Petersburg, frozen market at, 8.
Summer, preparations for, 87.
Sunset and sunrise, 270.
Superstitions, Russian, 286.
Swallow, barn, 122.
Swamps, willow, 164.
Swan, Bewick's, 2, 195, 214.
———, skin of, 213.

T.

Tarns in the woods, 138.
Teal, 104.
Tenure of land, 86.

Terck sandpiper, 148.
Tern, Arctic, 163.
Thunder-storm, 290.
Timber rafts, 175.
Time, confusion of, 279.
Titmouse, Lapp, 144.
———, marsh, 14, 21, 61.
Toads, 129.
Traffic, 13.
Trees, snipe in, 157.
Triad, the, 264, 288.
Trip, results of the, 294.
Tundra, 55, 170, 267, 276.
———, birds seen on the, 180, 185.
———, march of geese on, 282.
———, midnight on, 210.
———, near Stanavialachta, 189.
——————— the Yooshina river, 186.
———, sailing for the, 177.
———, vegetation of the, 179.

U.

Umskia, 36, 58.
Unknown breeding-grounds, 1.
Ust-Zylma, 38.
———, churches of, 43.
———, farms of, 43.
———, fire at, 85.
———, houses of, 41.
———, last days at, 155.
———, manure of, 42.
———, population of, 43.
———, return to, 152.
———, streets of, 40, 43.
———, Sunday at, 84.

V.

Velvet scoter, nest of the, 211.
Verakin, M., 9.
Via diabolica, the, 32.
Villages, 34.

Viski, 166.
Vocabulary, Samoyede, 19.
Vologda, 9.
———, sledging from, to Archangel, 10.

W.

Waders, arrival of, 121.
Wagtail, green, 103.
———, white, 91.
———, yellow-headed, 141.
Warbler, Arctic willow, 159.
———, blue-throated, 127.
———, reed, 245.
———, sedge, 160.
———, Transvaal, 246.
———, willow, 108.
———, yellow-browed, 256.
Waterspout, 291.
Wasilkova, excursion to, 195.
Waxwing, 9, 21, 144.
Weather, 13, 30, 88, 138, 284.
Wedding of the engineer's son, 152.
Wheatear, 116.
Whimbrel, 103.
White whales, shoal of, 227.
Widgeon, 107, 149.

Wild goose chase, a, 93.
Willow grouse, abundance of, 154, 191.
——— swamps, 164.
Winter, 55.
———, return of, 92.
Woodpecker, black, 97.
———, great spotted, 14, 27.
———, lesser spotted, 21.
———, Siberian lesser spotted, 109.
———, three-toed, 109.
Woods, rambles in the, 134.
———, tarns in the, 138.
Wolley, John, 2.

Y.

Yellow-hammer, 14, 52.
Yellow-headed wagtail, 141.
Yemschik, 10.
Yoking horses, modes of, 12.
Yooshina river, tundra near the, 186.

Z.

Zylma river, break up of ice on the, 110.
Zyriani, 206.

THE END.

LONDON: PRINTED BY WILLIAM CLOWES AND SONS, LIMITED, STAMFORD STREET
AND CHARING CROSS.

50, ALBEMARLE STREET, LONDON,
February, 1883.

MR. MURRAY'S
GENERAL LIST OF WORKS.

ALBERT MEMORIAL. A Descriptive and Illustrated Account of the National Monument erected to the PRINCE CONSORT at Kensington. Illustrated by Engravings of its Architecture, Decorations, Sculptured Groups, Statues, Mosaics, Metalwork &c. With Descriptive Text. By DOYNE C. BELL. With 24 Plates. Folio. 12*l.* 12*s.*

——— HANDBOOK TO. Post 8vo. 1*s.*; or Illustrated Edition. 2*s.* 6*d.*

— (PRINCE) SPEECHES AND ADDRESSES. Fcap. 8vo. 1*s.*

ABBOTT (REV. J.). Memoirs of a Church of England Missionary in the North American Colonies. Post 8vo. 2*s.*

ABERCROMBIE (JOHN). Enquiries concerning the Intellectual Powers and the Investigation of Truth. Fcap. 8vo. 3*s.* 6*d.*

ACLAND (REV. CHARLES). Popular Account of the Manners and Customs of India. Post 8vo. 2*s.*

ÆSOP'S FABLES. A New Version. By Rev. THOMAS JAMES. With 100 Woodcuts, by TENNIEL and WOLF. Post 8vo. 2*s.* 6*d.*

AGRICULTURAL (ROYAL) JOURNAL. (*Published half-yearly.*)

AIDS TO FAITH: a Series of Essays. Miracles; Evidences of Christianity; Prophecy and Mosaic Record of Creation; Ideology and Subscription; The Pentateuch; Inspiration; Death of Christ; Scripture and its Interpretation. By various Authors. 8vo. 9*s.*

ALBERT DÜRER; his Life, with a History of his Art. By DR. THAUSING, Keeper of Archduke Albert's Art Collection at Vienna. Translated from the German. With Portrait and Illustrations. 2 vols. Medium 8vo. [*In the Press.*

AMBER-WITCH (THE). A most interesting Trial for Witchcraft. Translated by LADY DUFF GORDON. Post 8vo. 2*s.*

APOCRYPHA: With a Commentary Explanatory and Critical, by various Writers. Edited by REV. PROFESSOR WACE. 2 Vols. Medium 8vo. [*In the Press.*

ARISTOTLE. See GROTE, HATCH.

ARMY LIST (THE). *Published Monthly by Authority.*

——— (THE NEW OFFICIAL). *Published Quarterly.* Royal 8vo. 15*s.*

ARTHUR'S (LITTLE) History of England. By LADY CALLCOTT. *New Edition, continued to* 1872. With 36 Woodcuts. Fcap. 8vo. 1*s.* 6*d.*

ATKINSON (DR. R.) Vie de Seint Auban. A Poem in Norman-French. Ascribed to MATTHEW PARIS. With Concordance, Glossary and Notes. Small 4to. 10*s.* 6*d.*

AUSTIN (JOHN). LECTURES ON GENERAL JURISPRUDENCE; or, the Philosophy of Positive Law. Edited by ROBERT CAMPBELL. 2 Vols. 8vo. 32*s.*

——— STUDENT'S EDITION, compiled from the above work, by ROBERT CAMPBELL. Post 8vo. 12*s.*

——— Analysis of. By GORDON CAMPBELL. Post 8vo. 6*s.*

LIST OF WORKS

ADMIRALTY PUBLICATIONS; Issued by direction of the Lords Commissioners of the Admiralty:—

CHALLENGER EXPEDITION, 1873—1876: Report of the Scientific Results of. Vol. I. Zoology. 4to. 37s. 6d.

A MANUAL OF SCIENTIFIC ENQUIRY, for the Use of Travellers. Fourth Edition. Edited by ROBERT MAIN, M.A. Woodcuts. Post 8vo. 3s. 6d.

GREENWICH ASTRONOMICAL OBSERVATIONS, 1841 to 1847, and 1847 to 1877. Royal 4to. 20s. each.

GREENWICH ASTRONOMICAL RESULTS, 1847 to 1877. 4to. 3s. each.

MAGNETICAL AND METEOROLOGICAL OBSERVATIONS, 1844 to 1877. Royal 4to. 20s. each.

MAGNETICAL AND METEOROLOGICAL RESULTS, 1848 to 1877. 4to. 3s. each.

APPENDICES TO OBSERVATIONS.
   1837. Logarithms of Sines and Cosines in Time. 3s.
   1842. Catalogue of 1439 Stars, from Observations made in 1836. 1841. 4s.
   1845. Longitude of Valentia (Chronometrical). 3s.
   1847. Description of Altazimuth. 3s.
       Description of Photographic Apparatus. 2s.
   1851. Maskelyne's Ledger of Stars. 3s.
   1852. I. Description of the Transit Circle. 3s.
   1853. Bessel's Refraction Tables. 3s.
   1854. I. Description of the Reflex Zenith Tube. 3s.
       II. Six Years' Catalogue of Stars, from Observations, 1848 to 1853. 4s.
   1860. Reduction of Deep Thermometer Observations. 2s.
   1862. II. Plan of Ground and Buildings of Royal Observatory, Greenwich. 3s.
       III. Longitude of Valentia (Galvanic). 2s.
   1864. I. Moon's Semi-diameter, from Occultations. 2s.
       II. Reductions of Planetary Observations. 1831 to 1835. 2s.
   1868. I. Corrections of Elements of Jupiter and Saturn. 2s.
       II. Second Seven Years' Catalogue of 2760 Stars, 1861-7. 4s.
       III. Description of the Great Equatorial. 3s.
   1871. Water Telescope. 3s.
   1873. Regulations of the Royal Observatory. 2s.
   1876. II. Nine Years' Catalogue of 2263 Stars. (1861-67.) 4s.

Cape of Good Hope Observations (Star Ledgers): 1856 to 1863. 2s.
——————————————— 1856. 5s.
——————— Astronomical Results. 1857 to 1858. 5s.
Cape Catalogue of 1159 Stars, reduced to the Epoch 1860. 3s.
Cape of Good Hope Astronomical Results. 1859 to 1860. 5s.
——————————————————— 1871 to 1873. 5s.
——————— 1874 to 1876. 5s. each.
Report on Teneriffe Astronomical Experiment. 1856. 5s.
Paramatta Catalogue of 7385 Stars. 1822 to 1826. 4s.

REDUCTION OF THE OBSERVATIONS OF PLANETS. 1750 to 1830. Royal 4to. 20s. each.
——————————————— LUNAR OBSERVATIONS. 1750 to 1830. 2 Vols. Royal 4to. 20s. each.
——————— 1831 to 1851. 4to. 10s. each.

——————— GREENWICH METEOROLOGICAL OBSERVATIONS. Chiefly 1847 to 1873. 5s.

ARCTIC PAPERS. 13s. 6d.

BERNOULLI'S SEXCENTENARY TABLE. 1779. 4to. 5s.

BESSEL'S AUXILIARY TABLES FOR HIS METHOD OF CLEARING LUNAR DISTANCES. 8vo. 2s.

ENCKE'S BERLINER JAHRBUCH, for 1830. Berlin, 1828. 8vo. 9s.

HANNYNGTON'S HAVERSINES.

HANSEN'S TABLES DE LA LUNE. 4to. 20s.

LAX'S TABLES FOR FINDING THE LATITUDE AND LONGITUDE. 1821. 8vo. 10s.

ADMIRALTY PUBLICATIONS—*continued*.
    LUNAR OBSERVATIONS at GREENWICH. 1783 to 1819. Compared with the Tables, 1821. 4to. 7s. 6d.
    MACLEAR ON LACAILLE'S ARC OF MERIDIAN. 2 Vols. 20s. each.
    MAYER'S DISTANCES of the MOON'S CENTRE from the PLANETS. 1822, 3s.; 1823, 4s. 6d. 1824 to 1835. 8vo. 4s. each.
    ————— TABULÆ MOTUUM SOLIS ET LUNÆ. 1770. 5s.
    ————— ASTRONOMICAL OBSERVATIONS MADE AT GÖTTINGEN, from 1756 to 1761. 1826. Folio. 7s. 6d.
    NAUTICAL ALMANACS, from 1767 to 1883. 2s. 6d. each.
    ————— SELECTIONS FROM, up to 1812. 8vo. 5s. 1834-54. 5s.
    ————— SUPPLEMENTS, 1828 to 1833, 1837 and 1838. 2s. each.
    ————— TABLE requisite to be used with the N.A. 1781. 8vo. 5s.
    SABINE'S PENDULUM EXPERIMENTS to DETERMINE THE FIGURE OF THE EARTH. 1825. 4to. 40s.
    SHEPHERD'S TABLES for CORRECTING LUNAR DISTANCES. 1772. Royal 4to. 21s.
    ————— TABLES, GENERAL, of the MOON'S DISTANCE from the SUN, and 10 STARS. 1787. Folio. 5s. 6d.
    TAYLOR'S SEXAGESIMAL TABLE. 1780. 4to. 15s.
    ————— TABLES OF LOGARITHMS. 4to. 60s.
    TIARK'S ASTRONOMICAL OBSERVATIONS for the LONGITUDE of MADEIRA. 1822. 4to. 5s.
    ————— CHRONOMETRICAL OBSERVATIONS for DIFFERENCES of LONGITUDE between DOVER, PORTSMOUTH, and FALMOUTH. 1823. 4to. 5s.
    VENUS and JUPITER: OBSERVATIONS of, compared with the TABLES. London, 1822. 4to. 2s.
    WALES AND BAYLY'S ASTRONOMICAL OBSERVATIONS. 1777. 4to. 21s.
    ————— REDUCTION OF ASTRONOMICAL OBSERVATIONS MADE IN THE SOUTHERN HEMISPHERE. 1764–1771. 1788. 4to. 10s. 6d.

BARBAULD (Mrs.). Hymns in Prose for Children. With 100 Illustrations. 16mo. 3s. 6d.

BARCLAY (BISHOP). Selected Extracts from the Talmud, chiefly illustrating the Teaching of the Bible. With an Introduction. Illustrations. 8vo. 14s.

BARKLEY (H. C.). Five Years among the Bulgarians and Turks between the Danube and the Black Sea. Post 8vo. 10s. 6d.

—— —— —— Bulgaria Before the War; during a Seven Years' Experience of European Turkey and its Inhabitants. Post 8vo. 10s. 6d.

—— —— —— My Boyhood: a True Story. A Book for Schoolboys and others. With Illustrations. Post 8vo. 6s.

BARROW (JOHN). Life, Exploits, and Voyages of Sir Francis Drake. Post 8vo. 2s.

BARRY (CANON). The Manifold Witness for Christ. Being an Attempt to Exhibit the Combined Force of various Evidences, Direct and Indirect, of Christianity. 8vo. 12s.

—————— (EDW.), R.A. Lectures on Architecture, delivered before the Royal Academy. With Illustrations. 8vo. [*In Preparation.*

BATES (H. W.). Records of a Naturalist on the Amazons during Eleven Years' Adventure and Travel. Illustrations. Post 8vo. 7s. 6d.

BAX (CAPT.). Russian Tartary, Eastern Siberia, China, Japan, &c. A Cruise in H.M.S. Dwarf. Illustrations. Cr. 8vo. 12s.

BELCHER (LADY). Account of the Mutineers of the 'Bounty,' and their Descendants; with their Settlements in Pitcairn and Norfolk Islands. Illustrations. Post 8vo. 12s.

B 2

LIST OF WORKS

BELL (Sir Chas.). Familiar Letters. Portrait. Post 8vo. 12s.

——— (Doyne C.). Notices of the Historic Persons buried in the Chapel of St. Peter ad Vincula, in the Tower of London, with an account of the discovery of the supposed remains of Queen Anne Boleyn. With Illustrations. Crown 8vo. 14s.

BERTRAM (Jas. G.). Harvest of the Sea: an Account of British Food Fishes, including Fisheries and Fisher Folk. Illustrations. Post 8vo. 9s.

BIBLE COMMENTARY. The Old Testament. Explanatory and Critical. With a Revision of the Translation. By BISHOPS and CLERGY of the ANGLICAN CHURCH. Edited by F. C. Cook, M.A., Canon of Exeter. 6 Vols. Medium 8vo. 6l. 15s.

Vol. I. 30s. { Genesis. Exodus. Leviticus. Numbers. Deuteronomy. }

Vols. II. and III. 36s. { Joshua, Judges, Ruth, Samuel, Kings, Chronicles, Ezra, Nehemiah, Esther. }

Vol. IV. 24s. { Job. Psalms. Proverbs. Ecclesiastes. Song of Solomon. }

Vol. V. 20s. { Isaiah. Jeremiah. }

Vol. VI. 25s. { Ezekiel. Daniel. Minor Prophets. }

——— The New Testament. 4 Vols. Medium 8vo.

Vol. I. 18s. { Introduction. St. Matthew. St. Mark. St. Luke. }

Vol II. 20s. { St. John. Acts. }

Vol. III. { Romans, Corinthians, Galatians, Philippians, Ephesians, Colossians, Thessalonians, Philemon, Pastoral Epistles, Hebrews. }

Vol. IV. { St. James, St. Peter, St. John, St. Jude, Revelation. }

——— The Student's Edition. Abridged and Edited by John M. Fuller, M.A., Vicar of Bexley. (To be completed in 6 Volumes.) Vols. I. to III. Crown 8vo. 7s. 6d. each.

BIGG-WITHER (T. P.). Pioneering in South Brazil; Three Years of Forest and Prairie Life in the Province of Parana. Map and Illustrations. 2 vols. Crown 8vo. 21s.

BIRCH (Samuel). A History of Ancient Pottery and Porcelain: Egyptian, Assyrian, Greek, Roman, and Etruscan. With Coloured Plates and 200 Illustrations. Medium 8vo. 42s.

BIRD (Isabella). Hawaiian Archipelago; or Six Months among the Palm Groves, Coral Reefs, and Volcanoes of the Sandwich Islands. Illustrations. Crown 8vo. 7s. 6d.

——— Unbeaten Tracks in Japan: Travels of a Lady in the interior, including Visits to the Aborigines of Yezo and the Shrines of Nikko and Ise. With Map and Illustrations. 2 Vols. Crown 8vo. 24s.

——— A Lady's Life in the Rocky Mountains. Illustrations. Post 8vo. 10s. 6d.

BISSET (Sir John). Sport and War in South Africa from 1834 to 1867, with a Narrative of the Duke of Edinburgh's Visit. With Map and Illustrations. Crown 8vo. 14s.

BLUNT (Lady Anne). The Bedouins of the Euphrates Valley. With some account of the Arabs and their Horses. With Map and Illustrations. 2 Vols. Crown 8vo. 24s.

——— A Pilgrimage to Nejd, the Cradle of the Arab Race, and a Visit to the Court of the Arab Emir. With Map and Illustrations. 2 Vols. Post 8vo.

BLUNT (Rev. J. J.). Undesigned Coincidences in the Writings of the Old and New Testaments, an Argument of their Veracity. Post 8vo. 6s.
——— History of the Christian Church in the First Three Centuries. Post 8vo. 6s.
——— Parish Priest; His Duties, Acquirements, and Obligations. Post 8vo. 6s.
——— University Sermons. Post 8vo. 6s.

BOOK OF COMMON PRAYER. Illustrated with Coloured Borders, Initial Letters, and Woodcuts. 8vo. 18s.

BORROW (George). Bible in Spain; or the Journeys, Adventures, and Imprisonments of an Englishman in an Attempt to circulate the Scriptures in the Peninsula. Post 8vo. 5s.
——— Gypsies of Spain; their Manners, Customs, Religion, and Language. With Portrait. Post 8vo. 5s.
——— Lavengro; The Scholar—The Gypsy—and the Priest. Post 8vo. 5s.
——— Romany Rye—a Sequel to "Lavengro." Post 8vo. 5s.
——— Wild Wales: its People, Language, and Scenery. Post 8vo. 5s.
——— Romano Lavo-Lil; Word-Book of the Romany, or English Gypsy Language; with Specimens of their Poetry, and an account of certain Gypsyries. Post 8vo. 10s. 6d.

BOSWELL'S Life of Samuel Johnson, LL.D. Including the Tour to the Hebrides. Edited by Mr. Croker. *Seventh Edition*. Portraits. 1 vol. Medium 8vo. 12s.

BRACE (C. L.). Manual of Ethnology; or the Races of the Old World. Post 8vo. 6s.

BREWER (Rev. J. S.). English Studies. Contents. New Sources of English History. Green's History. Royal Supremacy. Hatfield House. The Stuarts. Shakespeare. How to Study English History. Erasmus. Ancient London. 8vo. 14s.

BRITISH ASSOCIATION REPORTS. 8vo.

York and Oxford, 1831-32, 13s. 6d.
Cambridge, 1833, 12s.
Edinburgh, 1834, 15s.
Dublin, 1835, 13s. 6d.
Bristol, 1836, 12s.
Liverpool, 1837, 16s. 6d.
Newcastle, 1838, 15s.
Birmingham, 1839, 13s. 6d.
Glasgow, 1840, 15s.
Plymouth, 1841, 13s. 6d.
Manchester, 1842, 10s. 6d.
Cork, 1843, 12s.
York, 1844, 20s.
Cambridge, 1845, 12s.
Southampton, 1846, 15s.
Oxford, 1847, 18s.
Swansea, 1848, 9s.
Birmingham, 1849, 10s.
Edinburgh, 1850, 15s.
Ipswich, 1851, 16s. 6d.
Belfast, 1852, 15s.
Hull, 1853, 10s. 6d.
Liverpool, 1854, 18s.
Glasgow, 1855, 15s.
Cheltenham, 1856, 18s.
Dublin, 1857, 15s.
Leeds, 1858, 20s.
Aberdeen, 1859, 15s.
Oxford, 1860, 25s.
Manchester, 1861, 15s.
Cambridge, 1862, 20s.
Newcastle, 1863, 25s.
Bath, 1864, 18s.
Birmingham, 1865, 25s.
Nottingham, 1866, 24s.
Dundee, 1867, 26s.
Norwich, 1868, 25s.
Exeter, 1869, 22s.
Liverpool, 1870, 18s.
Edinburgh, 1871, 16s.
Brighton, 1872, 24s.
Bradford, 1873, 25s.
Belfast, 1874, 25s.
Bristol, 1875, 25s.
Glasgow, 1876, 25s.
Plymouth, 1877, 24s.
Dublin, 1878, 24s.
Sheffield, 1879, 24s.
Swansea, 1880, 24s.

BRUGSCH (Professor). A History of Egypt, under the Pharaohs. Derived entirely from Monuments, with a Memoir on the Exodus of the Israelites. Translated by Philip Smith, B.A., with new preface and notes by the author. Maps. 2 vols. 8vo. 32s.

LIST OF WORKS

BUNBURY (E. H.). A History of Ancient Geography, among the Greeks and Romans, from the Earliest Ages till the Fall of the Roman Empire. With Index and 20 Maps. 2 Vols. 8vo. 42s.

BURBIDGE (F. W.). The Gardens of the Sun: or A Naturalist's Journal on the Mountains and in the Forests and Swamps of Borneo and the Sulu Archipelago. With Illustrations. Crown 8vo. 14s.

BURCKHARDT'S Cicerone; or Art Guide to Painting in Italy. Translated from the German by Mrs. A. Clough. New Edition, revised by J. A. Crowe. Post 8vo. 6s.

BURN (Col.). Dictionary of Naval and Military Technical Terms, English and French—French and English. Crown 8vo. 15s.

BUTTMANN'S Lexilogus; a Critical Examination of the Meaning of numerous Greek Words, chiefly in Homer and Hesiod. By Rev. J. R. Fishlake. 8vo. 12s.

BUXTON (Charles). Memoirs of Sir Thomas Fowell Buxton, Bart. Portrait. 8vo. 16s. *Popular Edition*. Fcap. 8vo. 5s.

—————— (Sydney C.). A Handbook to the Political Questions of the Day; with the Arguments on Either Side. 8vo. 5s.

BYLES (Sir John). Foundations of Religion in the Mind and Heart of Man. Post 8vo. 6s.

BYRON'S (Lord) LIFE AND WORKS :—

    Life, Letters, and Journals. By Thomas Moore. *Cabinet Edition*. Plates. 6 Vols. Fcap. 8vo. 18s.; or One Volume, Portraits. Royal 8vo., 7s. 6d.

    Life and Poetical Works. *Popular Edition*. Portraits. 2 vols. Royal 8vo. 15s.

    Poetical Works. *Library Edition*. Portrait. 6 Vols. 8vo. 45s.

    Poetical Works. *Cabinet Edition*. Plates. 10 Vols. 12mo. 30s.

    Poetical Works. *Pocket Ed.* 8 Vols. 16mo. In a case. 21s.

    Poetical Works. *Popular Edition*. Plates. Royal 8vo. 7s. 6d.

    Poetical Works. *Pearl Edition*. Crown 8vo. 2s. 6d.

    Childe Harold. With 80 Engravings. Crown 8vo. 12s.

    Childe Harold. 16mo. 2s. 6d.

    Childe Harold. Vignettes. 16mo. 1s.

    Childe Harold. Portrait. 16mo. 6d.

    Tales and Poems. 16mo. 2s. 6d.

    Miscellaneous. 2 Vols. 16mo. 5s.

    Dramas and Plays. 2 Vols. 16mo. 5s.

    Don Juan and Beppo. 2 Vols. 16mo. 5s.

    Beauties. Poetry and Prose. Portrait. Fcap. 8vo. 3s. 6d.

CAMPBELL (Lord). Lord Chancellors and Keepers of the Great Seal of England. From the Earliest Times to the Death of Lord Eldon in 1838. 10 Vols. Crown 8vo. 6s. each.

—————— Chief Justices of England. From the Norman Conquest to the Death of Lord Tenterden. 4 Vols. Crown 8vo. 6s. each.

—————— Life and Letters: Based on his Autobiography, Journals, and Correspondence. Edited by his daughter, Mrs. Hardcastle. Portrait. 2 Vols. 8vo. 30s.

—————— (Thos.) Essay on English Poetry. With Short Lives of the British Poets. Post 8vo. 3s. 6d.

CARNARVON (Lord). Portugal, Gallicia, and the Basque Provinces. Post 8vo. 3s. 6d.

—————— The Agamemnon: Translated from Æschylus. Sm. 8vo. 6s.

CARNOTA (Conde da). Memoirs of the Life and Eventful Career of F.M. the Duke of Saldanha; Soldier and Statesman. With Selections from his Correspondence. 2 Vols. 8vo. 32s.

CARTWRIGHT (W. C.). The Jesuits: their Constitution and Teaching. An Historical Sketch. 8vo. 9s.

CAVALCASELLE'S WORKS. [See Crowe.]

CESNOLA (Gen.). Cyprus; its Ancient Cities, Tombs, and Temples. Researches and Excavations during Ten Years' Residence in that Island. With 400 Illustrations. Medium 8vo. 50s.

CHILD (Chaplin). Benedicite; or, Song of the Three Children; being Illustrations of the Power, Beneficence, and Design manifested by the Creator in his Works. Post 8vo. 6s.

CHISHOLM (Mrs.). Perils of the Polar Seas; True Stories of Arctic Discovery and Adventure. Illustrations. Post 8vo. 6s.

CHURTON (Archdeacon). Poetical Remains, Translations and Imitations. Portrait. Post 8vo. 7s. 6d.

CLASSIC PREACHERS OF THE ENGLISH CHURCH. St. James's Lectures.

—— 1877, Donne, by Bishop of Durham; Barrow, by Prof. Wace; South, by Dean Lake; Beveridge, by Rev. W. R. Clark; Wilson, by Canon Farrar; Butler, by Dean Goulburn. With Introduction by J. E. Kempe. Post 8vo. 7s. 6d.

—— 1878, Bull, by Rev. W. Warburton; Horsley, by Bishop of Ely; Taylor, by Canon Barry; Sanderson, by Bishop of Derry; Tillotson, by Rev. W. G. Humphry; Andrewes, by Rev. H. J. North. Post 8vo. 7s. 6d.

CLIVE'S (Lord) Life. By Rev. G. R. Gleig. Post 8vo. 3s. 6d.

CLODE (C. M.). Military Forces of the Crown; their Administration and Government. 2 Vols. 8vo. 21s. each.

—— Administration of Justice under Military and Martial Law, as applicable to the Army, Navy, Marine, and Auxiliary Forces. 8vo. 12s.

COLERIDGE'S (Samuel Taylor) Table-Talk. Portrait. 12mo. 3s. 6d.

COLONIAL LIBRARY. [See Home and Colonial Library.]

COMPANIONS FOR THE DEVOUT LIFE. A Series of Lectures on well-known Devotional Works. Crown 8vo. 6s.

De Imitatione Christi, Canon Farrar.
Pensées of Blaise Pascal. Dean Church.
S. François de Sales. Dean Goulburn.
Baxter's Saints' Rest. Archbishop of Dublin.
S. Augustine's Confessions. Bishop of Derry.
Jeremy Taylor's Holy Living and Dying. Rev. Dr. Humphry.
Theologia Germanica. Canon Ashwell.
Fénelon's Œuvres Spirituelles. Rev. T. T. Carter.
Andrewes' Devotions. Bishop of Ely.
Christian Year. Canon Barry.
Paradise Lost. Rev. E. H. Bickersteth.
Pilgrim's Progress. Dean Howson.
Prayer Book. Dean Burgon.

CONVOCATION PRAYER-BOOK. (See Prayer-Book.)

COOKE (E. W.). Leaves from my Sketch-Book. Being a Selection from Sketches made during many Tours. With Descriptive Text. 50 Plates. 2 Vols. Small folio. 31s. 6d. each.

COOKERY (Modern Domestic). Founded on Principles of Economy and Practical Knowledge. By a Lady. Woodcuts. Fcap. 8vo. 5s.

CRABBE (Rev. George). Life and Poetical Works. With Illustrations. Royal 8vo. 7s.

CRAWFORD & BALCARRES (Earl of). Etruscan Inscriptions. Analyzed, Translated, and Commented upon. 8vo. 12s.

CRIPPS (Wilfred). Old English Plate: Ecclesiastical, Decorative, and Domestic, its Makers and Marks. With a Complete Table of Date Letters, &c. New Edition. Illustrations. Medium 8vo.

—— Old French Plate; Furnishing Tables of the Paris Date Letters, and Fac-similes of Other Marks. With Illustrations. 8vo. 8s. 6d.

CROKER (J. W.). Progressive Geography for Children. 18mo. 1s. 6d.

—— Boswell's Life of Johnson. Including the Tour to the Hebrides. *Seventh Edition.* Portraits. 8vo. 12s.

—— Historical Essay on the Guillotine. Fcap. 8vo. 1s.

CROWE and CAVALCASELLE. Lives of the Early Flemish Painters. Woodcuts. Post 8vo, 7s. 6d.; or Large Paper, 8vo, 15s.

—— History of Painting in North Italy, from 14th to 16th Century. With Illustrations. 2 Vols. 8vo. 42s.

—— Life and Times of Titian, with some Account of his Family, chiefly from new and unpublished records. With Portrait and Illustrations. 2 vols. 8vo. 42s.

CUMMING (R. Gordon). Five Years of a Hunter's Life in the Far Interior of South Africa. Woodcuts. Post 8vo. 6s.

CUNYNGHAME (Sir Arthur). Travels in the Eastern Caucasus, on the Caspian and Black Seas, in Daghestan and the Frontiers of Persia and Turkey. With Map and Illustrations. 8vo. 18s.

CURTIUS' (Professor) Student's Greek Grammar, for the Upper Forms. Edited by Dr. Wm. Smith. Post 8vo. 6s.

—— Elucidations of the above Grammar. Translated by Evelyn Abbot. Post 8vo. 7s. 6d.

—— Smaller Greek Grammar for the Middle and Lower Forms. Abridged from the larger work. 12mo. 3s. 6d.

—— Accidence of the Greek Language. Extracted from the above work. 12mo. 2s. 6d.

—— Principles of Greek Etymology. Translated by A. S. Wilkins, M.A., and E. B. England, M.A. 2 vols. 8vo. 15s. each.

—— The Greek Verb, its Structure and Development. Translated by A. S. Wilkins, M.A., and E. B. England, M.A. 8vo. 12s.

CURZON (Hon. Robert). Visits to the Monasteries of the Levant. Illustrations. Post 8vo. 7s. 6d.

CUST (General). Warriors of the 17th Century—The Thirty Years' War. 2 Vols. 16s. Civil Wars of France and England. 2 Vols. 16s. Commanders of Fleets and Armies. 2 Vols. 18s.

—— Annals of the Wars—18th & 19th Century. With Maps. 9 Vols. Post 8vo. 5s. each.

DAVY (Sir Humphry). Consolations in Travel; or, Last Days of a Philosopher. Woodcuts. Fcap. 8vo. 3s. 6d.

—— Salmonia; or, Days of Fly Fishing. Woodcuts. Fcap. 8vo. 3s. 6d.

DARWIN (CHARLES) WORKS:—
    JOURNAL OF A NATURALIST DURING A VOYAGE ROUND THE WORLD. Crown 8vo. 9s.
    ORIGIN OF SPECIES BY MEANS OF NATURAL SELECTION; or, the Preservation of Favoured Races in the Struggle for Life. Woodcuts. Crown 8vo. 7s. 6d.
    VARIATION OF ANIMALS AND PLANTS UNDER DOMESTICATION. Woodcuts. 2 Vols. Crown 8vo. 18s.
    DESCENT OF MAN, AND SELECTION IN RELATION TO SEX. Woodcuts. Crown 8vo. 9s.
    EXPRESSIONS OF THE EMOTIONS IN MAN AND ANIMALS. With Illustrations. Crown 8vo. 12s.
    VARIOUS CONTRIVANCES BY WHICH ORCHIDS ARE FERTILIZED BY INSECTS. Woodcuts. Crown 8vo. 9s.
    MOVEMENTS AND HABITS OF CLIMBING PLANTS. Woodcuts. Crown 8vo. 6s.
    INSECTIVOROUS PLANTS. Woodcuts. Crown 8vo. 14s.
    EFFECTS OF CROSS AND SELF-FERTILIZATION IN THE VEGETABLE KINGDOM. Crown 8vo. 12s.
    DIFFERENT FORMS OF FLOWERS ON PLANTS OF THE SAME SPECIES. Crown 8vo. 10s. 6d.
    POWER OF MOVEMENT IN PLANTS. Woodcuts. Cr. 8vo. 15s.
    LIFE OF ERASMUS DARWIN. With a Study of his Works by ERNEST KRAUSE. Portrait. Crown 8vo. 7s. 6d.
    FACTS AND ARGUMENTS FOR DARWIN. By FRITZ MULLER. Translated by W. S. DALLAS. Woodcuts. Post 8vo. 6s.

DE COSSON (E. A.). The Cradle of the Blue Nile: a Journey through Abyssinia and Soudan, and a Residence at the Court of King John of Ethiopia. Map and Illustrations. 2 vols. Post 8vo. 21s.

DENNIS (GEORGE). The Cities and Cemeteries of Etruria. A new Edition, revised, recording all the latest Discoveries. With 20 Plans and 200 Illustrations. 2 vols. Medium 8vo. 42s.

DENT (EMMA). Annals of Winchcombe and Sudeley. With 120 Portraits, Plates and Woodcuts. 4to. 42s.

DERBY (EARL OF). Iliad of Homer rendered into English Blank Verse. With Portrait. 2 Vols. Post 8vo. 10s.

DERRY (BISHOP OF). Witness of the Psalms to Christ and Christianity. The Bampton Lectures for 1876. 8vo. 14s.

DEUTSCH (EMANUEL). Talmud, Islam, The Targums and other Literary Remains. With a brief Memoir. 8vo. 12s.

DILKE (SIR C. W.). Papers of a Critic. Selected from the Writings of the late CHAS. WENTWORTH DILKE. With a Biographical Sketch. 2 Vols. 8vo. 24s.

DOG-BREAKING. See HUTCHINSON.

DOMESTIC MODERN COOKERY. Founded on Principles of Economy and Practical Knowledge, and adapted for Private Families. Woodcuts. Fcap. 8vo. 5s.

DOUGLAS'S (Sir Howard) Theory and Practice of Gunnery. Plates. 8vo. 21s.

——— (Wm.) Horse-Shoeing; As it Is, and As it Should be. Illustrations. Post 8vo. 7s. 6d.

DRAKE'S (Sir Francis) Life, Voyages, and Exploits, by Sea and Land. By John Barrow. Post 8vo. 2s.

DRINKWATER (John). History of the Siege of Gibraltar, 1779-1783. With a Description and Account of that Garrison from the Earliest Periods. Post 8vo. 2s.

DUCANGE'S Mediæval Latin-English Dictionary. Re-arranged and Edited, in accordance with the modern Science of Philology, by Rev. E. A. Dayman and J. H. Hessels. Small 4to. [In Preparation.

DU CHAILLU (Paul B.). Equatorial Africa, with Accounts of the Gorilla, the Nest-building Ape, Chimpanzee, Crocodile, &c. Illustrations. 8vo. 21s.

——— Journey to Ashango Land; and Further Penetration into Equatorial Africa. Illustrations. 8vo. 21s.

DUFFERIN (Lord). Letters from High Latitudes; a Yacht Voyage to Iceland, Jan Mayen, and Spitzbergen. Woodcuts. Post 8vo. 7s. 6d.

——— Speeches and Addresses, Political and Literary, delivered in the House of Lords, in Canada, and elsewhere. 8vo. [In the Press.

DUNCAN (Major). History of the Royal Artillery. Compiled from the Original Records. Portraits. 2 Vols. 8vo. 18s.

——— English in Spain; or, The Story of the War of Succession, 1834-1840. Compiled from the Reports of the British Commissioners. With Illustrations. 8vo. 16s.

EASTLAKE (Sir Charles). Contributions to the Literature of the Fine Arts. With Memoir of the Author, and Selections from his Correspondence. By Lady Eastlake. 2 Vols. 8vo. 24s.

EDWARDS (W. H.). Voyage up the River Amazon, including a Visit to Para. Post 8vo. 2s.

ELDON'S (Lord) Public and Private Life, with Selections from his Diaries, &c. By Horace Twiss. Portrait. 2 Vols. Post 8vo. 21s.

ELGIN (Lord). Letters and Journals. Edited by Theodore Walrond. With Preface by Dean Stanley. 8vo. 14s.

ELLESMERE (Lord). Two Sieges of Vienna by the Turks. Translated from the German. Post 8vo. 2s.

ELLIS (W.). Madagascar Revisited. The Persecutions and Heroic Sufferings of the Native Christians. Illustrations. 8vo. 16s.

——— Memoir. By His Son. With his Character and Work. By Rev. Henry Allon, D.D. Portrait. 8vo. 10s. 6d.

——— (Robinson) Poems and Fragments of Catullus. 16mo. 5s.

ELPHINSTONE (Hon. Mountstuart). History of India—the Hindoo and Mahomedan Periods. Edited by Professor Cowell. Map. 8vo. 18s.

——— (H. W.). Patterns for Turning; Comprising Elliptical and other Figures cut on the Lathe without the use of any Ornamental Chuck. With 70 Illustrations. Small 4to. 15s.

ELTON (Capt.) and H. B. COTTERILL. Adventures and Discoveries Among the Lakes and Mountains of Eastern and Central Africa. With Map and Illustrations. 8vo. 21s.

ENGLAND. [See Arthur, Croker, Hume, Markham, Smith, and Stanhope.]

ESSAYS ON CATHEDRALS. Edited, with an Introduction. By Dean Howson. 8vo. 12s.

FERGUSSON (James). History of Architecture in all Countries from the Earliest Times. With 1,600 Illustrations. 4 Vols. Medium 8vo.
Vol. I. & II. Ancient and Mediæval. 63s.
Vol. III. Indian & Eastern. 42s. Vol. IV. Modern. 31s. 6d.
—— Rude Stone Monuments in all Countries; their Age and Uses. With 230 Illustrations. Medium 8vo. 24s.
—— Holy Sepulchre and the Temple at Jerusalem. Woodcuts. 8vo. 7s. 6d.
—— Temples of the Jews and other buildings in the Haram Area at Jerusalem. With Illustrations. 4to. 42s.
FLEMING (Professor). Student's Manual of Moral Philosophy. With Quotations and References. Post 8vo. 7s. 6d.
FLOWER GARDEN. By Rev. Thos. James. Fcap. 8vo. 1s.
FORBES (Capt. C. J. F. S.) British Burma and its People; Sketches of Native Manners, Customs, and Religion. Cr. 8vo. 10s. 6d.
FORD (Richard). Gatherings from Spain. Post 8vo. 3s. 6d.
FORSTER (John). The Early Life of Jonathan Swift. 1667-1711. With Portrait. 8vo. 15s.
FORSYTH (William). Hortensius; an Historical Essay on the Office and Duties of an Advocate. Illustrations. 8vo. 7s. 6d.
—— Novels and Novelists of the 18th Century, in Illustration of the Manners and Morals of the Age. Post 8vo. 10s. 6d.
FRANCE (History of). [See Jervis — Markham — Smith — Students'—Tocqueville.]
FRENCH IN ALGIERS; The Soldier of the Foreign Legion— and the Prisoners of Abd-el-Kadir. Translated by Lady Duff Gordon. Post 8vo. 2s.
FRERE (Sir Bartle). Indian Missions. Small 8vo. 2s. 6d.
—— Eastern Africa as a Field for Missionary Labour. With Map. Crown 8vo. 5s.
—— Bengal Famine. How it will be Met and How to Prevent Future Famines in India. With Maps. Crown 8vo. 5s.
—— (Miss M.). Old Deccan Days, or Fairy Legends current in Southern India, with Introduction by Sir Bartle Frere. Illustrations. Post 8vo. 7s. 6d.
GALTON (F.). Art of Travel; or, Hints on the Shifts and Contrivances available in Wild Countries. Woodcuts. Post 8vo. 7s. 6d.
GEOGRAPHY. [See Bunbury — Croker — Richardson — Smith -Students'.]
GEOGRAPHICAL SOCIETY'S JOURNAL. (Published Yearly.)
GEORGE (Ernest). The Mosel; a Series of Twenty Etchings, with Descriptive Letterpress. Imperial 4to. 42s.
—— Loire and South of France; a Series of Twenty Etchings, with Descriptive Text. Folio. 42s.
GERMANY (History of). [See Markham.]
GIBBON (Edward). History of the Decline and Fall of the Roman Empire. Edited by Milman, Guizot, and Dr. Wm. Smith. Maps. 8 Vols. 8vo. 60s.
—— The Student's Edition; an Epitome of the above work, incorporating the Researches of Recent Commentators. By Dr. Wm. Smith. Woodcuts. Post 8vo. 7s. 6d.
GIFFARD (Edward). Deeds of Naval Daring; or, Anecdotes of the British Navy. Fcap. 8vo. 3s. 6d.

GILL (Capt. William), R.E. The River of Golden Sand. Narrative of a Journey through China to Burmah. With a Preface by Col. H. Yule, C.B. Maps and Illustrations. 2 Vols. 8vo. 30s.

——— (Mrs.). Six Months in Ascension. An Unscientific Account of a Scientific Expedition. Map. Crown 8vo. 9s.

GLADSTONE (W. E.). Rome and the Newest Fashions in Religion. Three Tracts. 8vo. 7s. 6d.

——— Gleanings of Past Years, 1843-78. 7 vols. Small 8vo. 2s. 6d. each. I. The Throne, the Prince Consort, the Cabinet and Constitution. II. Personal and Literary. III. Historical and Speculative. IV. Foreign. V. and VI. Ecclesiastical. VII. Miscellaneous.

GLEIG (G. R.). Campaigns of the British Army at Washington and New Orleans. Post 8vo. 2s.

——— Story of the Battle of Waterloo. Post 8vo. 3s. 6d.

——— Narrative of Sale's Brigade in Affghanistan. Post 8vo. 2s.

——— Life of Lord Clive. Post 8vo. 3s. 6d.

——— Sir Thomas Munro. Post 8vo. 3s. 6d.

GLYNNE (Sir Stephen R.). Notes on the Churches of Kent: With Preface by W. H. Gladstone, M.P. Illustrations. 8vo. 12s.

GOLDSMITH'S (Oliver) Works. Edited with Notes by Peter Cunningham. Vignettes. 4 Vols. 8vo. 30s.

GOMM (Field-Marshal Sir Wm. M.), Commander-in-Chief in India, Constable of the Tower, and Colonel of the Coldstream Guards. 1784-1875. His Life, Letters, and Journals. Edited by F. C. Carr Gomm. With Portrait. 8vo.

GORDON (Sir Alex.). Sketches of German Life, and Scenes from the War of Liberation. Post 8vo. 3s. 6d.

——— (Lady Duff) Amber-Witch: A Trial for Witchcraft. Post 8vo. 2s.

——— French in Algiers. 1. The Soldier of the Foreign Legion. 2. The Prisoners of Abd-el-Kadir. Post 8vo. 2s.

GRAMMARS. [See Curtius; Hall; Hutton; King Edward; Leathes; Maetzner; Matthiæ; Smith.]

GREECE (History of). [See Grote—Smith—Students'.]

GROTE'S (George) WORKS:—

History of Greece. From the Earliest Times to the close of the generation contemporary with the Death of Alexander the Great. *Library Edition.* Portrait, Maps, and Plans. 10 Vols. 8vo. 120s. *Cabinet Edition.* Portrait and Plans. 12 Vols. Post 8vo. 6s. each.

Plato, and other Companions of Socrates. 3 Vols. 8vo. 45s.

Aristotle. With additional Essays. 8vo. 18s.

Minor Works. Portrait. 8vo. 14s.

Letters on Switzerland in 1847. 6s.

Personal Life. Portrait. 8vo. 12s.

GROTE (Mrs.). A Sketch. By Lady Eastlake. Crown 8vo. 6s.

HALL'S (T. D.) School Manual of English Grammar. With Copious Exercises. 12mo. 3s. 6d.

——— Manual of English Composition. With Copious Illustrations and Practical Exercises. 12mo. 3s. 6d.

——— Primary English Grammar for Elementary Schools. Based on the larger work. 16mo. 1s.

——— Child's First Latin Book, comprising a full Practice of Nouns, Pronouns, and Adjectives, with the Active Verbs. 16mo. 2s.

HALLAM'S (Henry) WORKS:—
    The Constitutional History of England, from the Accession of Henry the Seventh to the Death of George the Second. *Library Edition*, 3 Vols. 8vo. 30s. *Cabinet Edition*, 3 Vols. Post 8vo. 12s. *Student's Edition*, Post 8vo. 7s. 6d.
    History of Europe during the Middle Ages. *Library Edition*, 3 Vols. 8vo. 30s. *Cabinet Edition*, 3 Vols. Post 8vo. 12s. *Student's Edition*, Post 8vo. 7s. 6d.
    Literary History of Europe during the 15th, 16th, and 17th Centuries. *Library Edition*, 3 Vols. 8vo. 36s. *Cabinet Edition*, 4 Vols. Post 8vo. 16s.

HALLAM'S (Arthur) Literary Remains; in Verse and Prose. Portrait. Fcap. 8vo. 3s. 6d.

HAMILTON (Gen. Sir F. W.). History of the Grenadier Guards. From Original Documents, &c. With Illustrations. 3 Vols. 8vo. 63s.

—— (Andrew). Rheinsberg: Memorials of Frederick the Great and Prince Henry of Prussia. 2 Vols. Crown 8vo. 21s.

HART'S ARMY LIST. (*Published Quarterly and Annually.*)

HATCH (W. M.). The Moral Philosophy of Aristotle, consisting of a translation of the Nichomachean Ethics, and of the Paraphrase attributed to Andronicus, with an Introductory Analysis of each book. 8vo. 18s.

HATHERLEY (Lord). The Continuity of Scripture, as Declared by the Testimony of our Lord and of the Evangelists and Apostles. 8vo. 6s. *Popular Edition.* Post 8vo. 2s. 6d.

HAY (Sir J. H. Drummond). Western Barbary, its Wild Tribes and Savage Animals. Post 8vo. 2s.

HAYWARD (A.). Sketches of Eminent Statesmen and Writers, with other Essays. Reprinted from the "Quarterly Review," with Additions and Corrections. Contents: Thiers, Bismarck, Cavour, Metternich, Montalembert, Melbourne, Wellesley, Byron and Tennyson, Venice, St. Simon, Sevigné, Du Deffand, Holland House, Strawberry Hill. 2 Vols. 8vo. 28s.

HEAD'S (Sir Francis) WORKS:—
    The Royal Engineer. Illustrations. 8vo. 12s.
    Life of Sir John Burgoyne. Post 8vo. 1s.
    Rapid Journeys across the Pampas. Post 8vo. 2s.
    Bubbles from the Brunnen of Nassau. Illustrations. Post 8vo. 7s. 6d.
    Stokers and Pokers; or, the London and North Western Railway. Post 8vo. 2s.

HEBER'S (Bishop) Journals in India. 2 Vols. Post 8vo. 7s.

—— Poetical Works. Portrait. Fcap. 8vo. 3s. 6d.

—— Hymns adapted to the Church Service. 16mo. 1s. 6d.

HERODOTUS. A New English Version. Edited, with Notes and Essays, Historical, Ethnographical, and Geographical, by Canon Rawlinson, Sir H. Rawlinson and Sir J. G. Wilkinson. Maps and Woodcuts. 4 Vols. 8vo. 48s.

HERRIES (Rt. Hon. John). Memoir of his Public Life during the Reigns of George III. and IV., William IV., and Queen Victoria, Founded on his Letters and other Unpublished Documents. By his son, Edward Herries, C.B. 2 vols. 8vo. 24s.

HERSCHEL'S (Caroline) Memoir and Correspondence. By Mrs. John Herschel. With Portraits. Crown 8vo. 7s. 6d.

FOREIGN HANDBOOKS.

HAND-BOOK—TRAVEL-TALK. English, French, German, and Italian. 18mo. 3s. 6d.

—— HOLLAND AND BELGIUM. Map and Plans. Post 8vo. 6s.

—— NORTH GERMANY and THE RHINE,— The Black Forest, the Hartz, Thüringerwald, Saxon Switzerland, Rügen, the Giant Mountains, Taunus, Odenwald, Elass, and Lothringen. Map and Plans. Post 8vo. 10s.

—— SOUTH GERMANY,—Wurtemburg, Bavaria, Austria, Styria, Salzburg, the Alps, Tyrol, Hungary, and the Danube, from Ulm to the Black Sea. Maps and Plans. Post 8vo. 10s.

—— PAINTING. German, Flemish, and Dutch Schools. Illustrations. 2 Vols. Post 8vo. 24s.

—— LIVES AND WORKS OF EARLY FLEMISH Painters. Illustrations. Post 8vo. 7s. 6d.

—— SWITZERLAND, Alps of Savoy, and Piedmont. In Two Parts. Maps and Plans. Post 8vo. 10s.

—— FRANCE, Part I. Normandy, Brittany, the French Alps, the Loire, Seine, Garonne, and Pyrenees. Maps and Plans. Post 8vo. 7s. 6d.

—— Part II. Central France, Auvergne, the Cevennes, Burgundy, the Rhone and Saone, Provence, Nimes, Arles, Marseilles, the French Alps, Alsace, Lorraine, Champagne, &c. Maps and Plans. Post 8vo. 7s. 6d.

—— MEDITERRANEAN—its Principal Islands, Cities, Seaports, Harbours, and Border Lands. For travellers and yachtsmen. With nearly 50 Maps and Plans. Post 8vo. 20s.

—— ALGERIA AND TUNIS. Algiers, Constantine, Oran, the Atlas Range. Maps and Plans. Post 8vo. 10s.

—— PARIS, and its Environs. Maps and Plans. 16mo. 3s. 6d.

—— SPAIN, Madrid, The Castiles, The Basque Provinces, Leon, The Asturias, Galicia, Estremadura, Andalusia, Ronda, Granada, Murcia, Valencia, Catalonia, Aragon, Navarre, The Balearic Islands, &c. &c. Maps and Plans. Post 8vo. 20s.

—— PORTUGAL, Lisbon, Porto, Cintra, Mafra, &c. Map and Plan. Post 8vo. 12s.

—— NORTH ITALY, Turin, Milan, Cremona, the Italian Lakes, Bergamo, Brescia, Verona, Mantua, Vicenza, Padua, Ferrara, Bologna, Ravenna, Rimini, Piacenza, Genoa, the Riviera, Venice, Parma, Modena, and Romagna. Maps and Plans. Post 8vo. 10s.

—— CENTRAL ITALY, Florence, Lucca, Tuscany, The Marches, Umbria, &c. Maps and Plans. Post 8vo. 10s.

—— ROME AND ITS ENVIRONS. With more than 50 Maps and Plans. Post 8vo.

—— SOUTH ITALY, Naples, Pompeii, Herculaneum, and Vesuvius. Maps and Plans. Post 8vo. 10s.

—— PAINTING. The Italian Schools. Illustrations. 2 Vols. Post 8vo. 30s.

—— LIVES OF ITALIAN PAINTERS, FROM CIMABUE to BASSANO. By Mrs. JAMESON. Portraits. Post 8vo. 12s.

—— NORWAY, Christiania, Bergen, Trondhjem. The Fjelds and Fjords. Maps and Plans. Post 8vo. 9s.

—— SWEDEN, Stockholm, Upsala, Gothenburg, the Shores of the Baltic, &c. Maps and Plan. Post 8vo. 6s.

HANDBOOK—DENMARK, Sleswig, Holstein, Copenhagen, Jutland, Iceland. Maps and Plans. Post 8vo. 6s.
────── RUSSIA, St. Petersburg, Moscow, Poland, and Finland. Maps and Plans. Post 8vo. 18s.
────── GREECE, the Ionian Islands, Continental Greece, Athens, the Peloponnesus, the Islands of the Ægean Sea, Albania, Thessaly, and Macedonia. Maps, Plans, and Views. Post 8vo. 15s.
────── TURKEY IN ASIA—Constantinople, the Bosphorus, Dardanelles, Broussa, Plain of Troy, Crete, Cyprus, Smyrna, Ephesus, the Seven Churches, Coasts of the Black Sea, Armenia, Euphrates Valley, Route to India, &c. Maps and Plans. Post 8vo. 15s.
────── EGYPT, including Descriptions of the Course of the Nile through Egypt and Nubia, Alexandria, Cairo, and Thebes, the Suez Canal, the Pyramids, the Peninsula of Sinai, the Oases, the Fyoom, &c. In Two Parts. Maps and Plans. Post 8vo. 15s.
────── HOLY LAND—Syria, Palestine, Peninsula of Sinai, Edom, Syrian Deserts, Petra, Damascus; and Palmyra. Maps and Plans. Post 8vo. 20s. *,* Travelling Map of Palestine. In a case. 12s.
────── INDIA. Maps and Plans. Post 8vo. Part I. Bombay, 15s. Part II. Madras, 15s. Part III. Bengal.

ENGLISH HAND-BOOKS.

HAND-BOOK—ENGLAND AND WALES. An Alphabetical Hand-Book. Condensed into One Volume for the Use of Travellers. With a Map. Post 8vo. 10s.
────── MODERN LONDON. Maps and Plans. 16mo. 3s. 6d.
────── ENVIRONS OF LONDON within a circuit of 20 miles. 2 Vols. Crown 8vo. 21s.
────── ST. PAUL'S CATHEDRAL. 20 Illustrations. Crown 8vo. 10s. 6d.
────── EASTERN COUNTIES, Chelmsford, Harwich, Colchester, Maldon, Cambridge, Ely, Newmarket, Bury St. Edmunds, Ipswich, Woodbridge, Felixstowe, Lowestoft, Norwich, Yarmouth, Cromer, &c. Map and Plans. Post 8vo. 12s.
────── CATHEDRALS of Oxford, Peterborough, Norwich, Ely, and Lincoln. With 90 Illustrations. Crown 8vo. 18s.
────── KENT, Canterbury, Dover, Ramsgate, Sheerness, Rochester, Chatham, Woolwich. Maps and Plans. Post 8vo. 7s. 6d.
────── SUSSEX, Brighton, Chichester, Worthing, Hastings, Lewes, Arundel, &c. Maps and Plans. Post 8vo. 6s.
────── SURREY AND HANTS, Kingston, Croydon, Reigate, Guildford, Dorking, Boxhill, Winchester, Southampton, New Forest, Portsmouth, Isle of Wight, &c. Maps and Plans. Post 8vo. 10s.
────── BERKS, BUCKS, AND OXON, Windsor, Eton, Reading, Aylesbury. Uxbridge, Wycombe, Henley, the City and University of Oxford, Blenheim, and the Descent of the Thames. Maps and Plans. Post 8vo.
────── WILTS, DORSET, AND SOMERSET, Salisbury, Chippenham, Weymouth, Sherborne, Wells, Bath, Bristol, Taunton, &c. Map. Post 8vo. 10s.
────── DEVON, Exeter, Ilfracombe, Linton, Sidmouth, Dawlish, Teignmouth, Plymouth, Devonport, Torquay. Maps and Plans. Post 8vo. 7s. 6d.

LIST OF WORKS

HAND-BOOK—CORNWALL, Launceston, Penzance, Falmouth, the Lizard, Land's End, &c. Maps. Post 8vo. 6s.

——————CATHEDRALS of Winchester, Salisbury, Exeter, Wells, Chichester, Rochester, Canterbury, and St. Albans. With 130 Illustrations. 2 Vols. Cr. 8vo. 36s. St. Albans separately, cr. 8vo. 6s.

——————GLOUCESTER, HEREFORD, AND WORCESTER, Cirencester, Cheltenham, Stroud, Tewkesbury, Leominster, Ross, Malvern, Kidderminster, Dudley, Bromsgrove, Evesham. Map. Post 8vo.

——————CATHEDRALS of Bristol, Gloucester, Hereford, Worcester, and Lichfield. With 50 Illustrations. Crown 8vo. 16s.

——————NORTH WALES, Bangor, Carnarvon, Beaumaris, Snowdon, Llanberis, Dolgelly, Cader Idris, Conway, &c. Map. Post 8vo. 7s.

——————SOUTH WALES, Monmouth, Llandaff, Merthyr, Vale of Neath, Pembroke, Carmarthen, Tenby, Swansea, The Wye, &c. Map. Post 8vo. 7s.

——————CATHEDRALS OF BANGOR, ST. ASAPH, Llandaff, and St. David's. With Illustrations. Post 8vo. 15s.

——————NORTHAMPTONSHIRE AND RUTLAND—Northampton, Peterborough, Towcester, Daventry, Market Harborough, Kettering, Wallingborough, Thrapston, Stamford, Uppingham, Oakham. Maps. Post 8vo. 7s. 6d.

——————DERBY, NOTTS, LEICESTER, STAFFORD, Matlock, Bakewell, Chatsworth, The Peak, Buxton, Hardwick, Dove Dale, Ashborne, Southwell, Mansfield, Retford, Burton, Belvoir, Melton Mowbray, Wolverhampton, Lichfield, Walsall, Tamworth. Map. Post 8vo. 9s.

——————SHROPSHIRE AND CHESHIRE, Shrewsbury, Ludlow, Bridgnorth, Oswestry, Chester, Crewe, Alderley, Stockport, Birkenhead. Maps and Plans. Post 8vo. 6s.

——————LANCASHIRE, Warrington, Bury, Manchester, Liverpool, Burnley, Clitheroe, Bolton, Blackburn, Wigan, Preston, Rochdale, Lancaster, Southport, Blackpool, &c. Maps and Plans. Post 8vo. 7s. 6d.

——————YORKSHIRE, Doncaster, Hull, Selby, Beverley, Scarborough, Whitby, Harrogate, Ripon, Leeds, Wakefield, Bradford, Halifax, Huddersfield, Sheffield. Map and Plans. Post 8vo. 12s.

——————CATHEDRALS of York, Ripon, Durham, Carlisle, Chester, and Manchester. With 60 Illustrations. 2 Vols. Cr. 8vo. 21s.

——————DURHAM AND NORTHUMBERLAND, Newcastle, Darlington, Gateshead, Bishop Auckland, Stockton, Hartlepool, Sunderland, Shields, Berwick-on-Tweed, Morpeth, Tynemouth, Coldstream, Alnwick, &c. Map. Post 8vo. 9s.

——————WESTMORLAND AND CUMBERLAND—Lancaster, Furness Abbey, Ambleside, Kendal, Windermere, Coniston, Keswick, Grasmere, Ulswater, Carlisle, Cockermouth, Penrith, Appleby. Map. Post 8vo.

*** MURRAY'S MAP OF THE LAKE DISTRICT, on canvas. 3s. 6d.

——————SCOTLAND, Edinburgh, Melrose, Kelso, Glasgow, Dumfries, Ayr, Stirling, Arran, The Clyde, Oban, Inverary, Loch Lomond, Loch Katrine and Trossachs, Caledonian Canal, Inverness, Perth, Dundee, Aberdeen, Braemar, Skye, Caithness, Ross, Sutherland, &c. Maps and Plans. Post 8vo. 9s.

——————IRELAND, Dublin, Belfast, the Giant's Causeway, Donegal, Galway, Wexford, Cork, Limerick, Waterford, Killarney, Bantry, Glengariff, &c. Maps and Plans. Post 8vo. 10s.

PUBLISHED BY MR. MURRAY. 17

HOME AND COLONIAL LIBRARY. A Series of Works adapted for all circles and classes of Readers, having been selected for their acknowledged interest, and ability of the Authors. Post 8vo. Published at 2s. and 3s. 6d. each, and arranged under two distinctive heads as follows:—

CLASS A.
HISTORY, BIOGRAPHY, AND HISTORIC TALES.

1. SIEGE OF GIBRALTAR. By JOHN DRINKWATER. 2s.
2. THE AMBER-WITCH. By LADY DUFF GORDON. 2s.
3. CROMWELL AND BUNYAN. By ROBERT SOUTHEY. 2s.
4. LIFE OF SIR FRANCIS DRAKE. By JOHN BARROW. 2s.
5. CAMPAIGNS AT WASHINGTON. By REV. G. R. GLEIG. 2s.
6. THE FRENCH IN ALGIERS. By LADY DUFF GORDON. 2s.
7. THE FALL OF THE JESUITS. 2s.
8. LIVONIAN TALES. 2s.
9. LIFE OF CONDÉ. By LORD MAHON. 3s. 6d.
10. SALE'S BRIGADE. By REV. G. R. GLEIG. 2s.
11. THE SIEGES OF VIENNA. By LORD ELLESMERE. 2s.
12. THE WAYSIDE CROSS. By CAPT. MILMAN. 2s.
13. SKETCHES OF GERMAN LIFE. By SIR A. GORDON. 3s. 6d.
14. THE BATTLE OF WATERLOO. By REV. G. R. GLEIG. 3s. 6d.
15. AUTOBIOGRAPHY OF STEFFENS. 2s.
16. THE BRITISH POETS. By THOMAS CAMPBELL. 3s. 6d.
17. HISTORICAL ESSAYS. By LORD MAHON. 3s. 6d.
18. LIFE OF LORD CLIVE. By REV. G. R. GLEIG. 3s. 6d.
19. NORTH-WESTERN RAILWAY. By SIR F. B. HEAD. 2s.
20. LIFE OF MUNRO. By REV. G. R. GLEIG. 3s. 6d.

CLASS B.
VOYAGES, TRAVELS, AND ADVENTURES.

1. BIBLE IN SPAIN. By GEORGE BORROW. 3s. 6d.
2. GYPSIES OF SPAIN. By GEORGE BORROW. 3s. 6d.
3 & 4. JOURNALS IN INDIA. By BISHOP HEBER. 2 Vols. 7s.
5. TRAVELS IN THE HOLY LAND. By IRBY and MANGLES. 2s.
6. MOROCCO AND THE MOORS. By J. DRUMMOND HAY. 2s.
7. LETTERS FROM THE BALTIC. By A LADY.
8. NEW SOUTH WALES. By MRS. MEREDITH. 2s.
9. THE WEST INDIES. By M. G. LEWIS. 2s.
10. SKETCHES OF PERSIA. By SIR JOHN MALCOLM. 3s. 6d.
11. MEMOIRS OF FATHER RIPA. 2s.
12 & 13. TYPEE AND OMOO. By HERMANN MELVILLE. 2 Vols. 7s.
14. MISSIONARY LIFE IN CANADA. By REV. J. ABBOTT. 2s.
15. LETTERS FROM MADRAS. By A LADY. 2s.
16. HIGHLAND SPORTS. By CHARLES ST. JOHN. 3s. 6d.
17. PAMPAS JOURNEYS. By SIR F. B. HEAD. 2s.
18. GATHERINGS FROM SPAIN. By RICHARD FORD. 3s. 6d.
19. THE RIVER AMAZON. By W. H. EDWARDS. 2s.
20. MANNERS & CUSTOMS OF INDIA. By REV. C. ACLAND. 2s.
21. ADVENTURES IN MEXICO. By G. F. RUXTON. 3s. 6d.
22. PORTUGAL AND GALICIA. By LORD CARNARVON. 3s. 6d.
23. BUSH LIFE IN AUSTRALIA. By REV. H. W. HAYGARTH. 2s.
24. THE LIBYAN DESERT. By BAYLE ST. JOHN. 2s.
25. SIERRA LEONE. By A LADY. 3s. 6d.

*** Each work may be had separately.

HOLLWAY (J. G.). A Month in Norway. Fcap. 8vo. 2s.
HONEY BEE. By Rev. Thomas James. Fcap. 8vo. 1s.
HOOK (Dean). Church Dictionary. 8vo. 16s.
—— (Theodore) Life. By J. G. Lockhart. Fcap. 8vo. 1s.
HOPE (A. J. Beresford). Worship in the Church of England. 8vo. 9s., or, *Popular Selections from.* 8vo. 2s. 6d.
HORACE; a New Edition c. the Text. Edited by Dean Milman. With 100 Woodcuts. Crown 8vo. 7s. 6d.
HOUGHTON'S (Lord) Monographs, Personal and Social. With Portraits. Crown 8vo. 10s. 6d.
—— Poetical Works. *Collected Edition.* With Portrait. 2 Vols. Fcap. 8vo. 12s.
HOUSTOUN (Mrs.). Twenty Years in the Wild West of Ireland, or Life in Connaught. Post 8vo. 9s.
HUME (The Student's). A History of England, from the Invasion of Julius Cæsar to the Revolution of 1688. New Edition, revised, corrected, and continued to the Treaty of Berlin, 1878. By J. S. Brewer, M.A. With 7 Coloured Maps & 70 Woodcuts. Post 8vo. 7s. 6d.
HUTCHINSON (Gen.). Dog Breaking, with Odds and Ends for those who love the Dog and the Gun. With 40 Illustrations. Crown 8vo. 7s. 6d.
HUTTON (H. E.). Principia Græca; an Introduction to the Study of Greek. Comprehending Grammar, Delectus, and Exercise-book, with Vocabularies. *Sixth Edition.* 12mo. 3s. 6d.
HYMNOLOGY, Dictionary of. See Julian.
INDIA in 1880. By Sir Richard Temple, Bart. With 2 Maps. 8vo. 16s.
IRBY AND MANGLES' Travels in Egypt, Nubia, Syria, and the Holy Land. Post 8vo. 2s.
JAMESON (Mrs.). Lives of the Early Italian Painters— and the Progress of Painting in Italy—Cimabue to Bassano. With 50 Portraits. Post 8vo. 12s.
JAPAN. See Bird, Mossman, Mounsey, Reed.
JENNINGS (Louis J.). Field Paths and Green Lanes in Surrey and Sussex. Illustrations. Post 8vo. 10s. 6d.
—— Rambles among the Hills in the Peak of Derbyshire and on the South Downs. With sketches of people by the way. With 23 Illustrations. Post 8vo. 12s.
JERVIS (Rev. W. H.). The Gallican Church, from the Concordat of Bologna, 1516, to the Revolution. With an Introduction. Portraits. 2 Vols. 8vo. 28s.
JESSE (Edward). Gleanings in Natural History. Fcp. 8vo. 3s. 6d.
JEX-BLAKE (Rev. T. W.). Life in Faith: Sermons Preached at Cheltenham and Rugby. Fcap. 8vo. 3s. 6d.
JOHNSON'S (Dr. Samuel) Life. By James Boswell. Including the Tour to the Hebrides. Edited by Mr. Croker. 1 vol. Royal 8vo. 12s. *New Edition.* Portraits. 4 Vols. 8vo. (*In Preparation.*
JULIAN (Rev. John J.). A Dictionary of Hymnology. A Companion to Existing Hymn Books. Setting forth the Origin and History of the Hymns contained in the Principal Hymnals used by the Churches of England, Scotland, and Ireland, and various Dissenting Bodies, with Notices of their Authors. Post 8vo. [*In the Press.*
JUNIUS' Handwriting Professionally investigated. By Mr. Chabot, Expert. With Preface and Collateral Evidence, by the Hon. Edward Twisleton. With Facsimiles, Woodcuts, &c. 4to. £3 3s.

KERR (ROBERT). Small Country House. A Brief Practical Discourse on the Planning of a Residence from 2000l. to 5000l. With Supplementary Estimates to 7000l. Post 8vo. 3s.

——— Ancient Lights; a Book for Architects, Surveyors, Lawyers, and Landlords. 8vo. 5s. 6d.

——— (R. MALCOLM). Student's Blackstone. A Systematic Abridgment of the entire Commentaries, adapted to the present state of the law. Post 8vo. 7s. 6d.

KING EDWARD VITH's Latin Grammar. 12mo. 3s. 6d.

——— First Latin Book. 12mo. 2s. 6d.

KING (R. J.). Archæology, Travel and Art; being Sketches and Studies, Historical and Descriptive. 8vo. 12s.

KIRK (J. FOSTER). History of Charles the Bold, Duke of Burgundy. Portrait. 3 Vols. 8vo. 45s.

KIRKES' Handbook of Physiology. Edited by W. MORRANT BAKER, F.R.C.S. With 400 Illustrations. Post 8vo. 14s.

KUGLER'S Handbook of Painting.—The Italian Schools. Revised and Remodelled from the most recent Researches. By LADY EASTLAKE. With 140 Illustrations. 2 Vols. Crown 8vo. 30s.

——— Handbook of Painting.—The German, Flemish, and Dutch Schools. Revised and in part re-written. By J. A. CROWE. With 60 Illustrations. 2 Vols. Crown 8vo. 24s.

LANE (E. W.). Account of the Manners and Customs of Modern Egyptians. With Illustrations. 2 Vols. Post 8vo. 12s.

LAWRENCE (SIR GEO.). Reminiscences of Forty-three Years' Service in India; including Captivities in Cabul among the Affghans and among the Sikhs, and a Narrative of the Mutiny in Rajputana. Crown 8vo. 10s. 6d.

LAYARD (A. H.). Nineveh and its Remains; a Narrative of Researches and Discoveries amidst the Ruins of Assyria. With an Account of the Chaldean Christians of Kurdistan; the Yezedis, or Devil-worshippers; and an Enquiry into the Manners and Arts of the Ancient Assyrians. Plates and Woodcuts. 2 Vols. 8vo. 36s.

*** A POPULAR EDITION of the above work. With Illustrations. Post 8vo. 7s. 6d.

——— Nineveh and Babylon; the Narrative of Discoveries in the Ruins, with Travels in Armenia, Kurdistan and the Desert, during a Second Expedition to Assyria. With Map and Plates. 8vo. 21s.

*** A POPULAR EDITION of the above work. With Illustrations. Post 8vo. 7s. 6d.

LEATHES' (STANLEY). Practical Hebrew Grammar. With the Hebrew Text of Genesis i.—vi., and Psalms i.—vi. Grammatical Analysis and Vocabulary. Post 8vo. 7s. 6d.

LENNEP (REV. H. J. VAN). Missionary Travels in Asia Minor. With Illustrations of Biblical History and Archæology. With Map and Woodcuts. 2 Vols. Post 8vo. 21s.

——— Modern Customs and Manners of Bible Lands in Illustration of Scripture. With Coloured Maps and 300 Illustrations. 2 Vols. 8vo. 21s.

LESLIE (C. R.). Handbook for Young Painters. With Illustrations. Post 8vo. 7s. 6d.

——— Life and Works of Sir Joshua Reynolds. Portraits and Illustrations. 2 Vols. 8vo. 42s.

LETO (POMPONIO). Eight Months at Rome during the Vatican Council. With a daily account of the proceedings. Translated from the original. 8vo. 12s.

c 2

LETTERS From the Baltic. By a Lady. Post 8vo. 2s.
——— Madras. By a Lady. Post 8vo. 2s.
——— Sierra Leone. By a Lady. Post 8vo. 3s. 6d.
LEVI (Leone). History of British Commerce: and Economic Progress of the Nation, from 1763 to 1878. 8vo. 18s.
LEX SALICA; the Ten Texts with the Glosses and the Lex Emendata. Synoptically edited by J. H. Hessels. With Notes on the Frankish Words in the Lex Salica by H. Kern, of Leyden. 4to. 42s.
LIDDELL (Dean). Student's History of Rome, from the earliest Times to the establishment of the Empire. Woodcuts. Post 8vo. 7s. 6d.
LISPINGS from LOW LATITUDES; or, the Journal of the Hon. Impulsia Gushington. Edited by Lord Dufferin. With 24 Plates. 4to. 21s.
LIVINGSTONE (Dr.). Popular Account of his First Expedition to Africa, 1840-56. Illustrations. Post 8vo. 7s. 6d.
——— Second Expedition to Africa, 1858-64. Illustrations. Post 8vo. 7s. 6d.
——— Last Journals in Central Africa, from 1865 to his Death. Continued by a Narrative of his last moments and sufferings. By Rev. Horace Waller. Maps and Illustrations. 2 Vols. 8vo. 15s.
——— Memoirs of his Personal Life. From his unpublished Journals and Correspondence. By Wm. G. Blaikie, D.D. With Map and Portrait. 8vo. 15s.
LIVINGSTONIA. Journal of Adventures in Exploring Lake Nyassa, and Establishing a Missionary Settlement there. By E. D. Young, R.N. Maps. Post 8vo. 7s. 6d.
LIVONIAN TALES. By the Author of "Letters from the Baltic." Post 8vo. 2s.
LOCKHART (J. G.). Ancient Spanish Ballads. Historical and Romantic. Translated, with Notes. Illustrations. Crown 8vo. 5s.
——— Life of Theodore Hook. Fcap. 8vo. 1s.
LOUDON (Mrs.). Gardening for Ladies. With Directions and Calendar of Operations for Every Month. Woodcuts. Fcap. 8vo. 3s. 6d.
LYELL (Sir Charles). Principles of Geology; or, the Modern Changes of the Earth and its Inhabitants considered as illustrative of Geology. With Illustrations. 2 Vols. 8vo. 32s.
——— Student's Elements of Geology. With Table of British Fossils and 600 Illustrations. Third Edition, Revised. Post 8vo. 9s.
——— Geological Evidences of the Antiquity of Man, including an Outline of Glacial Post-Tertiary Geology, and Remarks on the Origin of Species. Illustrations. 8vo. 14s.
——— (K. M.). Geographical Handbook of Ferns. With Tables to show their Distribution. Post 8vo. 7s. 6d.
LYTTON (Lord). A Memoir of Julian Fane. With Portrait. Post 8vo. 5s
McCLINTOCK (Sir L.). Narrative of the Discovery of the Fate of Sir John Franklin and his Companions in the Arctic Seas. With Illustrations. Post 8vo. 7s. 6d.
MACDOUGALL (Col.). Modern Warfare as Influenced by Modern Artillery. With Plans. Post 8vo. 12s.
MACGREGOR (J.). Rob Roy on the Jordan, Nile, Red Sea, Gennesareth, &c. A Canoe Cruise in Palestine and Egypt and the Waters of Damascus. With Map and 70 Illustrations. Crown 8vo. 7s. 6d.
MAETZNER'S English Grammar. A Methodical, Analytical, and Historical Treatise on the Orthography, Prosody, Inflections, and Syntax. By Clair J. Grece, LL.D. 3 Vols. 8vo. 36s.

MAHON (Lord), see STANHOPE.
MAINE (Sir H. Sumner). Ancient Law: its Connection with the Early History of Society, and its Relation to Modern Ideas. 8vo. 12s.
———— Village Communities in the East and West. 8vo. 12s.
———— Early History of Institutions. 8vo. 12s.
MALCOLM (Sir John). Sketches of Persia. Post 8vo. 3s. 6d.
MANSEL (Dean). Limits of Religious Thought Examined. Post 8vo. 8s. 6d.
———— Letters, Lectures, and Reviews. 8vo. 12s.
MANUAL OF SCIENTIFIC ENQUIRY. For the Use of Travellers. Edited by Rev. R. Main. Post 8vo. 3s. 6d. (Published by order of the Lords of the Admiralty.)
MARCO POLO. The Book of Ser Marco Polo, the Venetian. Concerning the Kingdoms and Marvels of the East. A new English Version. Illustrated by the light of Oriental Writers and Modern Travels. By Col. Henry Yule. Maps and Illustrations. 2 Vols. Medium 8vo. 63s.
MARKHAM (Mrs.). History of England. From the First Invasion by the Romans. Woodcuts. 12mo. 3s. 6d.
———— History of France. From the Conquest by the Gauls. Woodcuts. 12mo. 3s. 6d.
———— History of Germany. From the Invasion by Marius. Woodcuts. 12mo. 3s. 6d.
———— (Clements R.). A Popular Account of Peruvian Bark and its introduction into British India. With Maps. Post 8vo. 14s.
MARRYAT (Joseph). History of Modern and Mediæval Pottery and Porcelain. With a Description of the Manufacture. Plates and Woodcuts. 8vo. 42s.
MARSH (G. P.). Student's Manual of the English Language. Edited with Additions. By Dr. Wm. Smith. Post 8vo. 7s. 6d.
MASTERS in English Theology. The King's College Lectures, 1877. Hooker, by Canon Barry; Andrews, by Dean Church; Chillingworth, by Prof. Plumptre; Whichcote and Smith, by Canon Westcott; Jeremy Taylor, by Canon Farrar; Pearson, by Archdeacon Cheetham. With Introduction by Canon Barry. Post 8vo. 7s. 6d.
MATTHIÆ'S Greek Grammar. Abridged by Blomfield. Revised by E. S. Crooke. 12mo. 4s.
MAUREL'S Character, Actions, and Writings of Wellington. Fcap. 8vo. 1s. 6d.
MAYO (Lord). Sport in Abyssinia; or, the Mareb and Tackazzee. With Illustrations. Crown 8vo. 12s.
MEADE (Hon. Herbert). Ride through the Disturbed Districts of New Zealand, with a Cruise among the South Sea Islands. With Illustrations. Medium 8vo. 12s.
MELVILLE (Hermann). Marquesas and South Sea Islands. 2 Vols. Post 8vo. 7s.
MEREDITH (Mrs. Charles). Notes and Sketches of New South Wales. Post 8vo. 2s.
MICHAEL ANGELO, Sculptor, Painter, and Architect. His Life and Works. By C. Heath Wilson. Illustrations. Royal 8vo. 26s.
MIDDLETON (Chas. H.) A Descriptive Catalogue of the Etched Work of Rembrandt, with Life and Introductions. With Explanatory Cuts. Medium 8vo. 31s. 6d.

MILLINGTON (Rev. T. S.). Signs and Wonders in the Land of Ham, or the Ten Plagues of Egypt. With Ancient and Modern Illustrations. Woodcuts. Post 8vo. 7s. 6d.

MILMAN'S (Dean) WORKS:—
HISTORY OF THE JEWS, from the earliest Period down to Modern Times. 3 Vols. Post 8vo. 18s.
EARLY CHRISTIANITY, from the Birth of Christ to the Abolition of Paganism in the Roman Empire. 3 Vols. Post 8vo. 18s.
LATIN CHRISTIANITY, including that of the Popes to the Pontificate of Nicholas V. 9 Vols. Post 8vo. 54s.
HANDBOOK TO ST. PAUL'S CATHEDRAL. Woodcuts. Crown 8vo. 10s. 6d.
QUINTI HORATII FLACCI OPERA. Woodcuts. Sm. 8vo. 7s. 6d.
FALL OF JERUSALEM. Fcap. 8vo. 1s.
——— (Capt. E. A.) Wayside Cross. Post 8vo. 2s.
——— (Bishop, D.D.,) late Metropolitan of India. His Life. With a Selection from his Correspondence and Journals. By his Sister. Map. 8vo. 12s.

MIVART (St. George). Lessons from Nature; as manifested in Mind and Matter. 8vo. 15s.
——— The Cat. An Introduction to the Study of Backboned Animals, especially Mammals. With numerous Illustrations. 8vo.

MOORE (Thomas). Life and Letters of Lord Byron. *Cabinet Edition.* With Plates. 6 Vols. Fcap. 8vo. 18s.; *Popular Edition*, with Portraits. Royal 8vo. 7s. 6d.

MORESBY (Capt.), R.N. Discoveries in New Guinea, Polynesia, Torres Straits, &c., during the cruise of H.M.S. Basilisk. Map and Illustrations. 8vo. 15s.

MOSSMAN (Samuel). New Japan; the Land of the Rising Sun; its Annals during the past Twenty Years, recording the remarkable Progress of the Japanese in Western Civilisation. With Map. 8vo. 15s.

MOTLEY (J. L.). History of the United Netherlands: from the Death of William the Silent to the Twelve Years' Truce, 1609. Portraits. 4 Vols. Post 8vo. 6s. each.
——— Life and Death of John of Barneveld, Advocate of Holland. With a View of the Primary Causes and Movements of the Thirty Years' War. Illustrations. 2 Vols. Post 8vo. 12s.

MOZLEY (Canon). Treatise on the Augustinian doctrine of Predestination. Crown 8vo. 9s.

MUIRHEAD (Jas.). The Vaux-de-Vire of Maistre Jean Le Houx, Advocate of Vire. Translated and Edited. With Portrait and Illustrations. 8vo. 21s.

MUNRO'S (General) Life and Letters. By Rev. G. R. Gleig. Post 8vo. 3s. 6d.

MURCHISON (Sir Roderick). Siluria; or, a History of the Oldest rocks containing Organic Remains. Map and Plates. 8vo. 18s.
——— Memoirs. With Notices of his Contemporaries, and Rise and Progress of Palæozoic Geology. By Archibald Geikie. Portraits. 2 Vols. 8vo. 30s.

MURRAY (A. S.). A History of Greek Sculpture, from the Earliest Times down to the Age of Pheidias. With Illustrations. Roy. 8vo. 21s.

MUSTERS' (Capt.) Patagonians; a Year's Wanderings over Untrodden Ground from the Straits of Magellan to the Rio Negro. Illustrations. Post 8vo. 7s. 6d.

NAPIER (Sir Wm.). English Battles and Sieges of the Peninsular War. Portrait. Post 8vo. 9s.

NAPOLEON AT FONTAINEBLEAU AND ELBA. Journal of Occurrences and Notes of Conversations. By Sir Neil Campbell. Portrait. 8vo. 15s.

NARES (Sir George), R.N. Official Report to the Admiralty of the recent Arctic Expedition. Map. 8vo. 2s. 6d.

NASMYTH AND CARPENTER. The Moon. Considered as a Planet, a World, and a Satellite. With Illustrations from Drawings made with the aid of Powerful Telescopes, Woodcuts, &c. 4to. 30s.

NAUTICAL ALMANAC (The). (*By Authority.*) 2s. 6d.

NAVY LIST. (Monthly and Quarterly.) Post 8vo.

NEW TESTAMENT. With Short Explanatory Commentary. By Archdeacon Churton, M.A., and the Bishop of St. David's. With 110 authentic Views, &c. 2 Vols. Crown 8vo. 21s. bound.

NEWTH (Samuel). First Book of Natural Philosophy; an Introduction to the Study of Statics, Dynamics, Hydrostatics, Light, Heat, and Sound, with numerous Examples. Small 8vo. 3s. 6d.

———— Elements of Mechanics, including Hydrostatics, with numerous Examples. Small 8vo. 8s. 6d.

———— Mathematical Examples. A Graduated Series of Elementary Examples in Arithmetic, Algebra, Logarithms, Trigonometry, and Mechanics. Small 8vo. 8s. 6d.

NICOLAS (Sir Harris). Historic Peerage of England. Exhibiting the Origin, Descent, and Present State of every Title of Peerage which has existed in this Country since the Conquest. By William Courthope. 8vo. 30s.

NILE GLEANINGS. See Stuart.

NIMROD, On the Chace—Turf—and Road. With Portrait and Plates. Crown 8vo. 5s. Or with Coloured Plates, 7s. 6d.

NORDHOFF (Chas.). Communistic Societies of the United States; including Detailed Accounts of the Shakers, The Amana, Oneida, Bethell, Aurora, Icarian and other existing Societies; with Particulars of their Religious Creeds, Industries, and Present Condition. With 40 Illustrations. 8vo. 15s.

NORTHCOTE'S (Sir John) Notebook in the Long Parliament. Containing Proceedings during its First Session, 1640. Edited, with a Memoir, by A. H. A. Hamilton. Crown 8vo. 9s.

OWEN (Lieut.-Col.). Principles and Practice of Modern Artillery, including Artillery Material, Gunnery, and Organisation and Use of Artillery in Warfare. With Illustrations. 8vo. 15s.

OXENHAM (Rev. W.). English Notes for Latin Elegiacs; designed for early Proficients in the Art of Latin Versification, with Prefatory Rules of Composition in Elegiac Metre. 12mo. 3s. 6d.

PAGET (Lord George). Extracts from the Diary of a Cavalry Officer during the Crimean War. Crown 8vo.

PALGRAVE (R. H. I.). Local Taxation of Great Britain and Ireland. 8vo. 5s.

PALLISER (Mrs.). Mottoes for Monuments, or Epitaphs selected General Use and Study. With Illustrations. Crown 8vo. 7s. 6d.

PARIS (Dr.) Philosophy in Sport made Science in Earnest; or, the First Principles of Natural Philosophy inculcated by aid of the Toys and Sports of Youth. Woodcuts. Post 8vo. 7s. 6d.

PARKYNS' (Mansfield) Three Years' Residence in Abyssinia: with Travels in that Country. With Illustrations. Post 8vo. 7s. 6d.

PEEL'S (Sir Robert) Memoirs. 2 Vols. Post 8vo. 15s.

PENN (Richard). Maxims and Hints for an Angler and Chessplayer. Woodcuts. Fcap. 8vo. 1s.

PERCY (JOHN, M.D.). METALLURGY. Fuel, Wood, Peat, Coal, Charcoal, Coke, Fire-Clays. Illustrations. 8vo. 30s.
—— Lead, including part of Silver. Illustrations. 8vo. 30s.
—— Silver and Gold. Part I. Illustrations. 8vo. 30s.
PERRY (REV. CANON). Life of St. Hugh of Avalon, Bishop of Lincoln. Post 8vo. 10s. 6d.
—— History of the English Church. See STUDENTS' MANUALS.
PHILLIPS (JOHN). Geology of Yorkshire, The Coast, and Limestone District. Plates. 2 Vols. 4to. 31s. 6d. each.
—— (SAMUEL). Literary Essays from "The Times." With Portrait. 2 Vols. Fcap. 8vo. 7s.
POPE'S (ALEXANDER) Works. With Introductions and Notes, by REV. WHITWELL ELWIN. Vols. I., II., VI., VII., VIII. With Portraits. 8vo. 10s. 6d. each.
PORTER (REV. J. L.). Damascus, Palmyra, and Lebanon. With Travels among the Giant Cities of Bashan and the Hauran. Map and Woodcuts. Post 8vo. 7s. 6d.
PRAYER-BOOK (ILLUSTRATED), with Borders, Initials, Vignettes, &c. Edited, with Notes, by REV. THOS. JAMES. Medium 8vo. 18s. cloth; 31s. 6d. calf; 36s. morocco.
—— (THE CONVOCATION), with altered rubrics, showing the book if amended in conformity with the recommendations of the Convocations of Canterbury and York in 1879. Post 8vo. 5s.
PRINCESS CHARLOTTE OF WALES. A Brief Memoir. With Selections from her Correspondence and other unpublished Papers. By LADY ROSE WEIGALL. With Portrait. 8vo. 8s. 6d.
PRIVY COUNCIL JUDGMENTS in Ecclesiastical Cases relating to Doctrine and Discipline. With Historical Introduction, by G. C. BRODRICK and W. H. FREMANTLE. 8vo. 10s. 6d.
PSALMS OF DAVID. With Notes Explanatory and Critical by the Dean of Wells, Canon Elliott, and Canon Cook. Medium 8vo. 10s. 6d.
PUSS IN BOOTS. With 12 Illustrations. By OTTO SPECKTER. 16mo. 1s. 6d. Or coloured, 2s. 6d.
QUARTERLY REVIEW (THE). 8vo. 6s.
RAE (EDWARD). Country of the Moors. A Journey from Tripoli in Barbary to the Holy City of Kairwan. Map and Etchings. Crown 8vo. 12s.
RAMBLES in the Syrian Deserts. Post 8vo. 10s. 6d.
RASSAM (HORMUZD). British Mission to Abyssinia. With Notices of the Countries from Massowah to Magdala. Illustrations. 2 Vols. 8vo. 28s.
RAWLINSON'S (CANON) Herodotus. A New English Version. Edited with Notes and Essays. Maps and Woodcut. 4 Vols. 8vo. 48s.
—— Five Great Monarchies of Chaldæa, Assyria, Media, Babylonia, and Persia. With Maps and Illustrations. 3 Vols. 8vo. 42s.
—— (SIR HENRY) England and Russia in the East; a Series of Papers on the Political and Geographical Condition of Central Asia. Map. 8vo. 12s.
REED (Sir E. J.) Iron-Clad Ships; their Qualities, Performances, and Cost. With Chapters on Turret Ships, Iron-Clad Rams, &c. With Illustrations. 8vo. 12s.
—— Letters from Russia in 1875. 8vo. 5s.
—— Japan: Its History, Traditions, and Religions. With Narrative of a Visit in 1879. Illustrations. 2 Vols. 8vo. 28s.
REJECTED ADDRESSES (THE). By JAMES AND HORACE SMITH. Woodcuts. Post 8vo. 3s. 6d.; or Popular Edition, Fcap. 8vo. 1s.

REMBRANDT. A Descriptive Catalogue of his Etched Work; with Life and Introductions. By Chas. H. Middleton, B.A. Woodcuts. Medium 8vo. 31s. 6d.

REYNOLDS' (Sir Joshua) Life and Times. By C. R. Leslie, R.A. and Tom Taylor. Portraits. 2 Vols. 8vo. 42s.

RICARDO'S (David) Political Works. With a Notice of his Life and Writings. By J. R. M'Culloch. 8vo. 16s.

RIPA (Father). Thirteen Years at the Court of Peking. Post 8vo. 2s.

ROBERTSON (Canon). History of the Christian Church, from the Apostolic Age to the Reformation, 1517. 8 Vols. Post 8vo. 6s. each.

ROBINSON (Rev. Dr.). Biblical Researches in Palestine and the Adjacent Regions, 1838—52. Maps. 3 Vols. 8vo. 42s.

—— (Wm.) Alpine Flowers for English Gardens. With 70 Illustrations. Crown 8vo. 7s. 6d.

—————— Sub-Tropical Garden. Illustrations. Small 8vo. 5s.

ROBSON (E. R.). School Architecture. Remarks on the Planning, Designing, Building, and Furnishing of School-houses. Illustrations. Medium 8vo. 18s.

ROME (History of). See Gibbon—Liddell—Smith—Students'.

ROYAL SOCIETY CATALOGUE OF SCIENTIFIC PAPERS. 8 vols. 8vo. 20s. each. Half morocco, 28s. each

RUXTON (Geo. F.). Travels in Mexico; with Adventures among Wild Tribes and Animals of the Prairies and Rocky Mountains. Post 8vo. 3s. 6d.

ST. HUGH OF AVALON, Bishop of Lincoln; his Life by G. G. Perry, Canon of Lincoln. Post 8vo. 10s. 6d.

ST. JOHN (Charles). Wild Sports and Natural History of the Highlands of Scotland. New, and beautifully illustrated Edition. Crown 8vo. 15s. *Cheap Edition*, Post 8vo. 3s. 6d.

—————— (Bayle) Adventures in the Libyan Desert. Post 8vo. 2s.

SALDANHA (Duke of). See Carnota.

SALE'S (Sir Robert) Brigade in Affghanistan. With an Account of the Defence of Jellalabad. By Rev. G. R. Gleig. Post 8vo. 2s.

SCEPTICISM IN GEOLOGY; and the Reasons for It. An assemblage of facts from Nature combining to refute the theory of "Causes now in Action." By Verifier. Woodcuts. Crown 8vo. 6s.

SCOTT (Sir Gilbert). Lectures on the Rise and Development of Mediæval Architecture. Delivered at the Royal Academy. With 400 Illustrations. 2 Vols. Medium 8vo. 42s.

—————— Secular and Domestic Architecture, Present and Future. 8vo. 9s.

SCHLIEMANN (Dr. Henry). Troy and Its Remains. A Narrative of Researches and Discoveries made on the Site of Ilium, and in the Trojan Plain. With 500 Illustrations. Medium 8vo. 42s.

—————— Discoveries on the Sites of Ancient Mycenæ and Tiryns. With 500 Illustrations. Medium 8vo. 50s.

—————— Ilios; A Complete History of the City and Country of the Trojans, including all Recent Discoveries and Researches made on the Site of Troy and the Troad. With an Autobiography of the Author. With nearly 2000 Illustrations. Imperial 8vo. 50s.

SCHOMBERG (General). The Odyssey of Homer, rendered into English blank verse. Books I—XII. 8vo. 12s.

SEEBOHM (Henry). Siberia in Europe; a Naturalist's Visit to the Valley of the Petchora in N.E. Russia. With notices of Birds and their migrations. With Map and Illustrations. Crown 8vo. 14s.

SELBORNE (Lord). Notes on some Passages in the Liturgical History of the Reformed English Church. 8vo. 6s.

SHADOWS OF A SICK ROOM. Preface by Canon LIDDON. 16mo. 2s. 6d.

SHAH OF PERSIA'S Diary during his Tour through Europe in 1873. Translated from the Original. By J. W. REDHOUSE. With Portrait and Coloured Title. Crown 8vo. 12s.

SHAW (T. B.), Manual of English Literature. Post 8vo. 7s. 6d.
—— Specimens of English Literature. Selected from the Chief Writers. Post 8vo. 7s. 6d.
—— (ROBERT). Visit to High Tartary, Yarkand, and Kashgar (formerly Chinese Tartary), and Return Journey over the Karakorum Pass. With Map and Illustrations. 8vo. 16s.

SIERRA LEONE; Described in Letters to Friends at Home. By A LADY. Post 8vo. 3s. 6d.

SIMMONS (CAPT.). Constitution and Practice of Courts-Martial. 8vo. 15s.

SMILES' (SAMUEL, LL.D.) WORKS:—
  BRITISH ENGINEERS; from the Earliest Period to the death of the Stephensons. With Illustrations. 5 Vols. Crown 8vo. 7s. 6d. each.
  LIFE OF A SCOTCH NATURALIST (THOS. EDWARD). Illustrations. Crown 8vo. 10s. 6d.
  LIFE OF A SCOTCH GEOLOGIST AND BOTANIST (ROBERT DICK). Illustrations. Crown 8vo. 12s.
  HUGUENOTS IN ENGLAND AND IRELAND. Crown 8vo. 7s. 6d.
  SELF-HELP. With Illustrations of Conduct and Perseverance. Post 8vo. 6s. Or in French, 5s.
  CHARACTER. A Sequel to "SELF-HELP." Post 8vo. 6s.
  THRIFT. A Book of Domestic Counsel. Post 8vo. 6s.
  DUTY. With Illustrations of Courage, Patience, and Endurance. Post 8vo. 6s.
  INDUSTRIAL BIOGRAPHY; or, Iron Workers and Tool Makers. Post 8vo. 6s.
  BOY'S VOYAGE ROUND THE WORLD. Illustrations. Post 8vo. 6s.

SMITH (DR. GEORGE) Student's Manual of the Geography of India. Post 8vo.

SMITH'S (DR. WM.) DICTIONARIES:—
  DICTIONARY OF THE BIBLE; its Antiquities, Biography, Geography, and Natural History. Illustrations. 3 Vols. 8vo. 105s.
  CONCISE BIBLE DICTIONARY. With 300 Illustrations. Medium 8vo. 21s.
  SMALLER BIBLE DICTIONARY. With Illustrations. Post 8vo. 7s. 6d.
  CHRISTIAN ANTIQUITIES. Comprising the History, Institutions, and Antiquities of the Christian Church. With Illustrations. 2 Vols. Medium 8vo. 3l. 13s. 6d.
  CHRISTIAN BIOGRAPHY, LITERATURE, SECTS, AND DOCTRINES; from the Times of the Apostles to the Age of Charlemagne. Medium 8vo. Vols. I. & II. 31s. 6d. each. (To be completed in 4 Vols.)
  GREEK AND ROMAN ANTIQUITIES. With 500 Illustrations. Medium 8vo. 28s.
  GREEK AND ROMAN BIOGRAPHY AND MYTHOLOGY. With 600 Illustrations. 3 Vols. Medium 8vo. 4l. 4s.
  GREEK AND ROMAN GEOGRAPHY. 2 Vols. With 500 Illustrations. Medium 8vo. 56s.
  ATLAS OF ANCIENT GEOGRAPHY—BIBLICAL AND CLASSICAL. Folio. 6l. 6s.

SMITH's (DR. WM.) DICTIONARIES—*continued.*
    CLASSICAL DICTIONARY OF MYTHOLOGY, BIOGRAPHY, AND GEOGRAPHY. 1 Vol. With 750 Woodcuts. 8vo. 18s.
    SMALLER CLASSICAL DICTIONARY. With 200 Woodcuts. Crown 8vo. 7s. 6d.
    SMALLER GREEK AND ROMAN ANTIQUITIES. With 200 Woodcuts. Crown 8vo. 7s. 6d.
    COMPLETE LATIN-ENGLISH DICTIONARY. With Tables of the Roman Calendar, Measures, Weights, and Money. 8vo. 21s.
    SMALLER LATIN-ENGLISH DICTIONARY. 12mo. 7s. 6d.
    COPIOUS AND CRITICAL ENGLISH-LATIN DICTIONARY. 8vo. 21s.
    SMALLER ENGLISH-LATIN DICTIONARY. 12mo. 7s. 6d.

SMITH'S (DR. WM.) ENGLISH COURSE:—
    SCHOOL MANUAL OF ENGLISH GRAMMAR, WITH COPIOUS EXERCISES. Post 8vo. 3s. 6d.
    PRIMARY ENGLISH GRAMMAR. 16mo. 1s.
    MANUAL OF ENGLISH COMPOSITION. With Copious Illustrations and Practical Exercises. 12mo. 3s. 6d.
    PRIMARY HISTORY OF BRITAIN. 12mo. 2s. 6d.
    SCHOOL MANUAL OF MODERN GEOGRAPHY, PHYSICAL AND POLITICAL. Post 8vo. 5s.
    A SMALLER MANUAL OF MODERN GEOGRAPHY. 16mo. 2s. 6d.

SMITH'S (DR. WM.) FRENCH COURSE:—
    FRENCH PRINCIPIA. Part I. A First Course, containing a Grammar, Delectus, Exercises, and Vocabularies. 12mo. 3s. 6d.
    APPENDIX TO FRENCH PRINCIPIA. Part I. Containing additional Exercises, with Examination Papers. 12mo. 2s. 6d.
    FRENCH PRINCIPIA. Part II. A Reading Book, containing Fables, Stories, and Anecdotes, Natural History, and Scenes from the History of France. With Grammatical Questions, Notes and copious Etymological Dictionary. 12mo. 4s. 6d.
    FRENCH PRINCIPIA. Part III. Prose Composition, containing a Systematic Course of Exercises on the Syntax, with the Principal Rules of Syntax. 12mo. [*In the Press.*
    STUDENT'S FRENCH GRAMMAR. By C. HERON-WALL. With Introduction by M. Littré. Post 8vo. 7s. 6d.
    SMALLER GRAMMAR OF THE FRENCH LANGUAGE. Abridged from the above. 12mo. 3s. 6d.

SMITH'S (DR. WM.) GERMAN COURSE:—
    GERMAN PRINCIPIA. Part I. A First German Course, containing a Grammar, Delectus, Exercise Book, and Vocabularies. 12mo. 3s. 6d.
    GERMAN PRINCIPIA. Part II. A Reading Book; containing Fables, Stories, and Anecdotes, Natural History, and Scenes from the History of Germany. With Grammatical Questions, Notes, and Dictionary. 12mo. 3s. 6d.
    PRACTICAL GERMAN GRAMMAR. Post 8vo. 3s. 6d.

SMITH'S (DR. WM.) ITALIAN COURSE:—
    ITALIAN PRINCIPIA. An Italian Course, containing a Grammar, Delectus, Exercise Book, with Vocabularies, and Materials for Italian Conversation. By Signor Ricci, Professor of Italian at the City of London College. 12mo. 3s. 6d.
    ITALIAN PRINCIPIA. Part II. A First Italian Reading Book, containing Fables, Anecdotes, History, and Passages from the best Italian Authors, with Grammatical Questions, Notes, and a Copious Etymological Dictionary. By SIGNOR RICCI. 12mo. 3s. 6d.
[*Nearly ready.*

SMITH'S (Dr. Wm.) LATIN COURSE:—

THE YOUNG BEGINNER'S FIRST LATIN BOOK: Containing the Rudiments of Grammar, Easy Grammatical Questions and Exercises, with Vocabularies. Being a Stepping-stone to Principia Latina, Part I., for Young Children. 12mo. 2s.

THE YOUNG BEGINNER'S SECOND LATIN BOOK: Containing an easy Latin Reading Book, with an Analysis of the Sentences, Notes, and a Dictionary. Being a Stepping-stone to Principia Latina, Part II., for Young Children. 12mo. 2s.

PRINCIPIA LATINA. Part I. First Latin Course, containing a Grammar, Delectus, and Exercise Book, with Vocabularies. 12mo. 3s. 6d.
*** In this Edition the Cases of the Nouns, Adjectives, and Pronouns are arranged both as in the ORDINARY GRAMMARS and as in the PUBLIC SCHOOL PRIMER, together with the corresponding Exercises.

APPENDIX TO PRINCIPIA LATINA. Part I.; being Additional Exercises, with Examination Papers. 12mo. 2s. 6d.

PRINCIPIA LATINA. Part II. A Reading-book of Mythology, Geography, Roman Antiquities, and History. With Notes and Dictionary. 12mo. 3s. 6d.

PRINCIPIA LATINA. Part III. A Poetry Book. Hexameters and Pentameters; Eclog. Ovidianæ: Latin Prosody. 12mo. 3s. 6d.

PRINCIPIA LATINA. Part IV. Prose Composition. Rules of Syntax with Examples, Explanations of Synonyms, and Exercises on the Syntax. 12mo. 3s. 6d.

PRINCIPIA LATINA. Part V. Short Tales and Anecdotes for Translation into Latin. 12mo. 3s.

LATIN-ENGLISH VOCABULARY AND FIRST LATIN-ENGLISH DICTIONARY FOR PHÆDRUS, CORNELIUS NEPOS, AND CÆSAR. 12mo. 3s. 6d.

STUDENT'S LATIN GRAMMAR. For the Higher Forms. Post 8vo. 6s.

SMALLER LATIN GRAMMAR. For the Middle and Lower Forms. 12mo. 3s. 6d.

TACITUS, Germania, Agricola, &c. With English Notes. 12mo. 3s. 6d.

SMITH'S (Dr. Wm.) GREEK COURSE:—

INITIA GRÆCA. Part I. A First Greek Course, containing a Grammar, Delectus, and Exercise-book. With Vocabularies. 12mo. 3s. 6d.

APPENDIX TO INITIA GRÆCA. Part I. Containing additional Exercises. With Examination Papers. Post 8vo. 2s. 6d.

INITIA GRÆCA. Part II. A Reading Book. Containing Short Tales, Anecdotes, Fables, Mythology, and Grecian History. 12mo. 3s. 6d.

INITIA GRÆCA. Part III. Prose Composition. Containing the Rules of Syntax, with copious Examples and Exercises. 12mo. 3s. 6d.

STUDENT'S GREEK GRAMMAR. For the Higher Forms. By CURTIUS. Post 8vo. 6s.

SMALLER GREEK GRAMMAR. For the Middle and Lower Forms. 12mo. 3s. 6d.

GREEK ACCIDENCE. 12mo. 2s. 6d.

PLATO, Apology of Socrates, &c. With Notes. 12mo. 3s. 6d.

SMITH'S (Dr. Wm.) SMALLER HISTORIES:—

SCRIPTURE HISTORY. Woodcuts. 16mo. 3s. 6d.
ANCIENT HISTORY. Woodcuts. 16mo. 3s. 6d.
ANCIENT GEOGRAPHY. Woodcuts. 16mo. 3s. 6d.
ROME. Modern Geography. Woodcuts. 16mo. 3s. 6d.

SMITH'S (Dr. Wm.) Smaller Histories—*continued*.
    Greece. Woodcuts. 16mo. 3s. 6d.
    Classical Mythology. Woodcuts. 16mo. 3s. 6d.
    England. Woodcuts. 16mo. 3s. 6d.
    English Literature. 16mo. 3s. 6d.
    Specimens of English Literature. 16mo. 3s. 6d.
SMITH (Geo.). Life of John Wilson, D.D. (of Bombay), Fifty Years Missionary and Philanthropist. Portrait. Post 8vo. 9s.
——— (Philip). History of the Ancient World, from the Creation to the Fall of the Roman Empire, A.D. 476. 3 Vols. 8vo. 31s. 6d.
SOMERVILLE (Mary). Personal Recollections from Early Life to Old Age. Portrait. Crown 8vo. 12s.
——————— Physical Geography. Portrait. Post 8vo. 9s.
——————— Connexion of the Physical Sciences. Portrait. Post 8vo. 9s.
——————— Molecular & Microscopic Science. Illustrations. 2 Vols. Post 8vo. 21s.
SOUTH (John F.). Household Surgery; or, Hints for Emergencies. With new Preface and Additions. With Woodcuts. Fcap. 8vo. 3s. 6d.
SOUTHEY (Robt). Lives of Bunyan and Cromwell. Post 8vo. 2s.
STAEL (Madame de). *See* Stevens.
STANHOPE'S (Earl) WORKS :—
    History of England from the Reign of Queen Anne to the Peace of Versailles, 1701-83. 9 vols. Post 8vo. 5s. each.
    Life of William Pitt. Portraits. 3 Vols. 8vo. 36s.
    British India, from its Origin to 1783. Post 8vo. 3s. 6d.
    History of "Forty-Five." Post 8vo. 2s.
    Historical and Critical Essays. Post 8vo. 3s. 6d.
    French Retreat from Moscow, other Essays. Post 8vo. 7s. 6d.
    Life of Belisarius. Post 8vo. 10s. 6d.
    Life of Condé. Post 8vo. 3s. 6d.
    Miscellanies. 2 Vols. Post 8vo. 13s.
    Story of Joan of Arc. Fcap. 8vo. 1s.
    Addresses on Various Occasions. 16mo. 1s.
STANLEY'S (Dean) WORKS :—
    Sinai and Palestine. Maps. 8vo. 14s.
    Bible in the Holy Land; Extracted from the above Work. Woodcuts. Fcap. 8vo. 2s. 6d.
    Eastern Church. Plans. 8vo. 12s.
    Jewish Church. From the Earliest Times to the Christian Era. 3 Vols. 8vo. 38s.
    Epistles of St. Paul to the Corinthians. 8vo. 18s.
    Life of Dr. Arnold, of Rugby. Portrait. 2 vols. Cr. 8vo. 12s.
    History of the Church of Scotland. 8vo. 7s. 6d.
    Memorials of Canterbury Cathedral. Post 8vo. 7s. 6d.
    Westminster Abbey. Illustrations. 8vo. 15s.
    Sermons during a Tour in the East. 8vo. 9s.
    Memoir of Edward, Catherine, and Mary Stanley. Cr. 8vo. 9s.
    Christian Institutions. Essays on Ecclesiastical Subjects. 8vo. 12s.

STEPHENS (Rev. W. R. W.). Life and Times of St. John Chrysostom. A Sketch of the Church and the Empire in the Fourth Century. Portrait. 8vo. 12s.

STEVENS (Dr. A.). Madame de Staël; a Study of her Life and Times. The First Revolution and the First Empire. Portraits. 2 Vols. Crown 8vo. 24s.

STRATFORD DE REDCLIFFE (Lord). The Eastern Question. Being a Selection from his Writings during the last Five Years of his Life. With a Preface by Dean Stanley. With Map. 8vo.

STREET (G. E.). Gothic Architecture in Spain. Illustrations. Royal 8vo. 30s.

—— ——. Italy, chiefly in Brick and Marble. With Notes on North of Italy. Illustrations. Royal 8vo. 26s.

STUART (Villiers). Nile Gleanings: The Ethnology, History, and Art of Ancient Egypt, as Revealed by Paintings and Bas-Reliefs. With Descriptions of Nubia and its Great Rock Temples, 58 Coloured Illustrations &c. Medium 8vo. 31s. 6d.

STUDENTS' MANUALS:—

  OLD TESTAMENT HISTORY: from the Creation to the Return of the Jews from Captivity. Maps and Woodcuts. Post 8vo. 7s. 6d.

  NEW TESTAMENT HISTORY. With an Introduction connecting the History of the Old and New Testaments. Maps and Woodcuts. Post 8vo. 7s. 6d.

  ECCLESIASTICAL HISTORY. The Christian Church during the First Ten Centuries; From its Foundation to the full establishment of the Holy Roman Empire and the Papal Power. Post 8vo. 7s. 6d.

  HISTORY OF THE EARLY ENGLISH CHURCH, from the planting of the Church in Britain to the Accession of Henry VIII. By Canon PERRY. Post 8vo.

  ENGLISH CHURCH HISTORY, from the accession of Henry VIII. to the silencing of Convocation in the 18th Century. By Canon PERRY. Post 8vo. 7s. 6d.

  ANCIENT HISTORY OF THE East; Egypt, Assyria, Babylonia, Media, Persia, Asia Minor, and Phoenicia. Woodcuts. Post 8vo. 7s. 6d.

  ANCIENT GEOGRAPHY. By Canon BEVAN. Woodcuts. Post 8vo. 7s. 6d.

  HISTORY OF GREECE; from the Earliest Times to the Roman Conquest. By WM. SMITH, D.C.L. Woodcuts. Crown 8vo. 7s. 6d.
    ⁎ Questions on the above Work, 12mo. 2s.

  HISTORY OF ROME; from the Earliest Times to the Establishment of the Empire. By DEAN LIDDELL. Woodcuts. Crown 8vo. 7s. 6d.

  GIBBON'S DECLINE AND FALL OF THE ROMAN EMPIRE. Woodcuts. Post 8vo. 7s. 6d.

  HALLAM'S HISTORY OF EUROPE during the Middle Ages. Post 8vo. 7s. 6d.

  HISTORY OF MODERN EUROPE, from the end of the Middle Ages to the Treaty of Berlin, 1878. Post 8vo. [In the Press.

  HALLAM'S HISTORY OF ENGLAND; from the Accession of Henry VII. to the Death of George II. Post 8vo. 7s. 6d.

  HUME'S HISTORY OF ENGLAND from the Invasion of Julius Caesar to the Revolution in 1688. Revised, corrected, and continued down to the Treaty of Berlin, 1878. By J. S. BREWER, M.A. With 7 Coloured Maps & 70 Woodcuts. Post 8vo. 7s. 6d.
    ⁎ Questions on the above Work, 12mo. 2s.

  HISTORY OF FRANCE; from the Earliest Times to the Establishment of the Second Empire, 1852. By H. W. JERVIS. Woodcuts. Post 8vo. 7s. 6d.

  ENGLISH LANGUAGE. By GEO. P. MARSH. Post 8vo. 7s. 6d.

STUDENTS' M[ANUAL]s—continued.
    ENGLISH LITERATURE. By T. B. SHAW, M.A. Post 8vo. 7s. 6d.
    SPECIMENS OF ENGLISH LITERATURE from the Chief Writers. By T. B. SHAW. Post 8vo. 7s. 6d.
    MODERN GEOGRAPHY; Mathematical, Physical and Descriptive. By CANON BEVAN. Woodcuts. Post 8vo. 7s. 6d.
    GEOGRAPHY OF INDIA. By Dr. GEORGE SMITH, LL.D.
    MORAL PHILOSOPHY. By WM. FLEMING. Post 8vo. 7s. 6d.
    BLACKSTONE'S COMMENTARIES ON THE LAWS OF ENGLAND. By MALCOLM KERR. Post 8vo. 7s. 6d.

SUMNER'S (BISHOP) Life and Episcopate during 40 Years. By Rev. G. H. SUMNER. Portrait. 8vo. 14s.

SWAINSON (CANON). Nicene and Apostles' Creeds; Their Literary History, together with some Account of "The Creed of St. Athanasius." 8vo. 16s.

SYBEL (VON) History of Europe during the French Revolution, 1789–1795. 4 Vols. 8vo. 48s.

SYMONDS' (REV. W.) Records of the Rocks; or Notes on the Geology, Natural History, and Antiquities of North and South Wales, Siluria, Devon, and Cornwall. With Illustrations. Crown 8vo. 12s.

TALMUD. See BARCLAY; DEUTSCH.

TEMPLE (SIR RICHARD). India in 1880. With 2 Maps. 8vo. 16s.

THIBAUT'S (ANTOINE) Purity in Musical Art. Translated from the German. With a prefatory Memoir by W. H. Gladstone, M.P. Post 8vo. 7s. 6d.

THIELMANN (BARON). Journey through the Caucasus to Tabreez, Kurdistan, down the Tigris and Euphrates to Nineveh and Babylon, and across the Desert to Palmyra. Translated by CHAS. HENEAGE. Illustrations. 2 Vols. Post 8vo. 18s.

THOMSON (ARCHBISHOP). Lincoln's Inn Sermons. 8vo. 10s. 6d.
——— Life in the Light of God's Word. Post 8vo. 5s.
——— Word, Work, & Will: Collected Essays. Crown 8vo. 9s.

TITIAN'S LIFE AND TIMES. With some account of his Family, chiefly from new and unpublished Records. By CROWE and CAVALCASELLE. With Portrait and Illustrations. 2 Vols. 8vo. 42s.

TOCQUEVILLE'S State of Society in France before the Revolution, 1789, and on the Causes which led to that Event. Translated by HENRY REEVE. 8vo. 14s.

TOMLINSON (CHAS.). The Sonnet; Its Origin, Structure, and Place in Poetry. With translations from Dante, Petrarch, &c. Post 8vo. 9s.

TOZER (REV. H. F.) Highlands of Turkey, with Visits to Mounts Ida, Athos, Olympus, and Pelion. 2 Vols. Crown 8vo. 24s.
——— Lectures on the Geography of Greece. Map. Post 8vo. 9s.

TRISTRAM (CANON). Great Sahara. Illustrations. Crown 8vo. 15s.
——— Land of Moab; Travels and Discoveries on the East Side of the Dead Sea and the Jordan. Illustrations. Crown 8vo. 15s.

TRURO (BISHOP OF). The Cathedral: its Necessary Place in the Life and Work of the Church. Crown 8vo. 6s.

TWENTY YEARS' RESIDENCE among the Greeks, Albanians, Turks, Armenians, and Bulgarians. By an ENGLISH LADY. Edited by STANLEY LANE POOLE. 2 Vols. Crown 8vo. 21s.

TWISS' (HORACE) Life of Lord Eldon. 2 Vols. Post 8vo. 21s.

TYLOR (E. B.) Researches into the Early History of Mankind, and Development of Civilization. 3rd Edition Revised. 8vo. 12s.

―――― ―――― Primitive Culture; the Development of Mythology, Philosophy, Religion, Art, and Custom. 2 Vols. 8vo. 24s.

VATICAN COUNCIL. See LETO.

VIRCHOW (PROFESSOR). The Freedom of Science in the Modern State. Fcap. 8vo. 2s.

WELLINGTON'S Despatches during his Campaigns in India, Denmark, Portugal, Spain, the Low Countries, and France. 8 Vols. 8vo. 20s. each.

―――― ―――― Supplementary Despatches, relating to India, Ireland, Denmark, Spanish America, Spain, Portugal, France, Congress of Vienna, Waterloo and Paris. 14 Vols. 8vo. 20s. each. ** An Index. 8vo. 20s.

―――― ―――― Civil and Political Correspondence. Vols. I. to VIII. 8vo. 20s. each.

―――― ―――― Speeches in Parliament. 2 Vols. 8vo. 42s.

WHEELER (G.). Choice of a Dwelling; a Practical Handbook of Useful Information on Building a House. Plans. Post 8vo. 7s. 6d.

WHITE (W. H.). Manual of Naval Architecture, for the use of Naval Officers, Shipowners, Shipbuilders, and Yachtsmen. Illustrations. 8vo. 24s.

WHYMPER (EDWARD). The Ascent of the Matterhorn. With 2 Maps and 100 Illustrations. Medium 8vo. 10s. 6d.

WILBERFORCE'S (BISHOP) Life of William Wilberforce. Portrait. Crown 8vo. 6s.

―――― ―――― (SAMUEL, LL.D.), Lord Bishop of Oxford and Winchester; his Life. By Canon ASHWELL, D.D. With Portrait and Woodcuts. Vols. I. and II. 8vo. 15s. each.

WILKINSON (SIR J. G.). Manners and Customs of the Ancient Egyptians, their Private Life, Laws, Arts, Religion, &c. A new edition. Edited by SAMUEL BIRCH, LL.D. Illustrations. 3 Vols. 8vo. 84s.

―――― ―――― Popular Account of the Ancient Egyptians. With 500 Woodcuts. 2 Vols. Post 8vo. 12s.

WILSON (JOHN, D.D.), of Bombay, Fifty Years a Philanthropist and Missionary in the East; his Life. By GEORGE SMITH, LL.D. Portrait. Post 8vo. 9s.

WOOD'S (CAPTAIN) Source of the Oxus. With the Geography of the Valley of the Oxus. By COL. YULE. Map. 8vo. 12s.

WORDS OF HUMAN WISDOM. Collected and Arranged by E. S. With a Preface by CANON LIDDON. Fcap. 8vo. 3s. 6d.

YORK (ARCHBISHOP OF). Collected Essays. Contents.—Synoptic Gospels, Death of Christ, God Exists, Worth of Life, Design in Nature, Sports and Pastimes, Emotions in Preaching, Defects in Missionary Work, Limits of Philosophical Enquiry. Crown 8vo. 9s.

YULE (COLONEL). Book of Marco Polo. Illustrated by the Light of Oriental Writers and Modern Travels. With Maps and 80 Plates. 2 Vols. Medium 8vo. 63s.

―――― A. F. A Little Light on Cretan Insurrection. Post 8vo. 2s. 6d.

www.ingramcontent.com/pod-product-compliance
Lightning Source LLC
Chambersburg PA
CBHW020234240426

43672CB00006B/523